Pivoting Government through Digital Transformation

"Designing and implementing the digital architecture across levels of government is a herculean task. As governments embark in their digital journey, they need to mitigate these risks and manage digitalization in a way that it serves its citizens. That is why this book couldn't be more timely."
—**Romina Bandura**, Senior Fellow, Center for
Strategic and International Studies

Affecting every sector and country in the world, digital technology is changing the way citizens engage in society, companies conduct business, and governments deliver public services. The COVID-19 pandemic accelerated the pace of digitalization and exposed such vulnerabilities as inadequate infrastructure, weak regulations, and a scarcity of skilled professionals capable of digitally transforming government. Not immune to the digital revolution, governments are slowly adapting to a digital world. Governments are implementing digital solutions to deliver services to their citizens, make payments, and engage the public.

Focusing on how government can transition more effectively through digital transformation, *Pivoting Government through Digital Transformation* covers the following key components:

- Setting the stage during the Great Resignation period
- Filling the digital talent pipeline
- Best practices and vignettes for applying digital transformation in government
- Looking ahead towards the future

Key chapter contributors from U.S. and foreign governments, as well as state and local governments, discuss how they are coping with today's environment and how they are using digital transformation efforts to enhance their organization's effectiveness and digital talent pipeline.

With chapters on theory and practice, this groundbreaking book offers an in-depth analysis of the most innovative approaches to e-government and discusses case studies from local, state, and federal government perspectives. This is an essential guide for government employees, scholars, and regular citizens who want to make government work more effectively and democratically in the digital age.

Data Analytics Applications
Edited by
Jay Liebowitz

Forthcoming

Developing the Intuitive Executive: Using Analytics and Intuition for Success
Jay Liebowitz
ISBN: 978-1-032-49820-1

Published

Actionable Intelligence in Healthcare
Jay Liebowitz
ISBN: 978-1-4987-7993-7

Analytics and Knowledge Management
Suliman Hawamdeh and Hsia-Ching Chang
ISBN: 978-1-138-63026-0

Big Data Analytics in Cybersecurity
Onur Savas and Julia Deng
ISBN: 978-1-4987-7212-9

Big Data and Analytics Applications in Government: Current Practices and Future Opportunities
Gregory Richards
ISBN: 978-1-4987-6434-6

Big Data in the Arts and Humanities: Theory and Practice
Giovanni Schiuma and Daniela Carlucci
ISBN: 978-1-4987-6585-5

Business Models: Innovation, Digital Transformation, and Analytics
Iwona Otola and Marlena Grabowska
ISBN: 978-0-367-86279-4

Closing the Analytics Talent Gap: An Executive's Guide to Working with Universities
Jennifer Priestley and Robert McGrath
ISBN: 978-0-367-48690-7

Data Analytics and AI
Jay Liebowitz
ISBN: 978-0-367-89561-7

Data Analytics Applications in Education
Jan Vanthienen and Kristof De Witte
ISBN: 978-1-4987-6927-3

Data Analytics Applications in Gaming and Entertainment
Günter Wallner
ISBN: 978-1-138-10443-3

Data Analytics Applications in Latin America and Emerging Economies
Eduardo Rodriguez
ISBN: 978-1-4987-6276-2

Data Analytics for Smart Cities
Amir Alavi and William G. Buttlar
ISBN: 978-1-138-30877-0

Pivoting Government through Digital Transformation

Edited by Jay Liebowitz
Inagural Executive-in-Residence for
Public Service Data Science Institute
Columbia University

CRC Press
Taylor & Francis Group
Boca Raton London

CRC Press is an imprint of the
Taylor & Francis Group, an **informa** business
AN AUERBACH BOOK

First edition published 2024
by CRC Press
2385 Executive Center Drive, Suite 320, Boca Raton FL 33431

and by CRC Press
4 Park Square, Milton Park, Abingdon, Oxon, OX14 4RN

CRC Press is an imprint of Taylor & Francis Group, LLC

© 2024 Taylor & Francis Group, LLC

ISBN: 9781032439907 (hbk)
ISBN: 9781032439891 (pbk)
ISBN: 9781003369783 (ebk)

DOI: 10.1201/9781003369783

Typeset in Garamond
by Apex CoVantage, LLC

To our civil servants who should be recognized for their
valiant efforts in shaping our country's future

To Jim Pastoriza, by his gift to Columbia University/Partnership for Public
Service, for realizing the need to improve the data science acumen of our federal
executives and further expand our future digital talent in the U.S. Government

Contents

Foreword

The digital revolution is impacting every sector and country in the world, changing the way citizens engage in society, companies conduct business, and governments deliver public services. In particular, the COVID-19 pandemic accelerated the pace of digitalization and exposed many of the existing vulnerabilities, including inadequate infrastructure, weak regulations, and scarce skills for the digital age.

Although governments have been slower to adapt to this digital wave, they are not immune to this trend. Governments are implementing digital solutions to deliver services to their citizens, make payments, and engage the public. From tax collection to welfare distribution to voting, these are some of the public services that benefit from digitalization.

Digital government or e-government is defined by the UN "as the use of ICTs to more effectively and efficiently deliver government services to citizens and businesses. It is the application of ICT in government operations, achieving public ends by digital means." Digitalizing government operations has many benefits in the form of *greater efficiency, transparency, and accountability*. By employing mobile technology, for example, local governments can text important information to people, such as notices on inclement weather or disease outbreaks, thereby reaching underserved communities quickly. Citizens and companies can make and receive payments from governments using online or mobile tools, providing added convenience, transparency, and security to financial transactions. At the same time, governments can use mobile apps to engage citizens by conducting surveys or polls to help build trust and participation in democratic processes.

These and other examples highlight the fundamental principle behind digital transformation within government: it must have a purpose and benefit regular people. If government employees and citizens see the advantages of digitalization, there will be buy-in from the community. In that same spirit, then-President Barack Obama expressed, "I want us to ask ourselves every day, how are we using technology to make a real difference in people's lives."

Most U.S. federal agencies have embarked on digitalization efforts. In 2012, the United States launched its first-ever e-government strategy, "Building a 21st Century Digital Government," to guide federal agencies in applying innovative technologies to public services delivery. There is also a flurry of digital activity taking place at the state and local levels of government. Arizona was the first U.S. state to allow residents to use Apple's wallet feature to digitally store their driver's licenses and state IDs. Florida is currently working on a Smart ID that would allow motorists to display their identification information on their phones, and Utah has a mobile driver's license program of its own. The state of New York launched the Excelsior Pass Plus to allow residents to digitally store COVID-19 vaccination records and negative test results. With the increase in scams and fraudulent activity during the COVID-19 pandemic, the U.S. government has begun to consider digital IDs as a safer and more private way to share the information needed for a transaction so that only the most necessary information is shared.

Like the United States, many governments are undergoing a profound digital transformation. Although there are wide disparities, about one third of countries in the world are very advanced in e-government development, according to the United Nations E-Government Survey. For example, during the COVID-19 crisis, countries that already possessed a strong digital enabling environment, like Bangladesh, India, and South Africa, had an easier time distributing Covid relief to people in need through digital means. Other countries, like Togo, had to quickly catch up.

Digital transformation is a systemic change for any organization and, in particular, for employees who bear the brunt of the process. Switching from paper records to electronic means requires a major overhaul in IT systems and internal processes as well as training of the bureaucracy. Digitalization is not an easy process, and it must be well designed, implemented, and managed. That is why having in place a *change management strategy* can help organizations and governments navigate this process and ensure that they are taking the right steps to avoid major disruptions in operations and improve staff morale. For digitalization, foundational *components* include planning, designing digital governance of systems, accounting for budgeting and staffing needs, and ensuring data security, among others.

When designing digital solutions, governments need to consider the inherent risks attached to technology, ensuring cybersecurity, and safeguarding people's data and privacy. At the same time, fundamental democratic principles may or may not be embedded in digital systems. Governments can use surveillance technology and artificial intelligence (AI) to pursue authoritarian practices and violate civil rights of digital users. At the same time, predictive technologies like AI and machine learning can end up reinforcing social biases if not properly designed.

For all these reasons, designing and implementing the digital architecture across levels of government is a herculean task. As governments embark on their digital journey, they need to mitigate these risks and manage digitalization in such a way that it serves its citizens. That is why this book couldn't be more timely. By combining chapters on theory and practice, this groundbreaking publication provides an in-depth analysis of the most innovative approaches to e-government and discusses case studies from local, state, and federal government perspectives. This is an essential guide for government employees, scholars, and regular citizens who want to make government work more effectively and democratically in the digital age.

Romina Bandura
Senior Fellow, Center for Strategic and
International Studies (CSIS)
Washington, D.C.
rbandura@csis.org

Preface

Compounded by the aging Baby Boomer generation, the Great Resignation period, and the continual job movement of our younger workforce, interesting times are ahead for the United States in various sectors. Even though the U.S. government may not have reached the "human capital crisis" as predicted over the years, there are still many gaps in various job classifications across the U.S. government. For example, even though there are Federal Chief Data Officers per the Evidence Act, as well as the recent (December 2021) "data scientist" OPM job billet, the U.S. government still faces a number of challenges in the digital talent pipeline for the years ahead. Through various programs, such as the U.S. Digital Corps early-career technologist program, as well as the Partnership for Public Service's Cybersecurity Talent Initiative, the U.S. government is trying to fill these gaps in creative ways. State and local governments, as well as federal governments globally, are also facing similar challenges.

This book focuses on how government can "pivot" more effectively through digital transformation. Specifically, the book covers the following key components: setting the stage during this Great Resignation period, filling the digital talent pipeline, best practices and vignettes, and looking ahead. Key chapter contributors from U.S. and foreign governments, as well as state and local governments, discuss how they are coping with today's environment and how they are using digital transformation efforts to enhance their organization's effectiveness and digital talent pipeline. I am very thankful to include these contributions from some of the leading individuals and organizations worldwide that are trying to address these key issues.

In my previous role as the Executive-in-Residence for Public Service at Columbia University's Data Science Institute, I was collaborating with the Partnership for Public Service (a nonpartisan, not-for-profit organization in Washington, D.C., specializing in federal executive leadership development). The focus was twofold: First, to further enhance the data-literacy acumen of federal senior executives, and second, to help develop the digital talent pipeline in the U.S. Government. We were also considering the formation of a new center, called CREATE (Center to Realize Expectations of Analytics for the Executive), to focus on how we can better educate the use of data and evidence (perhaps called "decision intelligence") to further inform the decision making of executives, especially those in the government.

I would like to thank the chapter contributors, reviewers, and Taylor & Francis for making this book a reality. I also express great appreciation to Romina Bandura, Senior Fellow at the Center for Strategic and International Studies, for her thoughtful foreword to the book. I would also like to thank my colleagues at both Columbia University's Data Science Institute and the Partnership for Public Service for helping to shape my ideas in this space. In addition, I am very thankful to Jim Pastoriza from TDF Ventures for providing his gift to endow my position. And, of course, I couldn't have organized this book without the support of my family—they keep me going, especially since I have now reached Medicare age!

I hope you enjoy the book!

—Jay Liebowitz, D.Sc.

Editor

Dr. Jay Liebowitz recently served as the inaugural executive-in-residence for Public Service at Columbia University's Data Science Institute. He was previously visiting professor in the Stillman School of Business and the MS-Business Analytics Capstone and Co-Program director (External Relations) at Seton Hall University. He previously served as the distinguished chair of Applied Business and Finance at Harrisburg University (HU) of Science and Technology. Before HU, he was the Orkand endowed chair of Management and Technology in the Graduate School at the University of Maryland University College (UMUC). He served as full professor in the Carey Business School at Johns Hopkins University. He was ranked one of the top 10 knowledge management researchers/practitioners out of 11,000 worldwide, and he was ranked #2 in KM Strategy worldwide according to the January 2010 *Journal of Knowledge Management*. At Johns Hopkins University, he was the founding program director for the Graduate Certificate in Competitive Intelligence and the Capstone director of the MS-Information and Telecommunications Systems for Business Program, where he engaged over 30 organizations in industry, government, and not-for-profits in capstone projects.

Prior to joining Hopkins, Dr. Liebowitz was the first knowledge management officer at NASA Goddard Space Flight Center. Before NASA, Dr. Liebowitz was the Robert W. Deutsch Distinguished Professor of Information Systems at the University of Maryland-Baltimore County, professor of Management Science at George Washington University, and chair of Artificial Intelligence at the U.S. Army War College.

Dr. Liebowitz is the founding editor-in-chief of *Expert Systems with Applications: An International Journal* (published by Elsevier and ranked as a top-tier journal; the Thomson Impact Factor from June 2021 is 8.665). He is a Fulbright scholar, IEEE-USA Federal Communications Commission executive fellow, and Computer Educator of the Year (International Association for Computer Information Systems). He has published over 45 books and myriad journal articles on knowledge management, analytics, financial literacy, intelligent systems, and IT management. Dr. Liebowitz served as the editor-in-chief of *Procedia Computer Science* (Elsevier).

He is also the series book editor of the *Data Analytics Applications* book series (Taylor & Francis Group) as well as the series book editor of the new *Digital Transformation: Accelerating Organizational Intelligence* book series (World Scientific Publishing). In October 2011, the International Association for Computer Information Systems named the "Jay Liebowitz Outstanding Student Research Award" for the best student research paper at the IACIS Annual Conference. Dr. Liebowitz was the Fulbright Visiting Research Chair in Business at Queen's University for summer 2017 and a Fulbright Specialist at Dalarna University in Sweden in May 2019. He is in the top 2% of the top scientists in the world, according to a 2019 Stanford Study. As of 2021, he is visiting distinguished professor at the International School for Social and Business Studies in Slovenia. His recent books are *Data Analytics and AI* (Taylor & Francis Group, 2021), *The Business of Pandemics: The COVID-19 Story* (Taylor & Francis Group, 2021), *A Research Agenda for Knowledge Management and Analytics* (Elgar Publishers, 2021), *Online Learning Analytics* (Taylor & Francis Group, 2022), and *Digital Transformation for the University of the Future* (World Scientific, 2022). He has lectured and consulted worldwide.

Contributors

Jennifer Anastasoff
Founder and Executive Director
Tech Talent Project
USA

Hila Axelrad
Senior Researcher
Aaron Institute for Economic Policy
Reichman University
Israel

Jennifer Bachner
Director
Center for Advanced Governmental Studies
Johns Hopkins University
USA

Romina Bandura
Senior Fellow
Center for Strategic and International
    Studies
USA

Marie-Eve Bedard
Analyst/Statistician
Statistics Canada
Canada

Esther Ruiz Ben
Faculty of Business, Computing, and
    Law
Technische Hochschule (TH) Wildau
Germany

Eric Egan
Policy Fellow for Digital
    Government
The Information Technology and
    Innovation Foundation
USA

Joshua Franzel
Managing Director
MissionSquare Research Institute
    (formerly The Center for
    State and Local Government
    Excellence)
USA

Jennifer Koester
Director of Enterprise Data
Department of Technology and
    Information, State of Delaware
USA

Mark Lerner
Senior Manager, Technology and
    Innovation
Partnership for Public Service
USA

Jay Liebowitz
Inaugural Executive-in-Residence for
    Public Service
Data Science Institute
Columbia University
USA

Saeid Molladavoudi
Senior Data Science Advisor
Statistics Canada
Canada

Sarah Philbrick
Research and Analysis Manager, Data
and Evidence
Partnership for Public Service
USA

Margit Christa Scholl
Faculty of Business, Computing, and
Law
Technische Hochschule (TH) Wildau
Germany

Rebecca Sharples
Managing Director of Academic
Programs and Outreach
The Data Mine
Purdue University
USA

Hiren Shukla
Global Neuro-Diverse Center of
Excellence Leader
Ernst & Young (EY)
USA

Sergei Sumkin
Aaron Institute for Economic Policy
Tiomkin School of Economics
Reichman University
Israel

Barbara-Chiara Ubaldi
Head, Digital Government and Data
Unit
Organisation for Economic
Co-operation and Development
(OECD)
France

Mark Daniel Ward
Director, The Data Mine
Purdue University
USA

Geanina Watkins
International Programme Officer, Data
Science Campus
Office for National Statistics
UK

Benjamin Welby
Policy Analyst
Digital Government and Data
Organisation for Economic
Co-operation and Development
(OECD)
UK

Jay L. Zagorsky
Clinical Associate Professor
Questrom School of Business
Boston University
USA

Chapter 1

Digital Government
The Future Is Already Here, It's Just Unevenly Distributed

Benjamin Welby and Barbara-Chiara Ubaldi

Content

1.1 Introduction

The use of technology and data as the basis to deliver transformed government is nothing new. Ambitious ideas of future possibilities that use computers stand on the shoulders of those who have had those same thoughts over the last 50 years, if not longer (Negroponte, 1996). For many years, public administration reform has

DOI: 10.1201/9781003369783-1

gravitated towards the role that technology can play in reducing bureaucracy, eliminating paperwork and simplifying the activity of government (Fadi Salem, 2013).

Indeed, in 2022, the ongoing operations of public services in several Organisation for Economic Co-operation and Development (OECD) countries relied on software written in some of the oldest computer coding languages, decades after first being developed and deep into the 'digital era'. For example, a 2015 information request by the United States Committee on Oversight and Government Reform defined around 1 billion lines of code as 'legacy', almost 30% of which were the 1960s languages of Common Business Oriented Language (COBOL) or Fortran (United States House of Representatives Committee on Oversight and Government Reform, 2017).

Software written in COBOL and Fortran represented an incredible paradigm shift from all that had gone before and, at the time, reflected a complete transformation of the internal practices of government. This was not the era of personal computing but a period when computers were the size of rooms. What might be considered ancient technologies today were seen as cutting-edge examples of the future at the time.

This highlights the challenge that what might be considered the future can easily become a legacy overhead if the pace of wider cultural change does not keep pace with the opportunities provided by developments in technology.

As such, efforts to build a better future that reflects the potential and opportunities offered by the digital age mean that governments must consider historic advancements as well as more recent developments. In many parts of the world, 'e-government' remains the default way of taking these ideas into account. And while e-government and digital government might be used interchangeably, they actually refer to different concepts.

E-government reflects the pursuit of moving analogue activities and underlying operations online and working out from technology in order to deliver for the needs of government (OECD, 2003; United Nations, 2004). Significant improvements in terms of accessibility for users and efficiency for public service providers have been achieved following investment in these activities, but over time a more developed and nuanced approach to the maturity of government use of technology and data to rethink government activities and respond to the needs of society has been found in the idea of digital government (OECD, 2014).

Digital government focuses on achieving a service design mentality with technology and data as enablers for transformation and where the user's need is made the priority. Considering how technology might be an enabler for transforming processes and operations through a user-driven and user-centred approach reshapes the way in which governments operate and serve the public. Digital government therefore has implications for the whole government, including the capability of all public servants, the overall culture, the philosophy and behaviours of leaders, and the underlying organizational principles. As the OECD puts it, digital government is "the use of digital technologies, as an integrated part of governments' modernization strategies, to create public value" (OECD, 2014).

The COVID-19 pandemic presented a unique set of challenges for governments around the world and prompted many of them to further accelerate their efforts at using technology and data to support transformation. Some of these efforts were focused internally to increase remote work and collaboration among government employees so that they could coordinate an effective response to the crisis and continue to operate despite disruptions to their usual work environments. Other efforts helped to fight the virus and keep people informed by using data and analytics to monitor the spread of the virus, identify hotspots, and inform decision-making about containment and mitigation strategies. A significant amount of the response to the pandemic focused on the public-facing experience in terms of contact tracing, proof of vaccination or infection status and the use of websites to keep the public informed.

The extent to which countries were able to move quickly and respond to this challenge with technology and data reflected their digital government maturity. The ones that had invested efforts and resources to strategically transform their operations, rather than simply move activities online, found themselves more ready to design new responses with agility in order to address emergency needs across societies. The ones who had adopted a less focused approach struggled to show the capability to react promptly and invest in new solutions that could last in the long run rather than simply being short-term answers.

This chapter will provide an overview of the current state of digital government maturity and explore the challenges and opportunities that lie ahead. It will also offer strategies for achieving greater digital government maturity and highlight the importance of looking towards the future.

The chapter is organized into four main sections. In the first section, we will provide an overview of the current state of digital government maturity, including trends and developments that are shaping the landscape. We will also provide examples of countries and organizations that are leading the way in digital government maturity.

The second section will focus on the future challenges and opportunities for digital government maturity. We will explore emerging technologies and their potential impact on the public sector and discuss the challenges and obstacles that governments may face in achieving greater digital government maturity.

In the third section, we will offer strategies for achieving greater digital government maturity. This will include best practices and case studies from successful implementations, as well as the role of leadership and governance in driving digital transformation.

Finally, we will conclude by summarizing the key points and implications of the chapter. We will also provide a call to action for government leaders to prioritize digital government maturity.

1.2 Understanding Digital Government Maturity

Digital government maturity refers to the extent to which government organizations are able to leverage digital technologies and data to improve their performance,

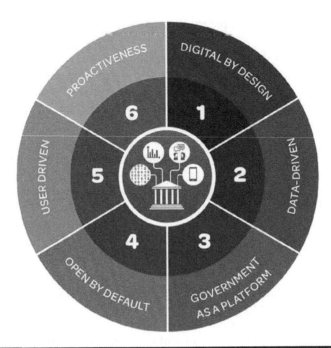

Figure 1.1   The OECD Digital Government Policy Framework.

Source: OECD (2020d). "The OECD Digital Government Policy Framework: Six Dimensions of a Digital Government".

efficiency and effectiveness. As the pace of technological change continues to accelerate, it is increasingly important for governments to prioritize digital transformation and strive for greater digital government maturity. By anticipating and planning for the future, governments can position themselves to capitalize on emerging technologies and trends and avoid being left behind.

To support governments in developing their maturity further, the OECD has developed the Digital Government Policy Framework (OECD, 2020d), as shown in Figure 1.1.

The six dimensions of the framework help governments better understand the potential benefits and challenges of digital transformation, and they provide a roadmap for implementing effective digital government strategies. These dimensions cover six areas:

■ **Digital by design:** The idea that digital technologies should be integrated into the governance, design and development of government policies, programmes and services from the outset. This means identifying opportunities to use digital technologies to improve the effectiveness and efficiency of government operations and considering the potential impacts and benefits of digital technologies as part of developing policies and services. It does not mean adopting a 'digital by default' approach, with the intent of moving all users online, but recognizes that there are transformative opportunities for technology to enable the interactions that take place offline and in person.

■ **Data-driven public sector:** The use of data as a strategic asset to inform decision-making and improve the efficiency and effectiveness of government services. This involves the collection and analysis of data from various sources to gain insights into the needs and preferences of citizens, as well as the performance and impact of government programs and policies. Data-driven public sectors also prioritize data quality, transparency, privacy and work to ensure that data is used ethically and responsibly. By using data and analytics to inform decision-making and drive continuous improvement, governments can better serve the needs of their citizens and contribute to the overall well-being of society (OECD, 2019).

■ **Government as a platform:** Providing clear and transparent sources of guidelines, tools, data and software that equip teams to deliver user-driven, consistent, seamless, integrated, proactive and cross-sectoral service delivery. These ecosystems of enablers are intended to support transformation at scale by prioritizing reusable and interoperable resources (guidelines, processes, resources and technical components). Government-as-a-platform ecosystems reduce duplication and enable more agile and responsive service delivery by fostering innovation and collaboration. To be successful, government as a platform requires strong governance and leadership, as well as ongoing and sustainable funding of these shared resources (OECD, 2020a; Welby & Hui Yan Tan, 2022).

■ **Open by default:** Government data and information should be made available to the public in a proactive and transparent way, unless there are compelling reasons for them to be kept confidential. This principle is based on the idea that open government data can contribute to economic growth, improve accountability and transparency and foster innovation and civic engagement (Ubaldi, 2013; OECD, 2018). It also recognizes that the policy-making and service design process should seek to be as open, accountable and participatory as possible, in line with fundamental principles and beliefs about open government (OECD, 2017).

■ **User driven:** Government services should be designed and delivered with the needs and preferences of citizens and businesses in mind. To support the implementation of user-driven approaches, governments should involve users in the design and development of services and regularly seek their feedback and input to inform continuous improvement. Governments should also work to ensure that services are easy to use and accessible to all and that they are available through a variety of channels, including online, mobile and in person (OECD, 2022).

■ **Proactiveness:** Proactiveness represents the ability of governments and civil servants to anticipate people's needs and respond to them rapidly so that users do not have to engage with the cumbersome process of data and service delivery. A proactive government pre-empts requests from citizens, seeking ways to answer queries and meet needs with the minimum of overheads resulting from interacting with public sector organizations (OECD, 2020c).

The current state of digital government maturity varies widely across different countries and organizations. Some governments have made significant progress in leveraging digital technologies and strategies to improve their performance, while others are still struggling to catch up.

Overall, there are several trends and developments that are shaping the current landscape of digital government maturity. One of the most significant trends is the way in which digital tools are being used to provide access to public services. The OECD Framework for Service Design and Delivery proposes that transformed public services should be approached in a channel-agnostic fashion and understood as follows (OECD, 2020a):

■ from when someone first attempts to solve a problem through to its resolution (end to end),
■ on a continuum from user experience to the processes for back-office staff (external to internal), and
■ across any and all of the channels involved (omnichannel) and platforms to deliver public services.

Another trend is the growing use of data and analytics to improve decision-making and performance. Governments are collecting and analyzing vast amounts of data to gain insights into citizen needs and preferences and to identify opportunities for improvement. This is enabling governments to anticipate needs, to make more informed decisions and to better target the use of their resources to show they are achieving results with transparency (OECD, 2019). Governments are becoming increasingly sophisticated in the publication of open government data and the opportunities available to private sector and third-sector actors to unlock the public value these datasets contain (OECD, 2018). As governments make more data available and invest in its use and reuse, this is a critical route to promoting transparency and accountability and, by extension, trust in government and democracy itself (Davies, 2019).

Public trust is easier to lose than to build, and Brezzi et al. (2021) indicate that the drivers of trust in public institutions to meet current and future challenges reflect a combination of competencies (in terms of responsiveness and reliability)

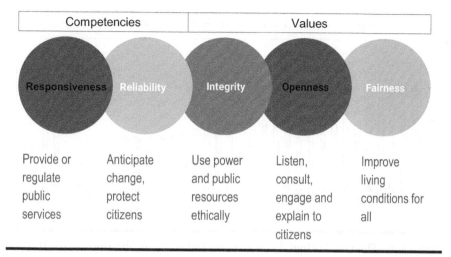

Figure 1.2   The drivers of trust in public institutions.

Source: Brezzi et al. (2021). "An Updated OECD Framework on Drivers of Trust in Public Institutions to Meet Current and Future Challenges".

and values (in terms of integrity, openness and fairness). Digital government maturity can help to support each of these five areas in different ways, as shown in Figure 1.2. This includes a recognition of digital security as a core consideration as governments become more reliant on digital technologies and with the increasing threat of cyberattacks and other security challenges.

There are also many opportunities for collaboration and innovation in terms of GovTech. Governments are increasingly partnering with the broad ecosystem of private sector companies and other organisations to develop and implement new technologies and solutions, leveraging in most of the cases the use of data coming from different sources (Ostrovskaya, 2022). This is enabling governments to tap into a wider pool of expertise and resources and to accelerate their digital transformation efforts.

Overall, the current state of digital government maturity is dynamic and evolving. Several tools exist for measuring the effectiveness of how governments are using digital technology and data, with the OECD's Digital Government Index reflecting the application of the Digital Government Policy Framework (OECD, 2020b). According to this instrument, it is the governments of Korea and the United Kingdom which are leading the way (see Figure 1.3), while others are still catching up. However, it is clear that digital technologies and data are playing an increasingly important role in the public sector and that governments need to prioritize digital transformation in order to stay competitive and effective.

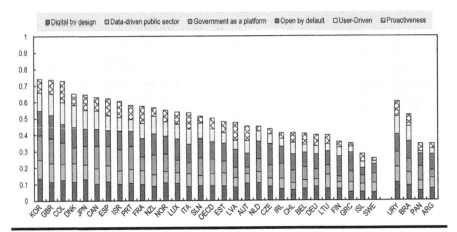

Figure 1.3 The OECD Digital Government Index composite results (2019).

Source: OECD Survey on Digital Government 1.0. Data are not available for Australia, Hungary, Mexico, Poland, Slovakia, Switzerland, Turkey and the United States.

1.3 Future Challenges and Opportunities

As governments around the world continue to embrace digital technologies and strategies, they face several challenges and opportunities that will shape the future of digital government and their capability to leverage digital means to truly achieve their transformation.

One of the biggest challenges is the rapid pace of technological change. New technologies and innovations are emerging all the time, and governments need to be able to adapt and keep pace with these changes in order to remain competitive and effective. Governments need the foundational cultures, behaviours and practices to be able to judge the value and relevance of new technologies and act to incorporate them as necessary and relevant, and not simply be attracted to the latest proposal (Lindman et al., 2020).

Another challenge is the need to develop the digital skills and competencies of government employees at all levels. In order for governments to fully leverage the potential of digital technologies, they need to invest in training and development programs that will equip their employees with the skills and knowledge they need (OECD, 2021c).

Associated with the challenges of developing a future-fit workforce is the need to overcome cultural and organizational barriers to change. The implications of digital transformation are extensive, and rely on the support and contribution of the whole of the public sector workforce. Governments need to overcome resistance to change and create cultures that are supportive of digital transformation in order to achieve greater digital government maturity (OECD, 2020a, 2021c).

Emerging technologies, such as artificial intelligence (AI) and the Internet of Things (IoT), are likely to have a significant impact on digital government maturity. These technologies have the potential to greatly enhance the efficiency and effectiveness of government operations and to improve the delivery of public services. For example, AI technologies can be used to automate many routine tasks and processes, freeing up government employees to focus on more complex and strategic tasks. This can help governments to improve their performance and efficiency and to deliver better services to citizens (Ubaldi et al., 2019). Governments that are able to effectively incorporate these technologies into their operations are likely to be more competitive and effective in the digital age.

While emerging technologies have the potential to greatly enhance the efficiency and effectiveness of government operations, it is also important for governments to be mindful of any potential negative implications, including unfair or biased results (Perez, 2019; O'Neill, 2017).

One potential negative implication of these technologies is the potential for job displacement. As AI and other automation technologies become more advanced, there is a risk that some government jobs may become redundant, leading to job losses and potentially negative social and economic impacts. One estimate of the impact of automation puts the number of jobs displaced by 2030 at 800 million and affecting up to 375 million workers globally (McKinsey Global Institute, 2017). The report also estimates that as many as 375 million new jobs could be created by the same technologies, which could offset some of the job losses. It is worth noting that the actual impact of automation on employment will depend on a variety of factors, including the pace of technological development, the adoption of automation technologies by businesses and the ability of workers to adapt to new technologies and acquire new skills.

Another potential negative implication strictly related to the use of emerging technologies, including AI, is the extent to which governments are effective in handling technology and data in a trusted and trustworthy way. This means not only being proactive in considering the potential for privacy and security breaches but also in considering any unintended consequences of particular deployments of technology to safeguard trust (OECD, 2019, 2021a, 2022).

Overall, achieving greater digital government maturity is a complex and challenging process that requires governments to overcome a number of obstacles and challenges. It is essential for governments to be prepared to adapt to changing technologies and trends and to invest in the skills and capabilities of their employees in order to stay competitive and effective in the digital age.

1.4 Achieving Greater Digital Government Maturity

The previous sections highlighted the importance for governments to take a strategic approach to the use of technology and data to achieve digital government maturity (OECD, 2014). While a future state that uses cutting-edge technology to provide seamless and proactive government in ways that bring science fiction to life is an enticing ambition, the priority for most, If not all, governments must be on creating the strongest possible foundations for the digital transformation.

The rest of this chapter will consider how countries are doing this through their efforts to develop leadership, governance, skills, shared resources and data.

1.4.1 Leadership and Vision to Set the Agenda and Build Momentum

Leadership plays a crucial role in driving digital transformation in the public sector. Effective leadership is necessary to create a vision for digital transformation, to mobilize resources and support and to overcome barriers and obstacles to change.

Digital government requires both political and administrative leadership. The most effective approaches create dedicated entities within governments that operate as the focal point for establishing a common approach and shared set of values in pursuit of digital transformation, such as the Digital Transformation Office in Türkiye, the Government Digital Service in the UK and the Agency for Digital Government in Sweden.

However, it is also absolutely critical that governments create networks of leadership throughout the public sector, identify those who might be champions for this agenda within the hierarchy of the government, and create momentum for change and transformation within individual public sector organisations.

These two factors complement one another and create an environment in which collaboration and coordination among different government agencies and other stakeholders can take place. Ensuring that there are focal points within organisations to work in partnership with a centrally coordinating function can help to reduce duplication and find routes to creating greater public value. This can also include GovTech partnerships with private sector companies and other organisations. As an example, during the COVID-19 pandemic, both the French and the Korean governments partnered with private sector companies and start-ups, reusing government data released as open data to develop apps that made it easier for citizens to identify the best locations to buy masks or book an appointment to be vaccinated.

In addition to collaboration and coordination, effective leadership in driving digital transformation also requires a focus on innovation and continuous improvement. This can include investing in the development of new technologies and approaches and fostering a culture of experimentation and risk-taking. The leadership to establish a digitally enabled state does not demand that leaders have deep technical expertise or be specialists in every aspect of digital transformation but relies on them being able to take the lead in visibly modelling a baseline understanding of digital government user skills and, more importantly, actively shaping an environment that encourages digital transformation (OECD, 2021c).

Overall, leadership plays a crucial role in driving digital transformation in the public sector. Effective leadership is necessary to create a vision for digital transformation, to mobilize resources and support and to empower civil servants to work differently and thus jointly collaborate to overcome barriers and obstacles to change.

1.4.2 Governance as the Engine of Digital Transformation

Good governance is crucial for driving digital transformation, achieving greater digital government maturity and fostering digital transformation at scale (Greenway, 2018). Governance refers to the mechanisms, processes and institutions through which governments are directed, controlled and held accountable. Effective governance is essential for ensuring that digital transformation efforts are well coordinated, transparent and accountable.

The *E-Leaders Handbook on the Governance of Digital Government* (OECD, 2021b) presents a framework that supports governments in developing and implementing strategies that underpin their efforts of establishing mature, digitally enabled states. The framework, per Figure 1.4, consists of three facets:

1. **Contextual factors**, which define country-specific characteristics—political, administrative, socio-economic, technological, policy and geographical—to be considered when designing policies to ensure a human-centred, inclusive and sustainable digital transformation of the public sector;

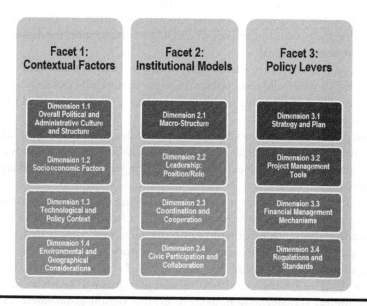

Figure 1.4   The OECD Framework on the Governance of Digital Government.

Source: OECD (2021b), The E-Leaders Handbook on the Governance of Digital Government.

2. **Institutional models** that present different institutional setups, approaches, arrangements and mechanisms within the public sector and digital ecosystem, which direct the design and implementation of digital government policies in a sustainable manner; and
3. **Policy levers**, which support governments to ensure a sound and coherent digital transformation of the public sector.

Good governance is vital for helping to ensure that digital transformation initiatives are aligned with broader government priorities and objectives. This can involve establishing clear goals and targets for digital transformation and setting up mechanisms to monitor and evaluate progress against these targets.

Good governance can help to ensure that digital transformation initiatives are well coordinated and integrated. This can involve establishing clear roles and responsibilities for different government agencies and other stakeholders and setting up mechanisms for collaboration and the sharing of best practices. With the launch of the Electronic Governance Strategy 2021–2025 and the creation of the Ministry for Digitalisation, the High Committee for Digital Transformation and the Inter-Ministerial Committee for Digitalisation, Luxembourg has established a solid foundation for governing and coordinating digital government policies. This governance approach can be pivotal to help align priorities among ministries and foster a coherent and sustainable digitalization.

Effective governance models also create the parameters by which teams in government that are focused on delivering value to their users are able to access the funding that they need. In this way, developing a robust model for digital government investments is critical.

Similarly, it is imperative that the governance for digital government creates an environment in which the expectations, in terms of the quality of services and the processes by which that quality is assessed, are clear to all those involved in providing public services.

Good governance can also help to ensure that digital transformation initiatives are transparent and accountable. This can involve establishing mechanisms for public participation and engagement and for providing regular updates and reporting on progress.

Overall, good governance is essential for driving digital transformation and achieving greater digital government maturity. Effective governance can help to ensure that digital transformation initiatives are well coordinated, transparent and accountable and can provide the framework and support that is necessary for digital transformation to be successful. Governments that are able to establish effective governance structures and practices will be better positioned to drive digital transformation, achieve greater digital government maturity and improve results but also to secure continuity and sustainability of efforts across time.

1.4.3 Investing in Talent and Skills to Create a Future-Fit Culture

Digital talent and skills are becoming increasingly important in the public sector as governments around the world seek to modernize and digitize their operations. The OECD Framework for Digital Talent and Skills in the Public Sector is a comprehensive guide that helps governments identify and address their digital talent and skills needs (OECD, 2021c). The framework consists of three pillars: establishing the right environment for public servants working on digital government, identifying the necessary skills for a digital government and implementing specific actions and enabling activities to build and maintain a workforce with the necessary digital skills.

In terms of establishing the right environment, the OECD framework emphasizes the importance of leadership, organizational structures, learning culture and ways of working in supporting a successful digital transformation. Governments should assess these areas in order to create a workplace environment that is conducive to a digital workforce, as highlighted previously in this chapter.

The second pillar of the OECD framework focuses on the necessary skills for a digital government. This includes user skills, such as the ability to use digital technologies effectively, as well as socio-emotional skills, such as teamwork and communication. Professional skills, such as data analytics and project management, and leadership skills, such as the ability to lead digital transformations, are also important. Governments should identify the areas in their organization's model of skills and competencies that need development in order to support the maturity of digital government.

The third pillar of the OECD framework addresses the specific actions and enabling activities required to build and maintain a workforce with the necessary digital skills. This includes redesigning recruitment methods, career planning, workplace mentoring and training, as well as considering the role of the public sector in developing digital talent and skills. Governments around the world have implemented a variety of strategies to address their digital talent and skills needs, including investing in training and professional development programs and implementing digital upskilling initiatives.

In order to effectively implement the OECD framework and address their digital talent and skills needs, governments must take a strategic and holistic approach. This means considering not only the technical skills needed for specific digital projects but also the broader cultural and organizational changes necessary to support a successful digital transformation.

One example of a government taking a strategic approach to developing digital talent and skills is the United Kingdom. In 2016, the UK government launched its Digital, Data, and Technology (DDaT) Profession, which aims to bring together digital, data and technology specialists from across the public sector and create a clear career path for these professionals (Government Digital Service, 2017). The DDaT Profession has established a set of professional standards and offers a range of training and development opportunities to help public sector employees develop the necessary skills for a digital government.

In Canada, the government has launched the Digital Academy, a program designed to provide public servants with the skills and knowledge needed to deliver digital services (Government of Canada, 2020). The academy offers a range of training and development opportunities, including online courses, workshops and mentorship programs. A similar model is being pursued by Denmark, Germany and Slovenia, among others, to embed the specific needs for digital transformation in the practice and activities of their Schools of Government.

The OECD Framework for Digital Talent and Skills in the Public Sector provides a valuable guide for governments looking to develop the necessary digital talent and skills in order to support their digital transformation efforts. By establishing the right environment, identifying the necessary skills and implementing specific actions and enabling activities, governments can effectively address their digital talent and skills needs and create a workforce that is equipped to succeed in the digital age.

1.4.4 Government as a Platform: Sharing Resources to Enable Transformation at Scale, and with Pace

Public services are administered by different organisations with varying governance, accountability to democratic structures or quality. As the ambition for digital transformation is improvement across the public sector, it is essential to find ways to design and deliver high-quality services at scale and with pace as opposed to slow, expensive and inefficient piecemeal approaches. As such, the OECD advocates for countries to explore the merit of government-as-a-platform approaches (see Figure 1.5) as a critical foundational dimension of a mature digital government, as described earlier in the chapter (OECD, 2020d).

According to the OECD, government as a platform can be thought about in terms of

- an ecosystem of enabling tools that supports service teams to meet needs,
- a marketplace for public services, and
- rethinking the relationship between citizens and state.

These opportunities are sequential, reflecting an iterative approach to digital transformation and the ambition for open government. Government as a platform is not solely focused on questions of technology but, in line with the digital government paradigm, considers the wider importance of creating an enabling environment to support public service teams to better meet citizen needs. Seven different areas of enabling activity have been identified as helping to effect changes to culture and philosophy while scaling the capacity to design and deliver public services that meet user needs.

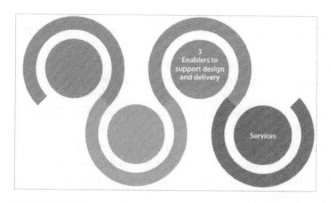

- Providing guidance and sharing good practice
- Governance processes that define and support quality public service design
- Commitment to an omnichannel strategy
- Combatting the digital divide through digital inclusion
- Long-term investment in common components and tools
- Establish data-driven public sector approaches
- Source the talent and skills for a digitally enabled state

Figure 1.5 The OECD Framework for Public Service Design And Delivery: enablers.

Source: OECD (2020a), "Digital Government in Chile—Improving Public Service Design and Delivery".

Government-as-a-platform ecosystems are the critical foundations that support and equip service design and delivery teams to meet the needs of their users. Building such foundations takes a significant commitment because the returns are not immediate, and as a result, it can be challenging to secure the necessary financial or political backing. Around the world, government-as-a-platform ecosystems showed their worth in ensuring that countries could respond to the challenges presented by COVID-19. Where governments could draw on these resources, they were a powerful demonstration of long-term digital government leadership and associated strategies to secure transformation (Welby, 2020).

A notable building block for digital government is service standards. Service standards refer to the policies, processes and practices that are used to ensure that government services are delivered consistently, effectively and efficiently. By establishing clear service standards and regularly reviewing and updating them, governments can improve the quality and reliability of their services and better meet the needs of their citizens. The OECD Good Practice Principles for Public Service Design and Delivery in the Digital Age propose that there are nine core principles which such service standards should usefully consider (OECD, 2022). They are as follows:

■ Build accessible, ethical and equitable public services that prioritize user needs rather than government needs
   1. Understand users and their needs
   2. Make the design and delivery of public services a participatory and inclusive process
   3. Ensure consistent, seamless and high-quality public services

■ Deliver with impact, at scale and with pace
4. Create conditions that help teams to design and deliver high-quality public services
5. Develop a consistent delivery methodology for public services
6. Curate an ecosystem of enabling tools, practices and resources

■ Be accountable and transparent in the design and delivery of public services to reinforce and strengthen public trust
7. Be open and transparent in the design and delivery of public services
8. Ensure the trustworthy and ethical use of digital tools and data
9. Establish an enabling environment for a culture and practice of public service design and delivery

While the nontechnical aspects of the government-as-a-platform ecosystem are absolutely critical for helping teams to focus on the value they can provide to their users, there are clear advantages to be able to rely on shared technical solutions developed to meet common needs. Areas in which such approaches can be advantageous include single government websites (such as GOV.BR, GOV.GR, GOV.IE, GOV.SI and GOV.UK), payment solutions or web infrastructure.

Digital identity is also an important building block. By investing in robust and secure digital identity systems, governments can support the delivery of digital services and ensure the protection of citizens' personal data. Creating the right conditions for the success of digital identity requires a significant technical focus, but it is also reliant on establishing a wider political and societal consensus over its potential value. The value of "secure, interoperable and trusted digital identity solutions that can provide better access to public and private sector services while promoting privacy and personal data protection" was recognized in the 2021 Declaration of the G20 Digital Ministers (G20, 2021).

1.4.5 Recognizing Data as a Strategic Asset for Unlocking Public Value

Data has become increasingly central to the digital transformation of governments around the world, and a growing number of governments are adopting whole-of-government data strategies. These include the U.S. Federal Data Strategy (FDS) that encompasses a 10-year vision for how the federal government can develop the data infrastructure for the future to accelerate the use of data and better deliver on its mission of serving the public while protecting security, privacy and confidentiality.

Digital technologies and data analytics are being used to improve the efficiency and effectiveness of government services and to better serve the needs of citizens and businesses. Data-driven approaches can help governments to better understand the needs and preferences of citizens and to design and deliver services that are more responsive to those needs (OECD, 2019).

By collecting and analyzing data from a variety of sources, governments can gain insights into the performance and impact of their programs and policies and identify opportunities for improvement. In addition to its role in improving the efficiency and effectiveness of government services, data can also contribute to transparency and accountability. The principle of "open by default" refers to the idea that government data and information should be made available to the public in a proactive and transparent manner unless there are compelling reasons for it to be kept confidential (OECD, 2020d). Open government data can help to promote accountability and transparency by providing the public with access to information about the activities of government (OECD, 2018; Ubaldi, 2013).

However, the effective use of data in driving digital transformation requires strong governance and leadership, as well as the development of clear standards and protocols for data sharing and interoperability. Governments need to ensure that data is collected and used ethically and responsibly and that appropriate safeguards are in place to protect personal data and other sensitive information.

The principle of "user-driven" design, which entails involving users in the design and development of services and regularly seeking their feedback, can also be important in ensuring that data-driven approaches meet the needs and preferences of citizens. By adopting "user-driven" and user-centred design approaches, governments can better understand the needs of their citizens and design services that are easy to use and accessible to all.

Finally, it is important for governments to be proactive in their use of data and analytics, seeking out opportunities to collect and use data to inform decision-making and drive continuous improvement. The principle of 'proactiveness' refers to the idea that governments should actively seek out and use data and analytics to inform decision-making and proactively share data and information with the public.

1.5 Conclusion

In conclusion, looking towards the future is crucial for government organizations and the broader public sector to understand how investments and decisions taken today should help achieve a sustainable digital government maturity that delivers long-lasting results for economies and societies at large with fairness and inclusiveness. Digital transformation is a complex and ongoing process that requires a long-term commitment to innovation and change, with a clear emphasis on how investments in technology will change the user experience of governments and, by extension, increase the levels of public trust and the support enjoyed by governments. Governments need to be proactive and strategic in their approach to digital transformation and must be willing to invest in the infrastructure, technology and skills that are necessary to support it.

Effective governance is crucial for driving a coherent digital transformation and achieving greater digital government maturity. Governance refers to the mechanisms, processes and institutions through which governments are directed, controlled and held accountable towards the achievement of shared objectives and based on common values. Given the horizontal nature of the digital transformation, effective governance is essential for ensuring that such transformation efforts are well-coordinated, coherent, transparent and shared. Despite being essential, establishing an adequate governance model that embraces principles of horizontality, integration and interoperability is not an easy task. As in most the cases, it is counterintuitive given the DNA of most public sectors, which are used to working vertically and in silos.

Based on the key points that have been discussed in this chapter, there are several specific recommendations for government leaders to address still-existing barriers in order to achieve digital government maturity:

■ Develop a long-term digital transformation strategy together with all parts of the public sector that is aligned with broader government priorities and objectives.
■ Invest in digital and data infrastructure and technology, such as high-speed broadband networks, cloud computing and data centres.
■ Develop the digital skills and competencies among leaders as well as government employees through training, upskilling and development programs.
■ Promote collaboration and sharing of best practices among different government agencies and with other public sector organizations.
■ Develop a digital culture that is supportive of innovation and change.
■ Establish effective governance structures and practices that support a coherent digital transformation.
■ Provide regular updates and reporting on progress towards digital government maturity.
■ Engage with citizens and other stakeholders in the broad ecosystem to promote public participation and collaboration.
■ Leverage emerging technologies, such as AI and the IoT, to improve the design and delivery of public services.
■ Monitor and evaluate the effectiveness of digital transformation initiatives, and adapt and adjust as necessary.

Overall, government organizations and the broader public sector need to achieve digital government maturity. By implementing these recommendations, government leaders can accelerate their digital transformation efforts and improve the delivery of public services.

References

Brezzi, M., González, S., Nguyen, D., & Prats, M. (2021). An updated OECD framework on drivers of trust in public institutions to meet current and future challenges. In *OECD working papers on public governance*. https://doi.org/10.1787/b6c5478c-en

Davies, T. W. (Ed.). (2019). *The state of open data: Histories and horizons*. Ottawa: African Minds and the International Development Research Centre (IDRC).

Fadi Salem, Y. J. (2013). Braving the future of government services: Paving the way forward. *The Government Summit Review*, 7–9.

G20. (2021). *G20 Italy—G20 Rome leaders' declaration*. Retrieved from https://www.g20.utoronto.ca/2021/211031-declaration.html

Government Digital Service. (2017). *Digital, Data and Technology (DDaT) profession*. Retrieved from https://www.gov.uk/government/collections/digital-data-and-technology-profession-capability-framework

Government of Canada. (2020). *Digital academy*. Retrieved from https://www.csps-efpc.gc.ca/About_us/Business_lines/digitalacademy-eng.aspx

Greenway, A., Terrett, B., Bracken, M. & Loosemore, T. (2018). *Digital transformation at scale: Why the strategy is delivery*. London: London Publishing Partnership.

Lindman, J., Berryhill, J., Welby, B., & Piccinin Barbieri, M. (2020). The uncertain promise of blockchain for government. In *OECD working papers on public governance*. Paris: OECD Publishing. https://doi.org/10.1787/d031cd67-en

McKinsey Global Institute. (2017). *Jobs lost, jobs gained: Workforce transitions in a time of automation*. Retrieved from https://www.mckinsey.com/featured-insights/future-of-work/jobs-lost-jobs-gained-what-the-future-of-work-will-mean-for-jobs-skills-and-wages

Negroponte, N. (1996). *Being digital*. New York: Vintage Books.

OECD. (2003). The e-Government imperative. In *OECD e-Government studies*. Paris: OECD Publishing. https://dx.doi.org/10.1787/9789264101197-en

OECD. (2014). *Recommendation of the council on digital government strategies, OECD/LEGAL/0406*. Paris: OECD. Retrieved from https://legalinstruments.oecd.org/en/instruments/OECD-LEGAL-0406

OECD. (2017). *Recommendation of the council on open government, OECD/LEGAL/0438*. Paris: OECD. Retrieved from https://legalinstruments.oecd.org/en/instruments/OECD-LEGAL-0438

OECD. (2018). Open government data report: Enhancing policy maturity for sustainable impact. In *OECD digital government studies*. Paris: OECD Publishing. https://dx.doi.org/10.1787/9789264305847-en

OECD. (2019). The path to becoming a data-driven public sector. In *OECD digital government studies*. Paris: OECD Publishing. https://doi.org/10.1787/059814a7-en

OECD. (2020a). Digital government in Chile—improving public service design and delivery. In *OECD digital government studies*. Paris: OECD Publishing. https://dx.doi.org/10.1787/b94582e8-en

OECD. (2020b). Digital government index: 2019 results. In *OECD public governance policy papers*. Paris: OECD Publishing. https://dx.doi.org/10.1787/4de9f5bb-en

OECD. (2020c). *Embracing innovation in government global trends 2020: Seamless government*. Retrieved from https://trends.oecd-opsi.org/wp-content/uploads/2020/11/OECD-Seamless-Government.pdf

OECD. (2020d). The OECD digital government policy framework: Six dimensions of a digital government. In *OECD public governance policy papers*. Paris: OECD Publishing. https://doi.org/10.1787/f64fed2a-en

OECD. (2021a). *OECD good practice principles for data ethics in the public sector*. Retrieved from https://www.oecd.org/gov/digital-government/good-practice-principles-for-data-ethics-in-the-public-sector.pdf

OECD. (2021b). The E-leaders handbook on the governance of digital government. In *OECD digital government studies*. Paris: OECD Publishing. https://doi.org/10.1787/ac7f2531-en

OECD. (2021c). The OECD framework for digital talent and skills in the public sector. In *OECD working papers on public governance*. Paris: OECD Publishing. https://doi.org/10.1787/4e7c3f58-en

OECD. (2022). OECD good practice principles for public service design and delivery in the digital age. In *OECD public governance policy papers*. Paris: OECD Publishing. https://doi.org/10.1787/2ade500b-en

O'Neill, C. (2017). *Weapons of math destruction*. New York: Crown Publishing Group.

Ostrovskaya, V. N. (2022). *Big data in the GovTech system*. London: Springer Nature.

Perez, C. C. (2019). *Invisible women*. New York: Abrams Press.

Ubaldi, B. (2013). Open government data: Towards empirical analysis of open government data initiatives. In *OECD working papers on public governance* (Vol. 2013). Paris: OECD Publishing. https://dx.doi.org/10.1787/5k46bj4f03s7-en

Ubaldi, B., Le Fevre, E., Petrucci, E., Marchionni, P., Biancalana, C., Hiltunen, N., . . . Yang, C. (2019). State of the art in the use of emerging technologies in the public sector. In *OECD working papers on public governance*. Paris: OECD.

United Nations. (2004). *United Nations e-Government survey*. New York: United Nations.

United States House of Representatives Committee on Oversight and Government Reform. (2017). *House report on the modernizing government technology act of 2017*. Washington, DC: United States House of Representatives.

Welby, B. (2020). *The value of 'government as a platform' in a crisis. Towards digital states*. Retrieved November 5, 2020, from https://medium.com/digital-states/the-value-of-government-as-a-platform-in-a-crisis-9556c2f2eec1

Welby, B., & Hui Yan Tan, E. (2022). Designing and delivering public services in the digital age. In *OECD going digital toolkit notes*. Paris: OECD Publishing. https://doi.org/10.1787/e056ef99-en

Chapter 2

Developing a Pipeline and Ecosystem for Digital Transformation

Our Federal Government

Jennifer Anastasoff, Sarah Philbrick, and Mark Lerner

Content

DOI: 10.1201/9781003369783-2

2.1 Introduction

The federal government is facing a stark workforce challenge with regard to technical talent. Less than 4% of the federal IT workforce is under the age of 30, while 52% of the IT workforce is over the age of 50. Only 25% of federal IT staff are identified as female compared to 44% of employees government-wide. Using more holistic measurements, the federal government's maturity with regard to the management of data and technical talent scores very low in comparison to both global public sector and global private sector measurements. These gaps in technical talent—which includes the skills and competencies needed to design, develop, operate, and manage software and digital products and services—have resulted in large-scale public failures of high impact public services, including well-known examples such as Healthcare.gov. Several strategies exist to improve the government's recruitment, management, and retention of technical talent. Furthermore, several promising pilots and initiatives across the federal government have demonstrated effective and efficient modern processes for closing the talent gap and are ready to be scaled across additional agencies.

We have experienced a profound technological revolution in the past decade. Just over 10 years ago, smartphones and tablets hit the market for the first time. Big data and working in the cloud were still in their infancy. Even with this immense technological change over the past decade, our federal government is still plagued with antiquated technical systems that make both working in the government and receiving its services frustrating. The Partnership for Public Service and Tech Talent Project's 2020 report, *Tech Talent for 21st Century Government*, highlights the importance of modern digital services and technology in the federal government in the report's introduction:

> Most federal policies and programs, from Social Security and health care to our nation's defense, rely on digital services and information technology platforms that are outdated and run ineffective software rife with security vulnerabilities. A lack of technological understanding by senior leaders in agencies—from Cabinet secretaries and deputy secretaries to explicitly technical executives—prevents much of the more than $90 billion spent

annually on technology by federal agencies from delivering results for the American people. There are numerous examples:

- *The 2013 rollout of Healthcare.gov shows how technical expertise can drive or derail policy outcomes.* Healthcare.gov initially faltered in large part due to technical systems, processes and regulations that did not focus on delivering outcomes. Unfortunately, it is only one of many such examples. It is a canary in the coal mine for presidential candidates who expect to make sweeping policy changes and are not preparing to engage the technical, digital and innovation leadership with the matching expertise to make those policies happen.
- *Social Security, which in fiscal 2019 paid almost $1.1 trillion to more than 71 million Americans, relies on antiquated and brittle systems, processes and regulations.* Protecting Social Security is often mentioned on the campaign trail. However, disability and retirement claims processing—the bread and butter of Social Security's mission—relies on 60 million lines of code written in a computer language that was created in 1959.
- *The 2014–2015 security breach at the Office of Personnel Management impacted 22.1 million federal employee records.* Not only did this breach make our country less safe, the time and focus required to recover impacted the federal government's ability to deliver on other priorities.

The federal government is aware of the need for thoughtful change. According to the 2018 President's Management Agenda, "modern information technology must function as the backbone of how Government serves the public in the digital age" (p. 7). For our government to be effective and move beyond the status quo, it must not only invest in modern digital service tools and systems but also hire and empower a skilled workforce who understand and know how to get the most from modern technology. This chapter explores the current state of the federal government's technical workforce and known gaps in talent. We also review recommendations for improving the tech expertise in government. Last, we highlight recent examples of best practices for recruiting and hiring technical talent.

2.2 What Do We Mean by Technical Talent?

In the private sector, technical talent often refers to those skillsets related to the software infrastructure, management, and design required to deliver digital services or products effectively to people. The traditional private sector triad of software engineers, product managers, and user experience designers largely covers this type of talent. Different companies may use different terms and titles or include different specializations of technical talent, such as site reliability engineers, information security engineers, interaction designers, user researchers, content strategists, software architects, sales engineers, mobile developers, web developers, and more. These distinctions also differ as seniority and responsibility increase, with titles such as "senior" or "staff" being amended to job titles or with more senior leaders in organizations taking on broader titles such as "director of product" or "vice president of creative design." While there are people working at technology companies who have skillsets outside of strictly technical skillsets (e.g., human resource managers), it's these technical competencies that enable private sector tech companies to develop innovative products and systems. Generally, this is the knowledge of how to design and build software systems, digital products, technical infrastructure, and even software projects and teams.

These same technical skills exist in government but often are labeled in ways that make them challenging to link together. Titles and labels such as IT managers, program managers, business analysts, and customer experience specialists are more common in the public sector and serve as the analogs for the technical skillsets from the private sector. In addition, when we talk about technical talent in the public sector, we also need to think about the types of technical skills and competencies that are unique to public sector contexts, such as procurement specialists, public service designers, and legislative analysts. Much like how there are nontechnical people in tech companies who make products happen, these types of skillsets are required in the public sector to deliver high-quality public services.

Public sector technical leadership structures tend to look quite different than what similar-scale tech companies use. Government agencies and offices leverage "chiefs" to lead large parts of the organization, particularly with regard to technology. Chief information officers (CIOs) are a congressionally mandated role within federal agencies who lead nearly every aspect of software usage within their agency. In addition to CIOs, it's very common to find chief technology officers, chief information security officers, and chief data officers, along with the relatively new chief customer experience officer, leading their respective areas in their agency. Each government agency has different ways of defining what the roles and responsibilities of these positions are, though they tend to be the most senior decision makers of technology and digital service delivery at the agency or component. In instances where there are identical titles in the private sector, such as chief technology officers, the similarly titled roles often both share technical competencies but differ significantly in responsibilities.

2.3 A Known Gap in Technical Talent

The technical and digital workforce in an agency, in partnership with program leaders and experts, is at the core of every agency's journey to become a modern workplace and to deliver modern digital public services. The success of any government agency's mission depends on having employees with the right technical skills in the right positions, at the right time, and with the right resources available to them. The

Partnership for Public Service and the Boston Consulting Group conducted a survey called the Federal Data and Digital Maturity Index in 2021 that assessed how federal agencies recruit, hire, develop, engage, reward, and retain their data and technical workforce. The goal of this survey was to help agencies understand where they were performing well and where they might allocate resources to improve.

The findings of that survey were published in the Partnership for Public Service's April 2022 report *Federal Data Maturity: Agencies Assess Where They Stand.* This report showed that agencies "aim to improve dramatically in the next 5 years." The overall score for federal agencies, which measured their current data and digital maturity against a model developed by the Partnership for Public Service, landed at 36 points out of 100. By comparison, the global public sector was at 47 of 100 and the global private sector at 54 of 100. For federal agencies to improve their standing, they will need to introduce dramatic changes in how they hire and support data and technical staff.

When it came to assessing human capital approaches to managing the data and technical workforce, scores across all survey components were low. The component measuring "Leadership and Cultural Change"[1] received the highest mark at 30 points out of 100. The "Leadership and Cultural Change" component of the survey evaluated how effectively agencies developed the leadership acumen of their data and technical workforce, promoted diversity and inclusion among this group of employees, and ensured that everyone in the organization has a base level of data and technical fluency. As shown in Table 2.1, the component measuring "Organizational Transformation," which scored the lowest at 25 points out of 100, assessed how thoroughly employees with data and technical expertise are involved in an agency's projects.

Thankfully, federal agencies have set lofty targets for their improved scores in this survey, demonstrating a desire to make the necessary drastic changes. In other words, federal agencies want to grow the maturity of their data and technical workforces over the next five years. As the report notes, "the average target maturity score for human capital was 67 points out of 100—a 39-point increase over the current level. And the target maturity scores for all six human capital building blocks were at least 37 points higher than current levels, according to the survey. Notably, the

Table 2.1 Federal Data and Digital Maturity Scores

Human Capital Building Block	Current Maturity Score	Target Maturity Score	Difference
Leadership and cultural change	30	68	38
Talent acquisition	29	66	37
People strategy	29	67	38
Performance, rewards, and engagement	28	66	38
People development	26	66	40
Organizational transformation	25	70	45

Organizational Transformation category has the lowest current maturity score, but the highest target score." These survey results and target scores highlight both the need and desire for transformative change in the federal technical workforce over the next five years.

2.4 Understanding the Gap in Technical Talent

The Partnership for Public Service discusses the federal government's workforce challenges in its report, *Roadmap for Renewing Our Federal Government*. As the roadmap notes, "The federal government struggles to recruit, hire, and retain diverse talent with the skills needed to meet the complex challenges facing our nation today and in the future." The challenges outlined in the roadmap are not unique to technical talent—across all kinds of talent, federal employee engagement lags behind that of the private sector, agencies do not maximize use of existing hiring authorities, and the federal compensation system is not aligned to the broader labor market. Additionally, hiring is a long and arduous process, as noted in the roadmap: "It takes government an average of 98 days to bring new talent onboard—more than double the time in the private sector."

The federal government also lags overall in recruiting and retaining early talent. The Partnership for Public Service highlights in the blog post "The Redesigned gogovernment.org and Why We Need More Young People in the Federal Government":

> Just over 7% of all permanent, full-time federal employees are under the age of 30, compared to more than 19.7% of all private sector employees. Of full-time employees under 30 who voluntarily quit federal service in fiscal year 2020, over 75% did so with less than two years of federal tenure. Meanwhile, about one in three federal workers are eligible to retire in the next five years.

Our government needs early-career talent to bring new skills that will help the country rise to the significant challenges of the day and prepare for what lies ahead. The gaps we see in early talent overall are even more staggering for the government's technical workforce. According to data published by the Office of Personnel Management and analyzed by the Tech Talent Project and Partnership for Public Service, less than 4% of the federal IT workforce is under the age of 30, while 52% of the IT workforce is over the age of 50 (Tech Talent Project, 2022).

In addition to age diversity challenges, the federal technical workforce also has gender and racial diversity challenges. The overwhelming majority of this workforce is male. Only 25% of federal IT staff identified as female compared to 44% of employees government-wide. Just over 60% of federal IT staff identify as White, consistent with 61% of employees government-wide.

Federal spending data also indicates there is room for the federal government to expand its internal IT capabilities, shown by the large amount of money spent on external IT labor costs. The US budgeted $20.8 billion for external labor costs in fiscal year 2022 compared to $8.35 billion budgeted for internal labor costs during the same year (Tech Talent Project, 2022). Federal agencies must attract, hire, and retain top talent from diverse backgrounds to tackle our country's most pressing challenges.

2.5 Strategies to Strengthen the Federal Government's Technical Workforce

The Partnership for Public Service's *Mobilizing Tech Talent* (2018) identified seven strategies to pivot our federal government through a technical talent transition and strengthen its technical workforce. These strategies are as follows:

1. Hire, appoint, and empower leaders with knowledge of modern technology.
2. Use private-sector best practices to recruit and hire tech talent.
3. Create the conditions for success.
4. Upgrade the technical skills and competencies of the existing workforce.
5. Build the brand and tell more stories.
6. Remove structural barriers and make operational excellence possible.
7. Consider ideas for future exploration.

Here, we have republished the first six strategies to highlight proven strategies for creating a digital transformation pipeline in government (Partnership for Public Service, 2018).

2.5.1 Hire, Appoint, and Empower Leaders with Knowledge of Modern Technology

It is difficult to think of any major government mission or agency responsibility, whether it's responding to an Ebola outbreak, delivering services to veterans, or formulating transportation policy, that doesn't rely on and benefit from technology expertise. Having senior leaders who understand technology and its importance to the mission is fundamental for ensuring a high level of government effectiveness.

Therefore, to roll out programs and policies, it is necessary to have a combination of political appointees and career leaders with successful track records using technology to accomplish goals on a large scale. It also is vital to hire technical experts into roles where they are integrally involved with both program execution and the core senior leadership team, and where they participate in policy discussions from day one. This ensures that those leading the development of critical policies understand the constraints and opportunities presented by existing and emerging technologies. Familiarity with and appreciation for modern technology in top leadership positions is so critical for success that such expertise should be no more than one step removed from an agency's leader.

This is true whether a program is being executed by government employees or contractors. Even when buying private-sector services, the government needs a critical mass of top in-house technical talent. Without these skills, agencies will not have the expertise to fully understand the solutions they need or evaluate which contractors are best to deliver those solutions. Agencies also need employees with the technical knowledge and skills to manage contractors efficiently and drive continuous improvement in agency operations.

The level of knowledge necessary, of course, depends on the person's leadership role. A Cabinet secretary or agency director, for instance, does not need to know how to write code, but should understand the importance of cloud storage. However, program directors and others responsible for moving the immigration system online, for example, will be most effective if they understand in great detail how to use the cloud and are fluent in security protocols and website reliability requirements.

Similarly, agency chief information officers should be highly skilled technological managers who can successfully handle existing technical operations, infrastructure and services. They should be able to work effectively with leaders across the organization to modernize service delivery and the approach to buying and implementing technology infrastructure. Crucially, they also should be able to alter the expectations of government digital services. These services should be useful, intuitive and available 24/7. Optimal candidates will have led organizational migrations from old systems to modern ones and have a track record of collaborating successfully with operations, product and engineering leaders to support the delivery of digital services.

While agency leaders must drive their own technology transformations, government-wide leadership also is critical. As former Office of Management and Budget Director Shaun Donovan noted in his 2017 exit memo, Agency and government-wide leadership [must] build, empower, and support these teams by knocking down roadblocks rather than by 'gatekeeping.' This includes leadership establishing rapid escalation procedures for teams to get help with roadblocks as they are encountered—to avoid wasting time. (Donovan, 2017)

Agencies also have a support system that can be of assistance, including the federal chief information officer and federal chief information security officer within OMB, the General Services Administration which offers a variety of shared technology services, and the Office of Personnel Management, which can assist agencies in the hiring of technical experts.

To tackle the complex problems facing our country, it is critical that the government hire and empower technical leaders. While progress has been made, the federal government is in the very early stages of developing its digital capacity and leadership. Ultimately, the goal is to raise the bar for what is expected of senior executives, and this starts by hiring people who know what is possible. According to the Donovan exit memo, "the probability of an agency being able to successfully modernize without such leaders is zero" (Partnership for Public Service, 2018, p. 13).

2.5.2 Use Private-Sector Best Practices to Recruit and Hire Tech Talent

Government hiring is often slow and painful for applicants, and jarringly different from the private sector. In the technology industry, the current best practice is that it should take no longer than 30 days from the time a candidate expresses interest in a role to making an offer.[2] In some cases, this can happen within a week. In the federal government, the Office of Personnel Management estimates that the average time to hire [in 2017 was] about 106 days, and it often can take much longer (Donovan, 2017).

From the perspective of a candidate, the length of the hiring process puts the government at an immediate disadvantage. This disadvantage is compounded by other factors, including the need to submit an extensive government-style resume and minimal communication from HR during the decision-making process. Those hired also have to fill out lengthy background investigation forms.

In addition, public-sector work has a poor reputation among potential technology candidates who have heard that government is intractable and that real impact is impossible. This makes potential candidates less inclined to apply or to stick around through setbacks in the hiring process. And even when highly qualified technical candidates apply, agencies often struggle to successfully identify those individuals because they do not have the adequate expertise to evaluate these skill sets. Thus, any agency that wants to compete with the private sector for top technology talent must exert considerable effort to counteract these disadvantages.

The U.S. Digital Services (USDS) found that the best way to do this was to create their own talent teams to manage the recruiting and hiring process in-house, meet all compliance requirements including veterans' preference and coordinate with agency HR teams when necessary, rather than rely on HR to manage the whole process. The teams are intimately familiar with effective industry practices, prioritize active recruiting, provide an excellent candidate experience and lead a rigorous selection process based on technical evaluation by subject matter experts.

Ultimately, through building an internal team to run recruiting and hiring, USDS hired nearly 300 high-caliber staff members in its first three years, about half of whom were actively recruited. USDS reduced time from application to offer from about 152 days to 34 days over that period of time—in line with the tech industry—and maintained a high candidate satisfaction rating even during the change of presidential administration and a government-wide hiring freeze (Partnership for Public Service, 2018 p. 16).

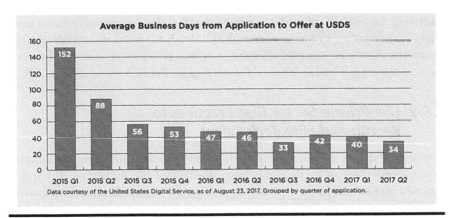

Figure 2.1 **Average business days from application to offer at U.S. Digital Services (USDS).**

2.5.3 *Create the Conditions for Success*

Bringing in the right people with the right technical expertise will have little impact if they aren't working on the right problems and empowered to be successful. To make this possible, the U.S. Digital Services worked not only to hire great people to partner with dedicated civil servants, but also created conditions that allowed them to make a difference.

Upon arrival at USDS, new employees are told that success is not guaranteed and failure is expected at least some of the time. At the same time, USDS leaders work with staff to do everything they can to set them up for success, such as securing top-level executive support and not sending anyone into a project alone. There are a set of baseline conditions without which any project is almost certainly doomed to fail. It is critical that government leaders ensure that all technical projects meet these baseline conditions to give all employees, including technical experts, the best possible chance of having an impact.

Through experience, USDS developed a few core principles:

- *Ensure executive air cover.* Approval and endorsement from senior agency leaders, particularly secretaries and deputy secretaries, is essential to institute technology changes that will affect services and internal operations. This includes a direct line to those who can make decisions and clear obstacles.
- *Never send anyone into agencies alone.* Always send in teams with the skills necessary to do the job.
- *Listen to the civil servants.* No problem can be solved without a partnership with civil servants. Many federal employees have been working on ambitious projects for years and bring vital expertise.
- *Create a sense of belonging, shared identity, culture and community.* The close-knit and collaborative ideals of the USDS culture generated interest from

talent within the technology industry as well as passion for the work and loyalty to the cause. The focus by USDS on values helped retain people longer than they intended to work in government, increasing impact.

Based on their experiences, USDS officials developed a set of values for leading successful projects across government. These tenets are core to how USDS teams approach their work and make decisions and have become vital conditions for success:

- *Hire and empower great people.* Both elements are prerequisites of success—hiring people with the technical ability needed to get the job done, and empowering both the new hires and the people already on the job to make informed changes. Skipping either of these steps will ultimately lead to failure.
- *Find the truth, tell the truth.* Understanding the actual status of a project, whether it is good, bad or ugly, is vital. USDS team members are committed to presenting the realities of a given situation in full transparency and holding each other accountable.
- *Optimize for results, not optics.* If how things look is more important than achieving positive outcomes, a project will probably fail. This also means accepting and even applauding failures that lead to future successes.
- *Go where the work is.* By working directly in and with agencies, the U.S. Digital Services can impact citizens who most need government services. This starts with working directly with civil servants.
- *Design with users, not for them.* Every project should start and end with the needs of the users, not the needs of the agency or the developer.
- *Create momentum.* Work toward incremental, achievable goals on tightly scoped, outcome-oriented projects. Any project that looks like it is trying to boil the ocean will probably fail, but you can achieve great things by starting small.

The work of transforming how the government handles technology projects is incredibly hard. There are those who are resistant to change, the tools available trail behind the private sector and success requires relentless persistence. But with the right conditions in place and the right team on the ground, these challenges become exciting opportunities to improve the lives of millions of Americans. In order to truly have an impact on the government's ability to implement its priorities, creating these conditions is essential (Partnership for Public Service, 2018, p. 20).

2.5.4 Upgrade the Technical Skills and Competencies of the Existing Workforce

The U.S. Digital Services model of recruiting a small number of people with technical skills is necessary but not sufficient to improve the federal government's capacity to design and execute technology projects. To make sustainable improvements, the government also needs to invest in and upgrade the skills of the existing technical workforce. This will require raising the expectations of political and career executives as to what can be achieved through technology as well as a concerted effort to improve the capabilities of the current IT workforce.

2.5.4.1 Raise Expectations for Senior Political and Career Executives

Senior executives should embrace the best practices of the technology industry when it comes to serving the needs of people, whether it involves obtaining health benefits, receiving Social Security checks, applying for student aid or getting a small business loan. Yet the people-facing technology standards in government lag far behind the private sector. It is up to senior executives to push for the higher standards. For example, major websites such as Google, Amazon and Microsoft Azure commit to at least 99.9 percent uptime for their websites—meaning the website would go down no more than 8.75 hours a year. When healthcare.gov launched, it had a 91 percent uptime rate. At the time, *The Atlantic* magazine described the situation this way: "Imagine if Google.com randomly stopped returning search requests for two hours, every day, and you would be imagining a more reliable website than the one that [was] introduced"(Meyer, 2015). According to a site that monitors uptime of 1,000 websites across industries, many government websites are unavailable for four days a year, an uptime rate of 98.9 percent. As long as this is seen as acceptable performance, it will not improve.

2.5.4.2 Invest in IT Employees

Tens of thousands of people work in federal government IT, many of whom do not yet have the modern technical experience to bring government technology into the 21st century. And with technology constantly changing, bringing existing technical workers up to date on what is possible [today] will be critical, but it won't be enough. Therefore, the government must build out the most important skills and competencies of the existing IT workforce, invest in training that works and create a culture of continuous learning.

Unfortunately, chief human capital officers (CHCOs) across government do not believe they have "reliable information on how much they spend on training and for what purposes," according to a 2012 General Accountability Office report. This makes it difficult to even begin comparing a professional development return on investment between the federal government and the private sector. Furthermore, GAO said some CHCOs reported they did not prioritize training so that the most important needs are met first and they did not evaluate the benefits of training.

In addition, in order to be promoted to more senior levels of project or program management, federal employees may have to receive certifications that teach and reinforce waterfall methodologies—a sequential, linear process of project management. This approach works for specific types of large projects such as buildings, bridges and battleships, but has been shown to be inefficient for building quality software and leading other types of rapidly evolving projects (18F, 2018).

The federal government can learn from large companies that are facing similar challenges and are investing heavily in reskilling. As Scott Smith, AT&T's senior vice president of human resources operations, said,

> You can go out to the street and hire for the skills, but we all know that the supply of technical talent is limited and everybody is going after it. Or you can do your best to step up and reskill your existing workforce to fill the gap.
>
> (Donovan & Benko, 2016)

AT&T has pursued several broad strategies to ensure that it has the workforce it needs to be competitive. AT&T created incentives for skill development by having managers clarify future roles and goals for teams and by aligning the people processes around those goals (Caminiti, 2018). AT&T managers documented gaps between the current profile of their teams and future role profiles for themselves and their teams. They focused performance metrics on how a role more directly meets business goals, raised performance expectations, and changed compensation plans to lower the impact of seniority and increase the impact of high demand skills to motivate high performers. AT&T is offering their employees tools such as tuition assistance; online courses, nano-certificates and master's degrees in high demand technical specialties such as software engineering and web development; career profile tools that allow workers to identify the skills they need for new jobs, and the ability to connect with nearby employees with similar skills; and career intelligence tools that allow workers to analyze hiring trends within the company.

The federal government should make similar investments to ensure wide employee understanding of the utility and tradeoffs of cloud computing, agile methodologies, human-centered design and the methods associated with building effective software over time (Partnership for Public Service & Accenture). Given the rapid pace of technological change, the federal government will need to make a commitment to support lifelong learning.

Lazlo Bock, former head of People for Google, identified three key areas of effective professional development. The federal government would be a much more attractive employer for technologists if it invested in all three.

■ *Build a culture of deliberate practice* in which the goal is continuous improvement over time with direct feedback.
■ *Have your best people teach.* For example, have those who have effectively built cloud platforms and products in government or utilized agile methodologies to develop useful software, share their experience and bring their colleagues

up to speed. The U.S. Digital Services has engaged civil servants in learning how to build effective software, first in the development of the Digital Services Playbook and then in the development of the Automated Testing Playbook.

■ *Only invest in courses that change behavior.* Bock identifies four levels of testing to determine if a behavior has changed, with the ideal test being whether the behavior change has improved outcomes. (Partnership for Public Service, 2018, pp. 21–22)

2.5.5 Build the Brand and Tell More Stories

When people think of top technical talent in government, they often think of organizations like NASA and the Defense Advanced Research Projects Agency because those are agencies with successful technology stories that have been chronicled in books and movies. But the federal government has many other compelling stories about technology it could and should tell if it hopes to recruit a critical mass of talented technologists. These stories fall into a number of categories:

A. *How technology has changed the way government delivers services. These stories inspire readers to see how their work could change the lives of millions of Americans:*
   - Redesigning the application process for Americans living in poverty to receive critical benefits[3]
   - Releasing FBI crime information through an interactive website that includes trend data, datasets for download and an open API so the public can build tools using the data.[4]
   - Digitizing the application for veterans to apply for health care from the Department of Veterans Affairs.[5]
   - Building tools to improve communication and coordination among NATO allies in Afghanistan.[6]

B. *Technology industry leaders who brought best practices to government, demonstrating the impact of these individuals:*
   - Kurt del Bene, former Microsoft executive, who became Chief Information Officer at the VA. [We added this to the text to provide a 2022 example.]
   - DJ Patil, who became the first chief data scientist of the United States after executive roles at LinkedIn, Greylock Partners, Skype and eBay.
   - Matt Cutts, former head of the web spam team at Google, who became acting administrator of the USDS.
   - Megan Smith, who served two years as chief technology officer of the United States after working as a vice president at Google X.

C. *Federal leaders who found success partnering with the Digital Services experts, showing the value technologists can add for career civil servants and agencies:*
- Former IRS Deputy Chief of Staff Elaine Ho, who helped the USDS team at IRS pull together various stakeholders and led the reorganization of the agency's research and data analytics office before becoming the USDS chief of staff.
- Renata Maziarz, the director for data transparency at the Department of the Treasury, who was responsible for implementing the DATA Act with assistance from 18F (18F.gsa.gov).
- Numerous VA civil servants partnering with USDS who have been vital to reaching and serving veterans through the Vets.gov platform.[7]
- The many alumni of the digital IT acquisition professional training program who are bringing best practices in procuring digital services to agencies around the government.[8]

D. *Stories of the successes that government will only be able to achieve with qualified technical expertise. Future technology professionals will have the opportunity to:*
- Protect the United States from critical threats such as cyber warfare and engineered pathogens.
- Allow Americans to live longer, healthier lives by improving our ability to diagnose, treat, prevent and cure diseases such as Alzheimer's and cancer. Initiatives like those furthering precision medicine have begun to explore ways to use data to tailor medicine to individuals and groups.[9]
- Provide veterans and their doctors with easily searchable and readable medical records during and after their service.
- Make paying for federal education loans as intuitive as paying a phone bill.

(Partnership for Public Service, 2018, p. 23)

2.5.6 Remove Structural Barriers and Make Operational Excellence Possible

The best technologists in the world will not be effective without the tools and an environment that allows them to be successful. The tools can be as simple as having an email, login and computer on the first day at work or as industry specific as having modern developer tools and an up-to-date tech stack—a combination of software products and programming languages used to create web or mobile applications.

An environment that allows a technologist to be successful also is one that allows professionals to purchase necessary goods or services, or launch and iterate on a product quickly in order to meet the needs of citizens. Yet in government, structural barriers in procurement and compliance requirements can undermine the productivity of technologists.

Former Office of Management and Budget Director Shaun Donovan noted that there should be a shift in approach that requires government to embrace secure and reliable cloud services, customer-centered design, agile development, shared services, a 'continuous upgrade' model of technology refresh and replacement, and enhanced cybersecurity while retaining the ability of agencies to focus on their mission goals and objectives.

Government should not only embrace these concepts, but also remove the barriers to realizing these goals. Below are a [couple of] examples where processes created to improve critical areas such as security and accountability have in practice led to a government that is less secure, accountable and effective

2.5.6.1 Procurement

Government procurement processes are unable to keep up with changing technical and user needs. Existing processes call for documenting all facets of a project in detail before a user ever engages with the product. This approach makes it exceedingly difficult to build easy-to-use, secure and effective digital products (USDS, 2016). In 2014, Dugan Petty, the former CIO and procurement director in the Oregon state government, noted that

> the alignment of technology and procurement has always had a lot of tension to it. Often, it's about whether the jurisdiction has met the procurement laws first, and perhaps secondly whether or not they actually achieved the outcomes they were looking for. (Brown, 2017)

Moreover, federal vendor approval processes are often based on a written proposal, not the demonstrated ability of the company to deliver results or create the needed product for citizens.

One solution is to adopt procurement vehicles that support iterative development like the agile blanket purchase agreement vendor pool piloted by 18F. The blanket purchase agreement helps agencies fill a repeated need for services or products with trusted suppliers. 18F created a pool of trusted agile vendors by requiring the companies to demonstrate their knowledge, create a technical product within a matter of weeks and show the code associated with that product rather than requiring hundreds of pages of written submissions. 18F's assessment team had the opportunity to see if a product worked and used that knowledge to choose vendors who had demonstrated their abilities.

Creating new procurement vehicles won't be enough without hiring in-house technical talent to buy and effectively manage technical products. Donovan made the case for reforming technology procurement. In an exit memo, he said the government needs a critical mass of top-flight in-house technical talent in order to be a good buyer of private sector services—otherwise, government will do a poor job of specifying the solutions it truly needs, won't be able to evaluate accurately which contractors are the best ones to deliver those solutions, will manage contractors badly, and won't be able to drive continuous iteration of how agencies work to support execution of the latest best practices (e.g., today, moving agencies from 'waterfall' to agile development, from monolithic systems to modular systems, from repetitive rebuilding of services to reuse of services, including extant, commercially available, cloud-based services).

2.5.6.2 Authority to Operate

A new product or service in government requires a designated authority to formally accept responsibility and the risk to agency operations. This is done via a process known as Authority to Operate. Within government, it is not unusual for this authorization process to take six to eighteen months, along with hundreds of pages of documentation. This means, for example, that there are often lengthy delays in securing approval to launch a website. The burdensome requirements of this system end up discouraging the creation of new systems and delaying the launch of those that are built. This also creates an environment which reinforces and locks projects into a relatively linear sequential design approach (USDS, 2016).

The Authority to Operate process requires an executive to sign off on a product, declaring that security and operational risks have been mitigated before the product can be launched. In practice, this makes executives very wary of signing an authorization unless all current and perceived future risks are mitigated, at times leading teams to spend months brainstorming and attempting to mitigate theoretical risks. In the private sector, understanding and addressing potential risks is usually an iterative process that involves testing products with a small number of users to identify weaknesses, fixing those weaknesses and then testing the product again. This is a much more efficient and effective way of identifying actual risks. 18F initially found that this process took an average of six months for every system that needed to be approved within its division of the General Services Administration. To shorten the time, 18F invested significant energy to reduce the time required to secure authorization from six months to one month. (Partnership for Public Service, 2018, pp. 24–25)

2.6 New Approaches for Identifying, Recruiting, and Hiring Tech Talent at Scale

The lessons outlined previously are largely from the experiences of federal digital service teams. In addition to the talent innovations from those teams, exciting recent work to build a transformational pipeline for technical talent has been happening through collaborations between the Office of Personnel Management (OPM), the General Services Administration (GSA), and other government agencies. For example, the GSA and OPM work together to publish a data dashboard on selection outcomes and assessments, allowing agencies to understand which assessments have been the most effective. Additionally, a new group at OPM has been created to focus on improving the hiring experience for candidates. In April 2021, OPM and the Office of Management and Budget invested in "talent teams," which former associate director of performance and personnel management at the Office of Management and Budget Pam Coleman explained will "connect agencies and hiring managers with the best talent to meet mission needs" (Alms, 2021). Furthermore, the GSA developed a new program, the U.S. Digital Corps, specifically geared towards hiring early career technical talent, closing one of the most pressing gaps in this space. These new collaborations and initiatives are paving the way for agencies to identify and hire technical talent at scale.

In addition to these initiatives for hiring large amounts of technical talent, new efforts have focused on building the bench of strong technical leadership roles across the federal government. One of the current effective methods for bringing in senior level technical leadership is to pair nontechnical senior leadership with technical advisors. For example, many federal agencies have prioritized strong data leadership by bringing in Chief Data Officers as a critical step towards leveraging machine learning or artificial intelligence in the future. In addition, the U.S. government created an official job classification as "Data Scientist" in December 2021 in order to attract data scientists as part of the digital talent pipeline. Other positions, including Chief Information Officers and Senior Advisors for Delivery, have been used to bring strong technical expertise and leadership skills in to directly support non-technical leadership to reach agencies' ambitious data and digital goals for the future.

Senior technical leaders and advisors cannot alone modernize their agencies. They need experienced technical talent at a scale large enough to manage digital services and infrastructure across their agencies. To build and maintain these modern technical workforces, government agencies must actively recruit qualified candidates while improving the speed of hiring to compete with the private sector. One of the ways the federal government has begun to do this is through piloting approaches to interview and qualify large numbers of technical experts simultaneously and allowing multiple agencies to hire from that shared pool of qualified candidates. The pilot, called Subject Matter Expertise Qualifications Assessments (SME-QA), has shown promising results in early tests, and is one of the most innovative hiring techniques developed by the Office of Personnel Management and the U.S. Digital Service.

2.7 Best Practice: The Use of SME-QA

Federal agencies and their HR specialists have historically struggled to determine whether applicants are qualified. Of all the job announcements that are made by every government agency, 93% of them use self-assessments to determine whether applicants are qualified and eligible for a role. Of those job announcements, only 51% result in a job offer to an applicant (GSA, 2022). This means that a significant amount of energy is put into assessing candidates for a job, and even after all of the assessments separate qualified candidates from unqualified ones, roughly half of those job announcements don't lead to a job offer from the hiring manager. Because of this, the level of effort it takes for one agency to hire a few strong technical experts can be high. However, agencies that use the SME-QA (usds.gov/projects/smeqa) process leverage reviews and assessments from technical experts, rather than self-assessments, to assess the technical qualifications of individuals who are applying for positions within the federal government. They evaluate an individual's skills and experience related to the subject matter area they are applying for and provide that information early in the hiring process. Multiple individuals that pass the assessment then are considered by multiple agencies for permanent positions, making the experience more effective and efficient for both the federal government and the candidate.

In 2019, the U.S. Digital Service tested the SME-QA process with both the Department of Health and Human Services, and the National Park Service at the Department of the Interior. They found that while fewer applicants were assessed to be qualified for the roles, more applicants were actually selected to be hired. In addition, the average number of days needed to make a candidate selection at the Department of the Interior dropped from 45 days to 16 days.[1]

One year later, the Office of Personnel Management, the U.S. Digital Service, and the Chief Data Officer Council ran an experiment in government-wide hiring of data scientists that attracted over 500 applicants. From this group of applicants, 105 data scientists were assessed as qualified, 50 were hired into roles across government agencies. The success of these efforts has led to some agencies incorporating SME-QA even further via hiring assessment measurement experts, often for the first time, into their talent teams.

2.8 Conclusion

The need for expanded and empowered technical talent in our federal government is clear. We cannot allow the continuation of the trend of failed high-impact digital services, which highlight all too well the need for technical talent. Technical talent may look slightly different in the context of the federal government—with language such as Digital Service Experts and IT Managers being used instead of private sector titles like Software Engineers and Product Managers—but the underlying skillsets of software development, information security, digital design, and technology infrastructure all remain as needed in the public sector as they do in the private sector. Agencies now have effective and repeatable measurements to understand their current state in comparison with each other, and with the global public and private sector. They understand where they lag behind, they know there is room for improvement, and most Importantly and reassuringly, they have set high goals for themselves in their improvement of hiring and managing technical talent.

The challenges ahead of these federal agencies are sizeable, particularly when it comes to ensuring that the gap in technical talent is filled with diverse talent. The tech talent gap is pronounced across multiple verticals of diversity, including age and gender. Additionally, the federal government's current investments in technical talent skew heavily towards outsourced talent rather than investments in in-house employees.

Fortunately, there are documented and effective strategies for improving the agency technical workforce. The federal government can and should seek to empower modern technical leaders, use best practices to recruit and hire tech talent, and upgrade the technical skills of the existing workforce, among other strategies. Some initiatives in government have already paved the way for others to follow, as well. Forward-leaning agencies are already making great progress via the adoption of modern best practices such as talent teams, transparent hiring process data, and subject matter expert assessments. While there is much more progress to be made—and many more agencies for it to be made in—the path is clear, and the desire is present. We have all the ingredients we need for a successful future of technical talent in our federal government.

Acknowledgment

This chapter is a compilation of work. The authors drew directly from the Partnership for Public Service and Tech Talent Project related writings: *Mobilizing Tech Talent* (Partnership for Public Service and Tech Talent Project, 2018), *Tech Talent for 21st Century Government* (Partnership for Public Service and Tech Talent Project, 2020), and *Federal Data and Digital Maturity: Agencies Assess Where They Stand* (Partnership for Public Service, 2022).

Notes

1 Survey questions were grouped into six categories, or building blocks, each reflecting a part of the human capital life cycle. A category score is calculated by taking the average score of its component questions.
2 It takes 30–60 days to process a strong candidate from first contact to formal offer, according to Dan Portillo, talent partner at Greylock Partners. Outside of 60 days, hiring a competitive candidate becomes difficult.
3 The U.S. Digital Service, "Redesigning the journey to critical benefits for Americans in poverty," Medium, January 5, 2017. Retrieved from https://bit.ly/2LlC8aP
4 18F, "Federal Bureau of Investigation: Opening up crime data," 2017. Retrieved from https://bit.ly/2Of I6Yk

5 The U.S. Digital Service, "Introducing a new digital application for health care at VA," Medium, July 1, 2016. Retrieved from https://bit.ly/2OdcF0K
6 Issie Lapowsky, "Meet the nerds coding their way through the Afghanistan War," Wired, May 27, 2017. Retrieved from https://bit.ly/2sjiBcV
7 The U.S. Digital Service, "Meet the Digital Service at VA Champions: May 2018," Medium, May 10, 2018. Retrieved from https://bit.ly/2LPlHzI
8 TechFAR Hub, "Digital IT Acquisition Professional Training (DITAP) Alumni." Retrieved from https://bit.ly/2OhCjBI
9 Centers for Disease Control and Prevention, "Precision Medicine: What Does it Mean for Your Health?" 2018. Retrieved from https://bit.ly/2QsrihN

References

18F. (2018). *Modern software product development.* Retrieved from https://agile.18f.gov/modern-software-product-development/

18F. *Agile blanket purchase agreement.* Retrieved from https://bit.ly/2CRPUhf

Alms, N. (2021, June 23). Biden HR strategy features new agency 'talent teams.' *FCW.* Retrieved from https://fcw.com/workforce/2021/06/biden-hr-strategy-features-new-agency-talent-teams/258335/

Anastasoff, J., & Smith, J. (2018, September). *Mobilizing tech talent: Hiring technologists to power better government.* Partnership for Public Service. Retrieved from https://ourpublicservice.org/wp-content/uploads/2018/09/Mobilizing_Tech_Talent-2018.09.26.pdf

Bock, L. (2015, April). *Work rules!: Insights from inside Google that will transform how you live and lead.* Grand Central Publishing.

Brown, J. (2014, March 4). *Bringing innovation to procurement.* Retrieved from https://bit.ly/1e5ZF3t

Bryan, K., & Pfund, A. (2022, May 16). The redesigned gogovernment.org and why we need more young people in the federal government. *Partnership for Public Service.* Retrieved from https://ourpublicservice.org/blog/redesigned-gogovernment-org-and-why-we-need-more-young-people-in-government/

Caminiti, S. (2018, March 13). *AT&T's $1 billion Gambit: Retraining nearly half its workforce.* Retrieved from www.cnbc.com/2018/03/13/atts-1-billion-gambit-retraining-nearly-half-its-workforce.html

Donovan, J., & Benko, C. (2016, October). AT&T's talent overhaul. *Harvard Business Review.* Retrieved from https://hbr.org/2016/10/atts-talent-overhaul

Donovan, S. (2017, January 5). *Office of management and budget cabinet exit memorandum.* U.S. Office of Management and Budget. Retrieved from https://obamawhitehouse.archives.gov/sites/default/files/omb/reports/cabinet_exit_memorandum.pdf

GSA. (2022). *Hiring assessment and selection outcomes dashboard* [Data set]. Data to Decisions. Retrieved from https://d2d.gsa.gov/report/hiring-assessment-and-selection-outcome-dashboard

Meyer, R. (2015, July 9). The secret startup that saved the worst website in America. *The Atlantic.* Retrieved from https://bit.ly/2o1650K

Partnership for Public Service. (n.d.). *Roadmap for renewing our Federal Government: Workforce*. Retrieved from https://ourpublicservice.org/our-solutions/roadmap-for-renewing-our-federal-government/workforce/

Partnership for Public Service & Accenture. *Customer experience*. Retrieved from https://bit.ly/2x8qk2m

Partnership for Public Service & Tech Talent Project. (2020, April). *Tech talent for 21st century government*. Retrieved from https://ourpublicservice.org/wp-content/uploads/2020/04/Tech-Talent-for-21st-Century-Government.pdf

Schulman, L. D., Garcia, D., & Powder, M. (2022, April). *Federal data maturity: Agencies assess where they stand*. Partnership for Public Service. Retrieved from https://ourpublicservice.org/publications/federal-data-and-digital-maturity/

Tech Talent Project. (2022). *Improve federal CX: Agency hiring data*. Retrieved from https://techtalentproject.org/improve-federal-cx/agency-hiring-data/

The U.S. Digital Service (USDS). (2016). *Transforming federal IT procurement*. Retrieved from www.usds.gov/report-to-congress/2016/procurement/

United States Government Accountability Office. (2012). *Information security: Improvements needed in NRC's oversight of contractor systems (Report No. GAO-12–878)*. Retrieved from www.gao.gov/assets/gao-12-878.pdf

U.S. Office of Management and Budget. (2018). *President's management agenda*. Retrieved from https://trumpadministration.archives.performance.gov/PMA/Presidents_Management_Agenda.pdf

Chapter 3

Capacity Building
The Federal Government's Efforts to Hire and Develop Analytics Staff

Jennifer Bachner

Content

3.1 Introduction

The availability of data and accessibility of powerful statistical methods have transformed how government officials make decisions. Today, there is a growing expectation that the development of public policies, rules, and regulations is informed by data. Many government agencies are seeking to grow their analytics staff and establish governance bodies to oversee the collection, management, analysis, and dissemination of data. Federal laws and accompanying guidance provide a roadmap and milestones as government agencies strive to upskill their employees and solidify the evidence base of their decision-making.

DOI: 10.1201/9781003369783-3

This chapter will first provide an overview of the federal government's efforts to hire analytics staff. The chapter will then discuss the results of the Government Analytics Survey, which asked government officials about how their organizations are using analytics and the challenges that are hindering efforts to expand the use of analytics for decision-making in government. The final section of the chapter will outline some of the specific ways government agencies are trying to recruit and retain analytics staff and offers some thoughts on how these efforts could be expanded in the years ahead.

3.2 Federal Government Hiring in Analytics

The Foundations for Evidence-Based Policymaking Act of 2018 (Evidence Act) was a landmark law passed with the intent of modernizing the federal government's approach to data and decision-making. This law, along with subsequent guidance from the Office of Management and Budget (OMB), including the Federal Data Strategy, established processes and policies to support the federal government's efforts to use statistical evidence as a key input in the policymaking process. The Evidence Act requires all agencies to craft plans to develop statistical evidence, build analytic capacity, and make more data publicly available. It also includes provisions to ensure that confidential information is protected and secure.

In addition, the Evidence Act specifies that government agencies should establish three key positions to support evidence-building activities (Roles and Responsibilities Under the Foundations for Evidence-Based Policymaking Act, 2020):

1. *Chief data officer (CDO)*: The CDO serves on the CDO Council and oversees data governance across an agency. The CDO is charged with ensuring that an agency follows best practices associated with data management, analysis, and dissemination. In addition, the CDO coordinates collaborative data activities with other government entities both at the federal level and with state and local agencies.
2. *Evaluation officer*: The evaluation officer oversees an agency's evaluation activities and ensures these efforts are aligned with an agency's mission and analytical best practices. The individual in this role serves as a senior advisor to top decision-makers on policy issues where evaluation results may be informative.
3. *Statistical official*: The statistical official provides oversight over data quality, data security, and statistical effectiveness. This role is charged with ensuring that an agency is leveraging its data to develop the best evidence possible using appropriate statistical tools and methods.

The Data Foundation and Grant Thornton Annual CDO Survey found, in 2021, that current CDOs tend to be long-time civil servants though new to their specific role (Hart et al., 2021). All 100% of responding CDOs reported having over five years of federal government experience, with 90% indicating that they had been employed at their current organization for at least one year. Nonetheless, over 40% reported serving in their role as CDO for less than one year. Moreover, over half of respondents reported having 10 or fewer full-time employees (FTEs) in their offices. There is some evidence, however, that efforts to grow these offices are bearing fruit, as the percentage of offices with more than 25 FTEs increased from 25% in 2020 to 40% in 2021.

Beyond the three leadership positions outlined in the Evidence Act, the legislation and subsequent guidance emphasize the need to hire data scientists and related positions. As the CDO Survey report explains, the need is not simply to add FTEs but to hire "specific highly-skilled data scientists, data architects, and data engineers required to successfully carry out data governance and management activities" (Hart et al., 2021, p. 12). In early 2021, OPM assisted a group of 10 agencies with a coordinated effort to hire data scientists (Heckman, 2021). Applicants were able to use a single application to apply for more than 50 positions. The effort was intended to bring in workers with high-demand skills at a much faster pace than is typical under the normal federal hiring process. Later that year, OPM developed a new occupational series for data scientists to support agencies in identifying applicants with skills in mathematics, statistics, and computer science. The creation of this series has helped agencies clearly indicate to prospective employees where there are positions that require data science skills at competitive compensation levels. It has been a critical piece in a constellation of federal initiatives to expand analytic capacity through hiring.

3.3 Recruiting and Retaining Analytics Staff: Results from the Government Analytics Survey

Since 2014, the Johns Hopkins University Center for Advanced Governmental Studies has partnered with REI Systems to host the Government Analytics Breakfast Forum. The purpose of this forum is to discuss how the public sector is using analytics to address complex challenges. Over the years, the forum has featured leaders from across government with roles such as chief data officer, chief risk officer and chief evaluation officer. With their insights in mind, REI Systems analysts and Johns Hopkins faculty decided to conduct a survey of those working in the field of government analytics to develop a systematic understanding of how government is using analytics to obtain value and the challenges it faces as it strives to expand evidence-based decision-making.

The second annual Government Analytics Survey was conducted in 2021.[1] The survey, conducted online using Qualtrics software, included 144 respondents working in the government analytics community for the federal government, state governments or private sector organizations adjacent to government. Most (57%) respondents had over 10 years of experience in the field, though many were newer to their roles. Table 3.1 displays a breakdown of the sector of employment and length of experience of the respondents.

As can be seen in Table 3.1, nearly half the respondents work in the federal government, while another 29% work in the private sector for a government contract or

Table 3.1 Summary of Government Analytics Survey Respondents (N = 144)

Attributes	Percentage of Respondents
Sector of employment	
Federal government	49
State/local government	15
Contracting/consulting firm	29
Other	7
Experience	
0–2 years	15
3–5 years	11
6–10 years	17
>10 years	57

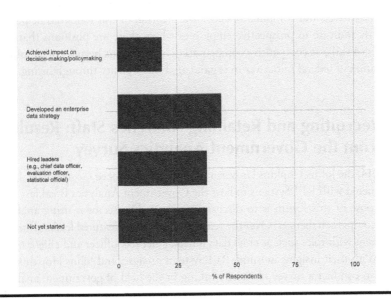

Figure 3.1   Implementation of the Evidence Act.

Source: Data are from the 2021 Government Analytics Survey. Respondents were asked to select all that apply.

consulting organization. Most respondents have significant (10+ years) experience, though there is representation from all experience levels.

Figure 3.1 displays the extent to which federal agencies have begun implementing the Evidence Act. While it is clear that many have made progress with respect to hiring leaders, developing an enterprise data strategy, and furthering data-driven decision-making, 38% of respondents indicated that their organization had not yet started the implementation process.

Analytics leaders have faced multiple challenges in their efforts to move their organizations forward. Conversations with experts in the field reveal three key hurdles leaders face:

1. securing leadership buy-in,
2. developing an effective organizational structure, and
3. cultivating an analytics culture.

In terms of securing leadership buy-in, the challenge is that those in decision-making positions are sometimes comfortable with their existing processes and resistant to new approaches. Experts suggest framing data-driven decision-making not as a 180-degree shift but as an extension of the decision-making processes already in place. Quantitative analyses, in other words, should supplement rather than replace other decision-making inputs. In pithier terms, data-driven decision-making should be presented as evolutionary rather than revolutionary.

A related challenge with bringing agency leaders onboard is that they are usually political appointees. Unlike career civil servants, who are experts in their area and largely insulated from political pressure, agency leaders play an important role in advancing the agenda of a president's administration. Over 60% of our survey respondents indicated that a significant challenge facing government analytics

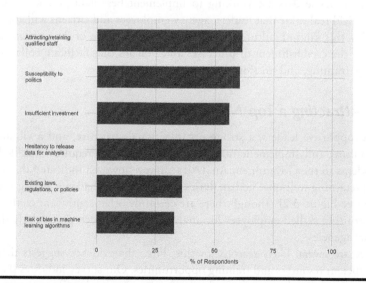

Figure 3.2 Challenges in government analytics.

Source: Data are from the 2021 Government Analytics Survey. Respondents were asked to select up to three choices.

is the risk that the analytic results will contradict political goals (see Figure 3.2). Nonetheless, most political appointees hope to pursue a successful career beyond their tenure as agency leaders and so will be open to an increased reliance on data for decision-making if analysts can demonstrate its value for advancing the organization's mission.

Once agency leaders are bought in, analytics leaders will want to develop a structure that best serves the broader organization's analytic needs. Experts increasingly suggest creating a centralized analytics unit in an agency/bureau such that it functions as an in-house consulting group. This is the approach taken by analytics leaders at the Consumer Financial Protection Bureau (CFPB), and it has served the organization well since its launch in 2011. Through this organizational structure, CFPB analysts are able to support data and analysis needs across the bureau, including by focusing on data literacy, such as teaching employees to use relational databases rather than traditional flat data files. Further, the CFPB's analytics group developed an enterprise platform such that employees can access self-service tools to analyze and visualize data themselves. This focus on providing employees with education and tools has greatly advanced the development of statistical evidence for policymaking.

And third, experts in the field point to the cultivation of an analytics culture as necessary for fully implementing the Evidence Act in a sustainable manner. This means not using analytics in a way that simply ensures that an agency is compliant with federal laws and regulations but, instead, leveraging data and tools for analysis because this leads to better outcomes. In other words, rather than just checking boxes, analytics leaders are working to implement best data practices such that analyses yield real value that leaders, agency employees and citizens will appreciate. Nurturing this kind of culture requires a clear articulation of the purpose of analytics and the establishment of processes and policies that facilitate collaboration, creativity, training, and mission-driven work.

3.3.1 Attracting a Top-Notch Staff

Beyond supportive leaders, a strong organizational structure, and a vibrant analytics culture, full implementation of the Evidence Act requires a skilled staff. Respondents to the Government Analytics Survey, however, indicated that attracting and retaining well-qualified analytics staff is the top challenge facing the community (see Figure 3.2). Though there are certainly other significant challenges as well, recruiting skilled employees for analytic work has been particularly difficult for many agencies.

There are several likely reasons for this. First, the evidence suggests that there are insufficient resources and training opportunities. Our survey indicates that there is wide variation in the extent to which organizations have sufficient resources to meet their analytic needs. Approximately 19% indicated that their organization's resources are "not at all" sufficient, while 10% indicated that their organization is

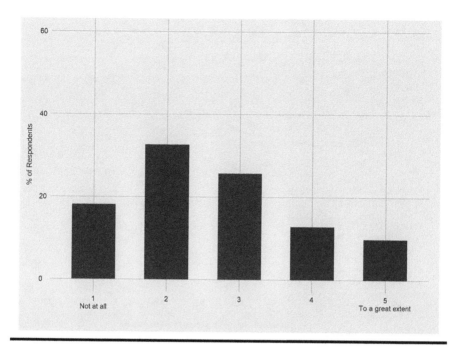

Figure 3.3   Sufficiency of resources to meet the organization's analytic needs.

Source: Data are from the 2021 Government Analytics Survey.

well resourced (see Figure 3.3). These results are not surprising to experts in the field, and they underscore that a lack of resources is deeply problematic from a recruitment standpoint. New employees are eager to both utilize their analytic skills using state-of-the-art tools and develop new abilities as they progress in their careers. To attract and keep top data analysts and data scientists, analytics groups need to offer opportunities for skill development using the latest tools and methods.

Part of the explanation for the sluggish implementation of new methods and tools might be rooted in hesitations about the ethical and privacy implications. We asked our survey respondents whether the use of artificial intelligence (AI) in facial recognition technology as an additional login verification mechanism presented these concerns. Approximately 71% of respondents expressed an ethical concern about this approach, and 83% expressed a privacy concern. Thus, while analysts may want to use cutting-edge techniques, there is clearly widespread apprehension about the use of AI methods. These concerns have spurred many in both government and the private sector to give more thought to governance issues surrounding analytics. The term *responsible AI* has come to refer to a set of best practices that ensure AI is designed and deployed in a way that values privacy, nondiscrimination, and transparency.

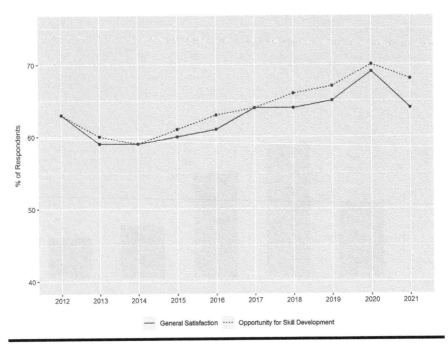

Figure 3.4   Perception of opportunity for skill improvement and general satisfaction in government agencies (2012–2021).

Source: Data are from the Federal Employee Viewpoint Survey. The graph shows the percentage of survey respondents who either (1) "strongly agree" or "agree" that they have an opportunity for skill improvement at their organization or (2) express satisfaction with their organization, pay, and job (as an index).

The finding about the insufficiency of analytic resources in some government agencies is echoed in data collected through the OPM's Federal Employee Viewpoint (FEV) Survey. This annual survey is offered electronically to federal employees to assess their workplace experiences and conditions. As part of the survey, respondents are asked whether they are "given a real opportunity to improve my skills in my organization," with a five-point response scale ranging from "strongly agree" to "strongly disagree" (*Federal Employee Viewpoint Survey Results*, 2021). Since 2012, the percentage of respondents expressing agreement has increased from 63% to 68%, hitting a peak of 70% in 2020 (see Figure 3.4). While this percentage is moving in the right direction, it is a modest increase and leaves room for improvement.

Looking at specific agencies, we see that the percentage of respondents who perceive that they have opportunities for skill improvement varies from approximately 59% at the Social Security Administration to 88% at the National Science Foundation (see Figure 3.5). That the Department of Homeland Security and the Department of Justice are among the lowest-performing agencies by this measure yet

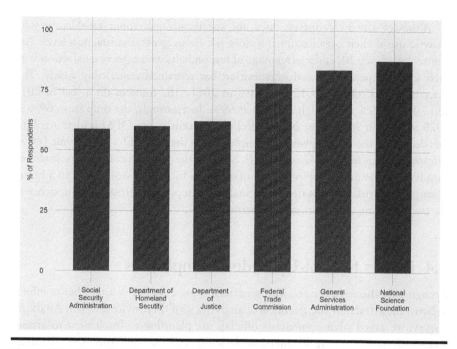

Figure 3.5 **Variation in perceived opportunity for skill improvement across agencies.**

Source: Data are from the Federal Employee Viewpoint Survey (2021).

are also among the largest agencies in terms of personnel highlights the magnitude of the opportunity to provide federal employees with more resources and training.

Our Government Analytics Survey also asked respondents about what should be done to make analytics a more prominent factor in decision-making at their organization and provided an open-ended response box. Common responses (in various forms) included "better training," "create . . . opportunities for advancement," and "invest in the tools and qualified personnel." It is clear that agencies can do better with providing staff with the software, hardware, and development opportunities needed to support professional growth.

A second reason why government might be struggling to attract analytic talent may be the slower-than-desired uptake in the use of analytics by organization leaders. In our survey, we asked respondents about the extent to which their organization's executives and managers use analytics on a scale of 1 to 5, with 1 being "not at all" and 5 being "to a great extent." Approximately 64% of respondents indicated a score of 3 or below; only 18% indicated that their leaders use analytics "to a great extent." This distribution leaves room for improvement. Employees want to work in an organization where their skills and output are appreciated by leadership and where the use of their expertise will lead to career advancement.

Although the FEV Survey does not specifically ask about satisfaction with analytic use at their organizations, it does ask about general satisfaction levels (see Figure 3.4). Since 2012, the percentage of respondents who express satisfaction with their job, compensation, and organization has remained remarkably steady. This percentage was 63% in 2012 and 64% in 2021. The number hit a low in 2013 and 2014 at 59% and a high in 2020 at 69%. Interestingly, the drop from 69% in 2020 to 64% in 2021 is the biggest decline in recent times. OPM leaders attribute this decline to the strains placed on employees by the COVID-19 pandemic (*OPM Releases Government-wide Results*, 2022). Some in the analytics community, however, wonder whether an uptick in the use of analytics by leaders would lead to a bump in employee satisfaction, as the use of analytics can promote trust and confidence in the policymaking and rulemaking processes.

3.4 Efforts to Tool-Up Federal Employees

Recognizing these challenges, hiring managers are engaged in a number of efforts to boost the attraction and retention of analytics staff. In the Government Analytics Survey, we asked what approaches officials are planning to implement to attract and retain staff who have advanced analytic capabilities (see Figure 3.6). The most frequent response was "encourage agency leadership to make data-driven decisions" (73%). Respondents indicated that creating improved data-sharing policies (49%) and developing a cloud-based platform with advanced technologies (44%) are also promising strategies. All of these responses echo earlier findings in support of the idea that high-quality analytics staff want to work in an environment where their work is valued, listened to, and well resourced.

Among current federal employees, there is wide recognition of the need for analytics training, both for analysts themselves and for all officials involved in the policymaking process. One survey respondent suggested creating a "program similar to 'Data Analytics for Dummies' that can be taught in 60 [minutes] or less to laypersons." Another respondent noted that "Data needs to not only be part of the ecosystem and culture, but it has to be 'hard wired,' like getting a cup of coffee every morning." There is clearly a sense that widespread analytics training for large swaths of the federal workforce would be highly beneficial.

This sentiment is reflected in the Federal Data Strategy (2021), developed by OMB. This document provides a 10-year, whole-of-government vision for how federal agencies should collect, manage, and use data. The 2021 Federal Data Strategy Action Plan outlines 11 concrete actions agencies should take to advance this effort, two of which relate specifically to staffing:

- action 4: increase staff data skills and
- action 9: data skills workforce development.

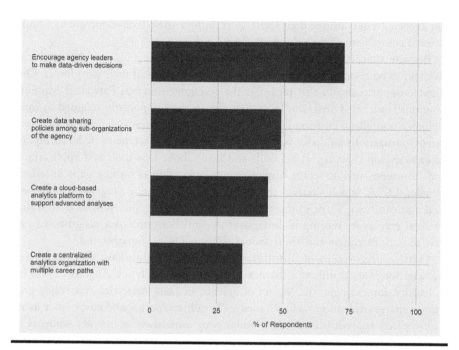

Figure 3.6   Efforts being taken to attract and retain analytics staff.

Source: Data are from the 2021 Government Analytics Survey. Respondents were asked to select up to two choices.

Action 4 indicates that agencies should work to address gaps in data literacy skills across all staff. The plan emphasizes that these skills should be widespread, meaning that agencies should work toward a "minimum level of data literacy among all staff" (*Federal Data Strategy*, 2021). Agencies are expected to implement rotational programs and professional development opportunities to help staff develop these skills, and they should measure their progress by setting clear goals using skills gap analyses and performance plans.

Action 9 was developed to support action 4, and it asks all agencies to document their training programs such that successful efforts can be shared and replicated. In addition, the plan calls for the Chief Data Officers Council to develop a data skills training guidebook for organizations seeking to implement new programs.

After agencies make substantial progress on upskilling their workforces, OMB next expects progress on federal government enterprise activities, such as data-use standards, data-related budgeting, and data-sharing coordination. Work on these efforts is expected to take place between 2023 and 2026, at which point OMB expects agencies to implement self-service for widespread use in data-driven activities (2026–2030). Throughout all stages of the 10-year vision, the expectation is that agencies will continue their focus on training and skill development as a foundational component of data-driven decision-making.

Because there was no new funding attached to the Evidence Act, agencies have had to be resourceful when identifying ways to upskill their workforces. One valuable opportunity in this regard is the Intergovernmental Personnel Mobility Program. Under this program, federal employees are temporarily assigned to work at eligible nonfederal entities, such as state governments, research centers, and non-profit organizations (and vice versa). Through strategic placements, federal employees can develop their analytical skills and learn about new tools and applications. And in reverse, private-sector employees can help address staffing gaps in federal agencies. OPM, which oversees the program, notes that the program is underutilized and can help "agencies meet their needs for 'hard-to-fill' positions" and that "Federal employees serving in Intergovernmental Personnel Act assignments can serve as both recruiters and ambassadors" (*Policy, Data, Oversight*, n.d.).

Outside of government, institutions of higher learning have also recognized the need for more training at the nexus of policy of analytics. At Johns Hopkins University, for example, the Master of Science in Data Analytics and Policy program prepares students to tackle challenges in politics, policy, and governance using sophisticated analytical methods. Similar programs likewise instruct students in statistics, data visualization, programming, and computational analysis for applications in policy, government, and security. Many students in these programs are seeking careers in government with an aim to improve policymaking, governance, and security using data-driven approaches.

There is significant opportunity for more collaboration between the federal government and universities with regard to upskilling workers. In the Intelligence Community, for example, the Office of the Director of National Intelligence has created Centers for Academic Excellence at colleges and universities to develop a qualified and diverse workforce to support the country's security initiatives. Similar centers are supported in the areas of cybersecurity and homeland security. A parallel effort could be undertaken in the area of analytics in light of the need for more skilled, knowledgeable, and diverse workers in this area. One challenge is that there is no obvious agency to oversee the program, as analytics skills are needed across all government organizations. It might therefore make sense for OMB to lead this kind of effort, as it is the agency tasked with overseeing implementation of the Evidence Act and developing the Federal Data Strategy.

In addition, agencies could consider working with colleges and universities on smaller-scale training opportunities for workers in specialized areas of analytics. Short courses on discrete topics in areas such as visualization, text analysis, geospatial analysis, data mining, and dashboarding may provide a way for agencies to fill skill gaps in areas critical to their work. These courses could be delivered in modalities that are convenient and accessible to workers, whether that is onsite, online, or in a hybrid format. The emphasis would be on the applied use of specific analytical skills; students may even engage in hands-on projects where they implement the methods being taught using their organizations' data. In short, there is enormous flexibility in designing these types of offerings in terms of content, structure, and delivery format, but building the communication and funding bridges between government and higher education has proven challenging. If universities continue to develop a better understanding of public sector skill needs and the federal government expands programs for partnering with institutions of higher learning, we may yet see these collaborations blossom and thrive.

Note

1 The first iteration of the survey was conducted in 2019 with similar results. See Bachner (2022) for more details about the survey and its findings across a broad range of topics related to government analytics.

References

Bachner, J. (2022). Optimizing analytics for policymaking and governance. *IBM Center for the Business of Government.* Retrieved from www.businessofgovernment.org/report/optimizing-analytics-policymaking-and-governance

Federal data strategy: 2021 action plan. (2021). Retrieved October 10, 2022, from https://strategy.data.gov/assets/docs/2021-Federal-Data-Strategy-Action-Plan.pdf

Federal employee viewpoint survey results. (2021). Retrieved October 13, 2022, from www.opm.gov/fevs/reports/governmentwide-reports/governmentwide-management-report/governmentwide-report/2021/2021-governmentwide-management-report.pdf

Hart, J., Lawton, S., & Willey. (2021, September). CDO insights: 2021 survey results on the maturation of data governance in U.S. Federal Agencies. *Data Foundation and Grant Thornton.* Retrieved October 22, 2022, from https://static1.squarespace.com/static/56534df0e4b0c2babdb6644d/t/614b4703cf9c893d903fa20e/1632323336994/CDO-Insights-Report-2021.pdf

Heckman, J. (2021, January 19). Data scientist hiring campaign maxes out applications in less than 2 days. *Federal News Network.* Retrieved October 21, 2022, from https://federalnewsnetwork.com/hiring-retention/2021/01/data-scientist-hiring-campaign-maxes-out-applications-in-less-than-2-days/

OPM releases government-wide results from 2021 OPM federal employee viewpoint survey. (2022, April 28). Retrieved October 10, 2022, from www.opm.gov/news/releases/2022/04/release-opm-releases-government-wide-results-from-2021-opm-federal-employee-viewpoint-survey/

Policy, Data, Oversight. (n.d.). Retrieved October 14, 2022, from www.opm.gov/policy-data-oversight/hiring-information/intergovernment-personnel-act/

Roles and responsibilities under the Foundations for Evidence-Based Policymaking Act. (2020, February 28). *The United States Department of Justice.* Retrieved October 21, 2022, from www.justice.gov/open/roles-and-responsibilities-under-foundations-evidence-based-policymaking-act

Chapter 4

How Did the Great Resignation Impact Government Jobs?

Jay L. Zagorsky

Content

In 2021, the U.S. labor market experienced a widespread surge in voluntary quitting. The media dubbed this mass exodus the "Great Resignation." For the first two decades of the 21st century, the typical month saw about 2.7 million U.S. workers quit their jobs. Then, at the end of 2021, this number jumped by almost 2 million more per month, to a seasonally adjusted peak of 4.5 million quitters in November and December.

Pundits quickly suggested that the COVID-19 epidemic caused massive numbers of people to re-evaluate their lives (Gulati, 2022). The popular explanation, based only on anecdotal data, was that people found their lives lacking and quit in droves to spend time in more meaningful, nonlabor market pursuits. Instead of the "Great Resignation," Fuller and Kerr (2022) suggested calling this shift a "Reconsideration." While the story of quitting to seek meaningful lifestyles got substantial amounts of notice, it turned out to not be true. Large numbers of quits happened, but many quitters were switching jobs, not dropping out of the labor force.

Whatever the reason for the Great Resignation, surges in quits are important to understand because labor turnover is costly (O'Connell & Kung, 2007). Replacing workers is an expensive, time-consuming, and inefficient process involving screening, interviewing, onboarding, and training new workers. Moreover, workers who quit often leave with institutional and job-specific knowledge that is hard to replace.

Because quits are important to understand, this chapter first overviews the literature on quits. Then it focuses on understanding the data on both economy-wide quits and also quits in federal, state, and local governments. Governments are important to understand because they are among the largest employers in the U.S. economy. During 2021, federal government workers comprised 2.0% of all civilian employment; state government workers comprised 3.6% and local government workers 9.5% (Bureau of Labor Statistics (BLS), 2022b). Combined, these three levels of governments employed 15.1% of civilian employment, which is about one out of every seven workers.

4.1 Previous Research on Why People Quit

While 2021 saw a dramatic increase in quitting, it is difficult for managers and policy makers to combat the rise in quitting without knowing why people quit. The earliest general research looked at the background of people who quit. Weiss (1984) found in two manufacturing plants that age, education, and complexity of tasks were associated with quits, with youth, less education, and being given more difficult tasks all leading to higher quit rates.

Later research focused on specific reasons people quit. Goler et al. (2018) looked at Facebook and found that people who quit were more likely to have not enjoyed their work, had jobs that did not play to their strengths, and felt they did have a career development path.

Other research focused on what managers can do to stop people from quitting. Firth et al. (2004) found that emotional support from supervisors reduced the intention to quit. Klatzke (2016) noted that people quit in stages. They often tell close co-workers of their intention before formally resigning. This gives managers who informally hear the news the ability to reverse the decision before it is official.

Beyond the general research into quitting, a number of researchers have been specifically focused on people quitting government jobs. One of the earliest papers was by Utgoff (1983), who noted that federal government workers rarely quit. Ippolito (1987) explained that one reason for these low quit rates is that federal workers have exceptionally large pensions. Quitting a job means losing a significant fraction of compensation. He shows that after 10 years of working, a federal employee who quits will lose almost three years of pension wages, compared to a private sector worker who will lose only one. Lacy (1987) pointed out that even the most highly talented inexperienced worker starts off at the bottom of the federal pay ladder. This means most federal quits should happen early in a person's career.

Selden and Moynihan (2000) investigated similar questions but focused on state government workers. They found that many state employees are represented by unions and receive better pay, which makes them less likely to quit. Hackman and Morath (2018) point out that not all state workers are immune from job dissatisfaction by pointing out the growing quit rates in public education.

Heywood et al. (2002), using British data, point out that another reason why government workers have lower quit rates is due to occupational sorting. They state that people who are more easily satisfied with their jobs are drawn into the public sector. Caillier (2011) explains this sorting by testing if people in government jobs have a public service motivation. He finds that they do. Surprisingly, he finds that the greater the motivation, the more likely someone is to quit once they feel the motivation is betrayed.

While this previous research is fascinating, none of it focuses specifically on the Great Resignation. To bridge this gap, Pew Research Center (Parker & Menasce Horowitz, 2022) asked participants in the American Trends Panel to explain the reasons why they quit a job in 2021. The top three reasons for quitting during 2021 were low pay (cited by 63% of respondents), no opportunities for advancement (also cited by 63%), and feeling disrespected at work (cited by 57%). The least-cited reasons were working too many hours, working too few hours, or being required to get a Covid vaccination.

Unfortunately, the Pew Panel asked only 1,000 people if they quit and found that just 10% had. This means the sample size was too small to be broken down by type of employer, which would have determined if government workers had different responses.

Based on the Pew Survey's findings, the Merit Systems Protection Board (MSPB) investigated the reasons for quits among federal workers (U.S. MSPB, 2022). The MSPB is an independent, quasi-judicial agency whose goal is to ensure that things like nepotism do not exist in the civil service and that government employees are not coerced into doing political activities. While the MSPB had a much larger sample size than Pew, they were only able to ask current employees about their likelihood of quitting. They did not survey government employees who had quit.

MSPB asked federal employees about the three drivers Pew identified by asking respondents if their organization provides employees with opportunities for growth and development, if they are treated with respect at work, and if their organization pays employees fairly. It also asked about respondents' quit intentions with three questions; "I plan to move to a different occupation or line of work," "I plan to move to a different organization or agency," and "I plan to resign from the federal government."

The survey received over 25,000 responses, out of approximately 100,000 surveys fielded. The results showed that over 12% of federal respondents had very high quit intentions. The analysis of responses showed that pay was not the key factor in planning to quit. Instead, the key factor was the ability to have growth and development opportunities. Unfortunately, low response rates combined with no actual quitters being sampled means this survey's data are only suggestive and not definitive. Moreover, research by Jung (2010) found there was little relationship between intention and actual turnover among federal government employees.

4.2 What Was the Great Resignation?

Data on overall quits in the U.S. economy come from the BLS Job Openings and Labor Turnover Survey (JOLTS). This survey produces data on job openings, hires, and separations. JOLTS breaks separations into three categories: quits; layoffs and discharges; and other separations, which are primarily retirements.

JOLTS figures showed that around 4.5 million people quit during November 2021 and that roughly the same number quit in December 2021 (Bureau of Labor Statistics, 2022c). This earned the title "Great" for two reasons. First, these figures were the highest number of monthly quits ever recorded in the U.S. Second, they are well above the long-term monthly average of 2.7 million quitters per month.

Comparing the absolute number of people who quit over time produces a biased view because the U.S. labor force is steadily growing. Using the percentage, or the rate of quitting, as shown in Figure 4.1, is more accurate. The rate in Figure 4.1 is the number who quit divided by the number of people employed in civilian jobs in each month. The figure's data are publicly available from the U.S. BLS (https://data.bls.gov/cgi-bin/srgate) as series JTS000000000000000QUR. Figure 4.1 shows that from 2000 to 2020, which was prior to the Covid pandemic, about 2% of workers quit during a typical month. During the Great Resignation, quit rates jumped to 3%.

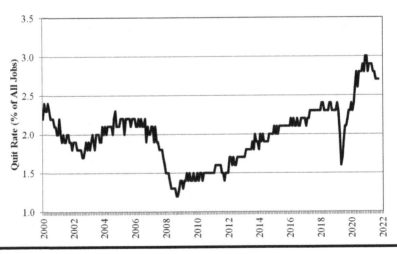

Figure 4.1   U.S. monthly quit rate as a percentage of all civilian jobs.

While the absolute jump from 2 to 3 percentage points is only 1 percentage point, this means monthly quit rates rose by 50%. More importantly, since the graph shows monthly quit rates, an extra percentage point per month translates into 12 percentage points a year. During 2021, an average of 1.3 million additional people quit each month. On a yearly basis, about 15.6 million more quits happened than expected during 2021. Given that there were 146 million people employed in the U.S. that year, a 1-percentage-point monthly jump in quit rates was quite significant.

4.3 Quits by Industry

The rate and absolute number of quits did not jump dramatically in all industries during 2021. Table 4.1 shows the quit rates in 19 high-level industries. The top of the table has the industries with the most turnover (food and lodging, at 4.11% per month) from 2000 to 2020. The industries at the bottom have the least turnover (federal government, at 0.53% per month) during the same period.

The fourth column of Table 4.1 shows what happened to each industry's average monthly quit rate during the Great Resignation. For many industries, the absolute quit rate spiked during that year. Comparing columns three and four shows the quit rate increased by 1.79 percentage points in food and lodging and 1.35 points among retailers. The quit rate did not change in mining and increased only slightly in real estate (0.04 percentage points) and finance (0.09 percentage points).

Using the absolute increase, however, misses understanding the true impact of the Great Resignation. Businesses at the top of the list with a high rank, like restaurants, hotels, and retail shops, have experienced high turnover for years. These industries are accustomed to workers quitting and many have procedures in place to manage rapid turnover. For example, fast food chains do not expect front-line workers to stay around a long time. Before the pandemic, "turnover at U.S. fast-food restaurants jumped to 150 percent—meaning a store employing 20 workers would go through 30 in one year" (Patton, 2018). Patton's figure is higher than the food and lodging figure reported in Table 4.1 for two reasons. First, Patton includes people who are fired, and second, he only looked at fast food restaurants, which is a portion of the food and lodging industry with one of the highest turnover rates.

The better way to understand the impact of the Great Resignation is to look at the percent change in the quit rate during 2021 compared to the average of prior years. This change shows which industries experienced the greatest shock from a changing quit rate.

For example, the federal government has consistently had an extremely low absolute quit rate and is at the bottom of Table 4.1. In a typical month, only about half of 1% of federal workers quit. During 2021, the quit rate jumped up to three quarters of 1%. In absolute terms, this quarter of a percentage point rise is not much, but the percent change is dramatic. The far-right column shows federal hiring managers needed to replace 44% more workers during the Great Resignation

Table 4.1 Average Monthly Quit Rates Before and During the Great Resignation by Industry

Industry	Rank	Quits 2000 to 2020	Quits 2021	Percent Change
Food and lodging	1	4.11	5.90	43%
Retail	2	2.84	4.19	48%
Arts	3	2.65	3.51	32%
Professional services	4	2.58	3.37	31%
Construction	5	1.97	2.47	25%
Other services	6	1.96	2.36	21%
Real estate	7	1.89	1.93	2%
Health	8	1.72	2.53	47%
Mining	9	1.72	1.72	0%
Transportation	10	1.58	2.61	66%
Information	11	1.50	1.83	23%
Nondurable	12	1.49	2.79	88%
Wholesale	13	1.30	1.97	52%
Finance	14	1.24	1.33	8%
Education	15	1.18	1.42	20%
Durable goods	16	1.11	2.07	87%
State and local government	17	0.72	1.01	39%
Public education	18	0.68	0.85	24%
Federal government	19	0.53	0.76	44%

than they had been replacing in prior years. This large change in turnover is difficult for a bureaucracy to handle (Lewis, 1991).

This substantial increase in turnover was also seen among state and local government employees as well as workers in public education. From 2000 to 2020, both state and local government (0.72%) and public education (0.68%) saw average quit rates of less than 1 percentage point per month. During 2021, the absolute rates rose for both groups. This resulted in a substantial percent change, with state and local governments seeing a 39% increase in quitting, while public education saw a 24% increase during the Great Resignation.

4.4 Details on JOLTS Quits

Knowing the details of quitters from the "Job Openings and Labor Turnover Survey" (Bureau of Labor Statistics, 2022a) improves understanding of what underlies Figure 4.1 and Table 4.1. Quits in the JOLTS survey are all employees who left an establishment voluntarily during the month. Quits exclude anyone who retired or transferred to another location within the same company. Quits also exclude workers who left voluntarily but were originally hired as a consultant or an outside contractor or were from a temporary help or employee leasing agency.

JOLTS data are based on interviews and the records of about 21,000 randomly selected businesses and government agencies each month. This high-quality survey attracts widespread attention from the business press (Cohen, 2022; Hilsenrath & Chaney Cambon, 2021) because it not only provides data on quits but also tracks the number of job openings plus the number of people hired, fired, laid off, and retired.

One of the primary drawbacks to JOLTS data is that they only begin in December 2000. This means that at the end of 2022, when this chapter was written, slightly more than two decades of quit information was available. Because the period is relatively short, it is difficult to take seriously the claim that during the Covid epidemic, the U.S. economy experienced the "Great Resignation." Typically, the word "great" is reserved for unique events. The adjective "great," which indicates something dramatically outside the normal range, would only apply if quits in 2021 were much higher than during 1999, the peak of the Internet Bubble, or during the 1940s, when World War II's massive economic expansion drove unemployment to unprecedented lows.

There are, in fact, data that show quits were much higher in the past. Turnover data were collected by the government for just manufacturing from the 1930s until the 1980s (Bauer, 2014). In 1945, the monthly quit rate in manufacturing was 6.1%. The quit rate in both November and December 2021, which was the peak of the "Great Resignation," saw a manufacturing quit rate of 2.6%. This modern figure was about two and a half times lower than the quit rate in the 1940s, suggesting there were other "Great Resignations" in the past that were larger than the modern event.

The business press often combines JOLTS data with the Current Population Survey (CPS) to analyze the ratio of job openings to unemployed workers (Pickert & Bloomberg News, 2022). This macroeconomic statistic provides data on the labor market's health and inflation. When the ratio is above 1, there are more open jobs in the economy than people seeking work. This signals a tight job market for employers with too few potential workers available. Ratios above 1 mean wages need to rise to attract more people into the workforce, typically triggering inflation. Conversely, ratios below 1 mean more people are seeking work than there are open jobs. In this situation, there is no upward pressure on wages or inflation.

During December 2021, the peak of the Great Resignation, JOLTS found 11.3 million open jobs (Bureau of Labor Statistics, 2022c) and the CPS, which tracks unemployment, found 6.3 million out-of-work people who were searching for work (Bureau of Labor Statistics, 2022b). This means that, at the peak of the Great Resignation, there were roughly two jobs for every available job seeker.

JOLTS showed that there were 1.1 million open jobs in all levels of government during December 2021, which was the peak of the Great Resignation. Unfortunately, the CPS does not track the type of industry in which job seekers are looking for work, since many apply to multiple industries simultaneously. This means it is not possible to calculate a job opening–to–unemployed worker ratio for government positions. Nevertheless, as Lee et al. (2018) point out, the extent of government job openings is important to track since they found that quit rates for federal workers plunge when federal jobs are scarce.

4.5 Government Quits in JOLTS

JOLTS data are useful for understanding quit rates in the government. Figure 4.2 shows the average monthly quit rate per 100 government workers for both the federal government (solid line) and for state and local governments (dotted line). The graph shows, from 2011 to 2022, steadily rising quit rates in both types of government. The rising rates indicate an increasing human resource problem. Unlike Figure 4.1, which showed a drop in quits for the entire U.S. economy in 2020, there appears to be no drop in government quits during the beginning of the pandemic.

While JOLTS provides figures on the absolute numbers who quit, again, it is better to use percentages, which adjust for the labor force's size. It is important to

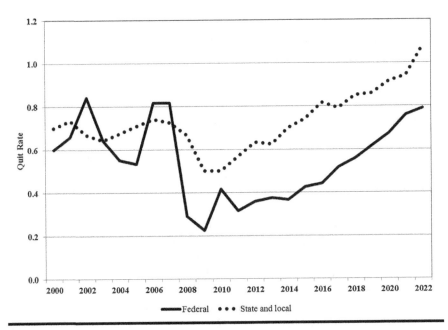

Figure 4.2   Average monthly quit rate per 100 government workers.

adjust for the labor force because in the two decades JOLTS has been tracking quits, the U.S. labor force grew from about 133 million to almost 150 million workers. A growing labor force sets new records for quits simply because there are more people working who can quit. This is like Hollywood movies constantly setting new box office records because ticket sales are not adjusted for inflation.

4.6 OPM Quit Data

The second data source on quits used in this chapter is information from the federal government's U.S. Office of Personnel Management (OPM). OPM is the master human resource agency for the federal government. This office sets federal personnel policies and serves as the administrative center for all civil service hiring. It also manages the federal government employee retirement, healthcare, and insurance programs.

Table 4.2 uses OPM data and shows both the absolute number of quits and the rate of quits from 2005 to 2022. The table shows that during the year 2021, there were over 94,000 federal employees who quit, a record number. One reason for the record is that the number of people working for the federal government has grown. When looked at in percentage terms, the 2021 quit rate of 4.3% is high, but this was surpassed by rates at or slightly below 5% from 2005 to 2008.

As the central human resource agency, OPM keeps careful records of all people who are hired, are fired, and quit. These records, which include demographic, salary, and tenure information, are publicly available online in a database called FedScope (www.fedscope.opm.gov). FedScope includes information from the largest cabinet-level agencies, like the Department of Homeland Security with over

Table 4.2 Number of Federal Employees Who Quit: 2005–2022

Year	Number of Quits	Federal Employment	Quit Rate	Year	Number of Quits	Federal Employment	Quit Rate
2005	91,123	1,830,000	5.0%	2014	73,148	2,033,000	3.6%
2006	91,643	1,833,000	5.0%	2015	73,451	2,042,000	3.6%
2007	90,161	1,832,000	4.9%	2016	76,851	2,057,000	3.7%
2008	89,870	1,875,000	4.8%	2017	79,316	2,062,000	3.8%
2009	74,774	1,978,000	3.8%	2018	80,641	2,061,000	3.9%
2010	75,261	2,128,000	3.5%	2019	83,434	2,085,000	4.0%
2011	76,709	2,102,000	3.6%	2020	73,800	2,180,000	3.4%
2012	76,248	2,091,000	3.6%	2021	94,252	2,183,000	4.3%
2013	74,374	2,058,000	3.6%	2022	85,444	2,206,000	3.9%

Source: Data for 2022 are estimated and based on information from the first three quarters.

200,000 workers, to the tiniest agencies, like the Council of Economic Advisors with about 25 people. FedScope also includes information on civilian workers in the military.

Administrative data, like OPM's FedScope, are clearly preferable to survey data, even high-quality data like JOLTS, since there are no questions about sample biases. Unfortunately, OPM data only cover the federal government and provide no information about state or local quit rates. Additionally, OPM data miss a number of important government agencies, like the Post Office, as well as all intelligence organizations like the CIA and NSA (Office of Personnel Management, 2014). These missing organizations employ roughly two thirds of a million workers. Because OPM data miss parts of the federal government and all state and local jobs, it is important to use multiple data sources to get a complete picture of government quits.

Table 4.3 uses FedScope data to show pay and tenure from 2018 to 2022, which covers the periods before, during, and after the Great Resignation. The top section of Table 4.3 shows that the salary for the average federal employee over this period was almost $90,000. However, the typical quitter made only $63,000, or 70% of the typical federal employee's pay. The bottom section of Table 4.3 shows that the average federal employee had worked for the government for slightly more than a dozen years. The tenure of the typical quitter was much shorter. Quitters lasted only 4.3 years, which is about one third of the average federal employee's time.

Table 4.3 Salary and Tenure Comparison between All Federal Employees and Those Who Quit

	2018	2019	2020	2021	2022	Average
Average quitter salary	$59,707	$61,188	$61,382	$65,287	$67,213	$62,955
Average employee salary	$85,519	$87,240	$90,098	$91,773	$94,156	$89,757
Ratio	70%	70%	68%	71%	71%	70%
Average quitter tenure, years	4.3	4.4	4.2	4.1	4.5	4.3
Average employee tenure, years	12.6	12.4	12.2	12.2	12.2	12.3
Ratio	34%	35%	34%	34%	37%	35%

Source: The 2022 data are estimated based on information from the first three quarters. Number of workers is as of September. Number of quitters is for the entire federal fiscal year, which starts October 1.

Table 4.4 Quit Rates for Federal Employees, 2018–2022

Gender and Education	Percentage of Quitters	Tenure	Percentage of Quitters	Age	Percentage of Quitters
Overall	3.9%	<1 year	15.4%	<20	31.1%
		1–2 years	8.1%	20–24	18.7%
Female	4.3%	3–4 years	5.3%	25–29	9.8%
Male	3.5%	5–9 years	3.4%	30–34	6.4%
		10–14 years	1.6%	35–39	4.4%
Less than college	0.4%	15–19 years	0.9%	40–44	3.4%
Associate's degree	0.3%	20–24 years	0.7%	45–49	2.8%
Bachelor's degree	5.0%	25–29 years	0.4%	50–54	2.3%
Master's degree	9.1%	30–34 years	0.3%	55–59	1.8%
Ph.D.	15.8%	35+ years	0.4%	60–64	1.5%
				65+	2.5%

Table 4.4 uses FedScope quit data to show the averages from 2018 to 2022 of four characteristics. The left side of Table 4.4 shows that female federal government employees are slightly more likely (4.3% vs. 3.5%) to quit than their male counterparts. This is opposite the pattern found by Moynihan and Landuyt (2008), who looked at quitting in the Texas state government.

The bottom left corner, which breaks quitters down by educational attainment, has interesting results. The more education a federal employee has, the more likely they are to quit. Among those employees who never went to college, the average quit rate from 2018 to 2022 was 0.4%. Those with an associate's degree had a similar 0.3% quit rate. However, 5% of employees with a bachelor's degree quit; over 9% of those with a master's degree quit; and among Ph.D.s, almost 16% quit the federal workforce each year.

The middle section of Table 4.4 shows the highest quit rates for those with the least tenure. Slightly more than 15% of quitters worked less than a year in their federal government jobs. However, after working 10 to 14 years, the quit rate fell to 1.6%. Those working beyond 14 years had quit rates well under 1%.

The far-right side of Table 4.4 contains FedScope data broken down by age. Quit rates fall precipitously as people age. Over 30% of employees under age 20 quit, while just 1.5% of employees in their early 60s quit.

Further analysis of OPM's FedScope data shows another factor, agency size, as being important. This factor was previously identified by Kellough and Osuna (1995).

Larger agencies have lower quit rates than smaller agencies. From 2018 to 2022, large independent agencies with 1,000 or more employees, like NASA or the Federal Reserve, had an annual quit rate of 2.9%. Medium independent agencies with 100 to 999 employees, like the Export-Import Bank or the Federal Election Commission, had an annual quit rate of 4.9%. Small independent agencies with fewer than 100 employees, like the Office of Government Ethics or the Commission on Civil Rights, had a quit rate of 7.2%. One reason for this relationship is that large agencies might do a better job finding candidates that better match the agencies' work.

4.7 Discussion

Quits are important to study because replacing workers is an expensive process that takes time away from remaining workers and prevents them from focusing on their primary tasks. Governments at the federal, state, and local levels typically have much lower quit rates than all other industries. Research has suggested three reasons for lower government quit rates. First, government workers get higher pay. Second, government workers get large pensions, which lock people into their jobs. Last is occupational sorting, which ensures that people who believe in the government's mission apply and are hired for particular jobs. FedScope data analyzed in this chapter show quits are more likely to occur among younger, more highly educated women with jobs in smaller agencies.

During the Great Resignation, JOLTS data show that government quit rates were still low in absolute terms. During 2021, the federal government saw a monthly quit rate of 0.76%. However, this was a dramatic percent increase compared to the average quit rate for the 20 years before the Great Resignation. The rise in quit rates meant federal hiring managers needed to replace 44% more workers during the Great Resignation than they had been replacing in prior years. State and local governments, with a 39% increase in quits, and public education, with a 24% increase, also saw substantial changes. The graph showing the quit rates in both federal and state/local governments since 2000 reveals that for the past decade, quit rates in both levels of government have been rising.

These changes mean governments at all levels have a number of options. The first is pointed out by the MSPB survey. One of the most important reasons people state they are going to quit a government job is that they feel there are no growth and development opportunities. Ensuring government workers have the ability to improve their skills and face new challenges will likely lower quit rates and boost retention (Cho & Lewis, 2012).

Another possibility for governments, especially government organizations that have repetitive bureaucratic work, is to deskill a job. Deskilling makes a job simpler, so it is easier to train new employees and ensures a larger pool of potential workers, since the less education and skill needed for a job, the more candidates who qualify for a position.

Another option is to automate the job by replacing humans with machines or computers. By automating a job, fewer workers are needed. Automation does not reduce the problem of quitting. However, in an automated world, the government needs fewer workers. When there are few workers, efficiency wages (Raff & Summers, 1987), which are when employers pay more than needed, is a possible way to lower quit rates and maintain the operation.

A last way is making jobs very bureaucratic, or rigid, with each job following a precise set of steps. Making jobs bureaucratic is not a good method of ensuring people want to work in an organization. However, it ensures replacements can easily be trained in advance of people quitting since the procedures that need to be followed are clearly laid out in all cases.

4.8 Summary

In 2021, there was a surge of involuntary quitting in many parts of the U.S. labor market. During the surge, almost 2 million more people each month left their jobs voluntarily than during the average month over the previous two decades. This surge was called "The Great Resignation" by the media.

Federal, state, and local governments did not see a huge increase in the absolute number of civilian employees quitting. However, governments at all levels did see a large increase in their quit rates, which means they, too, experienced a "Great Resignation." Federal quit rates jumped by 44%, and state and local worker quit rates jumped by 39%.

Increases in quit rates, like what happened during the Great Resignation, are not a new problem for either governments or businesses. High quit rates are simply a signal that workers are not satisfied with their job's pay, benefits, or working conditions and are showing it by voting with their feet. No matter what the causes, the steadily rising quit rates seen in government jobs since 2011 and the sharp jump during 2021 are a wakeup call for human resource managers at all levels of government. One set of potential solutions to these rising quits is to pivot government agencies through a digital transformation, which is outlined in this book's other chapters.

References

Bauer, K. (2014). Examination of state-level labor turnover survey data. *Monthly Labor Review, Jan., 137*(1). https://doi.org/10.21916/mlr.2014.5

Bureau of Labor Statistics. (2022a). *BLS handbook of methods.* Washington, DC: U.S. Government Printing Office. Retrieved from www.bls.gov/opub/hom/jlt/home.htm

Bureau of Labor Statistics. (2022b). *The employment situation: January 2022* (USDL-22-0155). Washington, DC: U.S. Department of Labor. Retrieved from www.bls.gov/news.release/archives/empsit_02042022.pdf

Bureau of Labor Statistics. (2022c). *Job openings and labor turnover—January 2022* (USDL-22–0413), Washington, DC: U.S. Department of Labor. Retrieved from www.bls.gov/news.release/archives/jolts_03092022.pdf

Caillier, J. G. (2011). I want to quit: A closer look at factors that contribute to the turnover intentions of state government employees. *State and Local Government Review*, *43*(2), 110–122. https://doi.org/10.1177/0160323X11403325

Cho, Y. J., & Lewis, G. B. (2012). Turnover intention and turnover behavior: Implications for retaining federal employees. *Review of Public Personnel Administration*, *32*(1), 4–23. https://doi.org/10.1177/0734371X11408701

Cohen, B. (2022, December 1–2). Business lessons from the world's best quitters. *Wall Street Journal*. Retrieved from www.wsj.com/articles/quit-annie-duke-book-slack-stewart-butterfield-11664387845

Firth, L., Mellor, D. J., Moore, K. A., & Loquet, C. (2004). How can managers reduce employee intention to quit? *Journal of Managerial Psychology*, *19*(2), 170–187. https://doi.org/10.1108/02683940410526127

Fuller, J., & Kerr, W. (2022). The great resignation didn't start with the pandemic. *Harvard Business Review Digital Articles*. Retrieved from https://hbr.org/2022/03/the-great-resignation-didnt-start-with-the-pandemic

Goler, L., Gale, J., Harrington, B., & Grant, A. (2018). Why people really quit their jobs. *Harvard Business Review Digital Articles*, 1–7.

Gulati, R. (2022, March 22). The great resignation or the great rethink? *Harvard Business Review Digital Articles*. Retrieved from https://hbr.org/2022/03/the-great-resignation-or-the-great-rethink

Hackman, M., & Morath, E. (2018). Teachers quit jobs at highest rate on record, article. *Wall Street Journal—Online Edition*, p. 1. Retrieved from www.wsj.com/articles/teachers-quit-jobs-at-highest-rate-on-record-11545993052

Heywood, J. S., Siebert, W. S., & Wei, X. (2002). Worker sorting and job satisfaction: The case of union and government jobs. *ILR Review*, *55*(4), 595–609. https://doi.org/10.1177/001979390205500402

Hilsenrath, J., & Chaney Cambon, S. (2021). The mismatch that is hammering job prospects. *The Wall Street Journal*. Retrieved from www.wsj.com/articles/job-openings-are-at-record-highs-why-arent-unemployed-americans-filling-them-11625823021

Ippolito, R. A. (1987). Why federal workers don't quit. *Journal of Human Resources*, *22*(2), 281–299. https://doi.org/10.2307/145906

Jung, C. S. (2010). Predicting organizational actual turnover rates in the U.S. Federal Government. *International Public Management Journal*, *13*(3), 297–317. https://doi.org/10.1080/10967494.2010.504124

Kellough, J. E., & Osuna, W. (1995). Cross-agency comparisons of quit rates in the federal service: Another look at the evidence. *Review of Public Personnel Administration*, *15*(4), 58–68. https://doi.org/10.1177/0734371X9501500406

Klatzke, S. R. (2016). I quit! The process of announcing voluntary organizational exit. *Qualitative Research Reports in Communication*, *17*(1), 44–51. https://doi.org/10.1080/17459435.2015.1088894

Lacy, L. W. (1987). Analyzing the link between compensation and the quit decisions of civil service employees. In R. J. Niehaus (Ed.), *Strategic human resource planning applications* (pp. 207–218). Boston, MA: Springer US.

Lee, S., Fernandez, S., & Chang, C. (2018). Job scarcity and voluntary turnover in the U.S. Federal Bureaucracy. *Public Personnel Management*, *47*(1), 3–25. https://doi.org/10.1177/0091026017732798

Lewis, G. B. (1991). Turnover and the quiet crisis in the federal civil service. *Public Administration Review, 51*(2), 145–155. https://doi.org/10.2307/977108

Moynihan, D. P., & Landuyt, N. (2008). Explaining turnover intention in state government: Examining the roles of gender, life cycle, and loyalty. *Review of Public Personnel Administration, 28*(2), 120–143. https://doi.org/10.1177/0734371X08315771

O'Connell, M., & Kung, M.-C. (2007). The cost of employee turnover. *Industrial Management, 49*(1), 14–19, 15.

Office of Personnel Management. (2014). *FedScope: Data definitions* (p. 20). Retrieved from www.fedscope.opm.gov/datadefn/DataDefinitions.pdf

Parker, K., & Menasce Horowitz, J. (2022). *Majority of workers who quit a job in 2021 cite low pay, no opportunities for advancement, feeling disrespected.* Retrieved from www.pewresearch.org/fact-tank/2022/03/09/majority-of-workers-who-quit-a-job-in-2021-cite-low-pay-no-opportunities-for-advancement-feeling-disrespected/

Patton, L. (2018, March 13). McDonald's high-tech makeover is stressing workers out. *Bloomberg News.* Retrieved from https://www.bloomberg.com/news/articles/2018-03-13/worker-exodus-builds-at-mcdonald-s-as-mobile-app-sows-confusion

Pickert, R., & Bloomberg News. (2022). Job openings surge unexpectedly in July, with about 2 positions open for every unemployed person. *Fortune.* Retrieved from https://fortune.com/2022/08/30/job-openings-surge-july-jolts-labor-department-layoffs-11-million/

Raff, D., & Summers, L. (1987). Did Henry Ford pay efficiency wages? *Journal of Labor Economics, 5*(4, Part 2), S57–S86. https://doi.org/10.1086/298165

Selden, S. C., & Moynihan, D. P. (2000). A model of voluntary turnover in state government. *Review of Public Personnel Administration, 20*(2), 63–74. https://doi.org/10.1177/0734371X0002000206

U.S. Merit Systems Protection Board (MSPB). (2022). *Why feds want to quit: Growth, respect, pay. "Issues of merit".* Washington, DC: Office of Policy and Evaluation. Retrieved from www.mspb.gov/studies/newsletters/Issues_of_Merit_September_2022_1963933.pdf

Utgoff, K. C. (1983). Compensation levels and quit rates in the public sector. *Journal of Human Resources, 18*(3), 394–406. https://doi.org/10.2307/145208

Weiss, A. (1984). Determinants of quit behavior. *Journal of Labor Economics, 2*(3), 371. https://doi.org/10.1086/298038

Chapter 5

Neurodiversity

An Important Contributor to the Government's Pivot through Digital Transformation

Hiren Shukla

Content

5.1 Diversity Is a Critical Success Factor for the Government's Journey through Digital Transformation

The government is a complex and multifaceted organization that serves the needs of a diverse population. In order to effectively carry out its duties and meet the evolving needs of society, it is important for the government to have a workforce that is equally diverse and representative of the communities it serves. This is especially

DOI: 10.1201/9781003369783-5

important as the government embarks on a digital transformation journey, as the use of technology and digital tools becomes increasingly integral to the way the government operates.

One reason why diversity is important in the government's digital transformation journey is that it helps to ensure that the government's technology and digital tools are inclusive and accessible to all members of society. When the government's workforce is diverse, it is more likely to have individuals with different backgrounds, perspectives, and experiences that can help identify potential barriers to accessibility and inclusivity and suggest ways to address them. For example, a government employee with a disability may have insights on how to make a digital tool more accessible for users with disabilities, or a government employee from a culturally or linguistically diverse background may be able to identify language or cultural considerations that need to be taken into account in order to make a digital tool more usable for a diverse population.

In addition, diversity is important in the government's digital transformation journey to foster innovation and creativity. When the government's workforce is diverse, it is more likely to have a range of ideas and perspectives that can be brought to bear on solving problems and developing new solutions. This diversity of thought can help the government to identify and pursue new opportunities for innovation and can also lead to more creative and effective solutions to problems. In addition, a diverse workforce can also help to create a more open and inclusive culture within the government, which can encourage collaboration and the sharing of ideas, leading to more innovative and effective outcomes.

Another important reason why the government needs a diverse workforce to support its digital transformation journey is that it helps to build trust and credibility with the public. When the government's workforce is diverse and representative of the communities it serves, it is more likely to be perceived as responsive to the needs and concerns of those communities. This can help to build trust and credibility with the public and can also help to foster a sense of belonging and connection between the government and the communities it serves. This is especially important in the digital age, when the government must be able to effectively communicate and engage with the public through digital channels and when the public is increasingly reliant on digital tools and services provided by the government.

5.2 What Is Neurodiversity?

One key aspect of the digital transformation journey is the recognition and inclusion of neurodivergent individuals in the design and implementation of technological systems.

Neurodiversity refers to the natural variations in the way the human brain functions and processes information. This can include diagnoses such as autism, dyslexia, ADHD, and dyscalculia, among others. These differences can affect an individual's ability to communicate, learn, and interact with the world around them. Neurodiversity is the diversity of the human brain and the different ways that it functions. This includes differences in how people think, learn, and process information, as well as differences in how they experience and express emotions. Neurodiversity is a natural part of the human experience and can be found in all populations and is present across all dimensions of the population regardless of race, age, gender, or sexual orientation.

It is estimated that the neurodivergent population makes up a significant portion of the global population, with some estimates suggesting that as many as 15% to 20% of people may be neurodivergent.

One of the challenges in accurately assessing the size of the neurodivergent population is the fact that many individuals may not be diagnosed or identified as having a neurodivergent condition. This can be due to a lack of access to appropriate medical and educational resources, stigma surrounding neurodiversity, or simply a lack of awareness about the signs and symptoms of these diagnoses.

There is also significant variability in the prevalence of different neurodivergent diagnosis around the world. For example, the prevalence of autism tends to be higher in certain countries, such as the United States, where recent CDC statistics estimated autism is present in approximately 1 in 44 children. In contrast, the prevalence of ADHD tends to be higher in other countries, such as Sweden, where it is estimated to affect approximately 8% of children.

Unfortunately, neurodivergent individuals often face unique challenges in the job market, leading to higher rates of unemployment compared to the general population. According to an article published by the UK's National Autistic Society (National Autistic Society, 2019) with data collected by the UK Office of National Statistics, only 22% of adults with ASD (autism spectrum disorder) in the UK are in any type of employment, despite the fact that many of these individuals have the skills and qualifications necessary to succeed in the workforce. In the United States, the unemployment rate for individuals with disabilities is more than double the rate for those without disabilities.

Despite the challenges in accurately assessing the size of the neurodivergent population, it is clear that neurodiversity is a significant and important aspect of human diversity. Many neurodivergent individuals have unique strengths and abilities that contribute to the richness and diversity of our society.

Traditionally, neurodiversity has been seen as a deficit or disorder that needs to be corrected. However, recent research has shown that neurodiversity is actually a source of strength and innovation, and many leading companies around the world have already proven this. Neurodivergent individuals often have unique perspectives and ways of thinking that can provide valuable insights and solutions to complex problems.

One of the key benefits of neurodiversity in the workplace is that it can lead to a more diverse and inclusive work environment. When a workplace is inclusive, it means that all employees feel valued, supported, and able to contribute to the organization. This can lead to increased job satisfaction, productivity, and retention of employees.

Another way in which neurodiversity can benefit the workplace is by providing a wider range of perspectives and approaches to problem-solving. Different brains think and process information in different ways, and this can lead to new and innovative solutions to problems. For example, an employee who has a different way of thinking about a problem might be able to come up with a solution that someone with a more traditional approach might not have considered.

In addition, neurodiversity in the workplace can lead to a more flexible and adaptable workforce. When a company has employees with a range of brain types and ways of thinking, it can be better equipped to adapt to changing circumstances and meet the needs of a diverse customer base. This can be particularly important in today's rapidly changing business environment.

There are also social and emotional benefits to neurodiversity in the workplace. When employees feel supported and included, they are more likely to feel a sense of belonging and connection to their colleagues and the organization. This can lead to better teamwork and collaboration and a more positive and supportive work culture.

5.3 How Can Neurodiversity Uniquely Accelerate Digital Transformation?

In the context of digital transformation, neurodiversity can contribute to the development of technology that is more inclusive, accessible, and effective. For example, neurodivergent individuals may have expertise in areas such as data analysis, pattern recognition, and problem-solving, which can be valuable in the creation of new technological systems.

In recent years, there has been a growing recognition of the important role that neurodivergent individuals can play in driving digital transformation. As neurodiversity refers to the diversity of brain function and neurological wiring, these variances can affect how individuals process information, communicate, and interact with others in both challenging and very positive ways.

There are several ways in which neurodiversity can contribute to digital transformation. One of the key ways is through the unique perspectives and approaches that neurodivergent individuals bring to problem-solving that are "out of the box." Neurodiversity can foster creativity and innovative thinking, as individuals with different brain wiring may approach problems in ways that others might not consider. For example, autistic individuals may have an aptitude for attention to detail and a strong ability to focus, which can be valuable in tasks such as data analysis or programming.

Neurodiversity can also contribute to digital transformation through the diversity of skills and abilities that neurodivergent individuals bring to the workplace. For example, individuals with dyslexia may have strong visual-spatial skills, which can be beneficial in tasks such as graphic design or user interface design. Similarly, individuals with ADHD may have strong multitasking abilities, which can be valuable in fast-paced, high-pressure environments.

In addition to the unique skills and abilities of neurodivergent individuals, their presence in the workplace can also contribute to a more inclusive and diverse culture. This can lead to a wider range of perspectives and ideas being considered, which can drive innovation and creativity. A diverse and inclusive culture can also lead to increased employee engagement and retention, as individuals feel valued and supported in the workplace.

There are many notable neurodivergent individuals, in addition to those more popularly known (Elon Musk, Bill Gates, Alan Turing, and Albert Einstein), who work in the realm of emerging technology and data. Here are a few examples:

1. Temple Grandin: Temple Grandin is an autism rights activist and professor of animal science at Colorado State University. She is known for her work in the field of animal behavior and her contributions to the understanding of autism. Grandin has also been involved in the development of new technologies for the livestock industry, including the design of more humane handling systems for animals.
2. Daniel Tammet: Daniel Tammet is a British author, essayist, and speaker on a variety of subjects, including mathematics and neuroscience. Tammet is known for his work on the concept of "thinking in numbers" and has written several books on the subject. He is also a high-functioning autistic individual and has been involved in research on the relationship between autism and math abilities.
3. John Elder Robison: John Elder Robison is an American author and speaker who has written extensively about his experiences as an individual with Asperger syndrome. Robison is also the cofounder of the TCS Auto Program at the Vermont Technical College, which provides education and training in automotive technology to students with autism.

One specific government neurodiversity model that has proven to be quite successful is the program created by the Israeli Defense Force (IDF) for neurodivergent individuals to support its cybersecurity needs. The program, called "Milky Way," was created in response to the growing need for skilled cybersecurity professionals and the recognition that neurodivergent individuals can bring unique skills and perspectives to the field.

The Milky Way program is designed to provide support and accommodations to neurodivergent individuals as they train and work in cybersecurity roles within the IDF. This includes providing assistive technology and other resources to help individuals with tasks such as coding and data analysis. The program also provides coaching and mentorship to help individuals develop their skills and succeed in their roles.

One of the key goals of the Milky Way program is to provide opportunities for neurodivergent individuals to contribute to the defense of Israel's cybersecurity.

The program has already produced several highly skilled professionals who have made significant contributions to the IDF's cybersecurity efforts. There has been improved efficiency and innovation in cybersecurity, and by leveraging the unique skills and abilities of neurodivergent individuals, the Milky Way program has helped to improve efficiency and drive innovation in the field of cybersecurity. Neurodiversity has shown here to foster creative and innovative thinking, and individuals with different brain wiring may approach problems in ways that others might not consider.

The success of the Milky Way program has attracted attention from other governments and organizations around the world, and it has been recognized as a model for how to support and leverage the unique skills and abilities of neurodivergent individuals in cybersecurity roles. The program demonstrates the important role that neurodiversity can play in driving innovation and improving efficiency in the field of cybersecurity.

5.4 Organization Adjustments to Create a More Neuro-Inclusive Environment

It's important to recognize that neurodiversity can also present challenges in the workplace. Some neurodivergent employees may need accommodations in order to fully participate in and contribute to the organization. This could include things like flexible work schedules, assistive technology, or modifications to the physical work environment. It's important for employers to be willing to make these accommodations and to work with employees to find solutions that meet their needs.

One way to support neurodivergent employees is through accommodations and modifications to the work environment. For example, an employee with ADHD may benefit from a standing desk or a quiet workspace to help them stay focused. An employee with dyslexia may need extra time to complete tasks or may benefit from using assistive technology such as text-to-speech software. These accommodations can be made through an interactive process between the employee, their supervisor, and a human resources representative.

Another way to support neurodivergent employees is through training and education for both the employee and their colleagues. This can include providing information about the specific neurological condition and how it may affect the employee's work, as well as teaching strategies for effective communication and collaboration. It can also be helpful for managers to learn about the strengths and challenges that neurodivergent employees may face and to create a supportive and inclusive work culture.

In addition to accommodations and education, it is important for neurodivergent employees to have access to support resources such as counseling or mentorship. This can help them navigate any challenges they may face in the workplace and feel supported in their career development.

Organizations need to adapt to be able to recognize and value the unique strengths and perspectives that neurodivergent employees can bring to the workplace. A deliberate change that has commitment is the only way to benefit from autistic employees, who may have a strong attention to detail and a unique ability to see patterns and analyze data, or employees with ADHD, who may be creative problem solvers and excel in fast-paced environments. By embracing the strengths of neurodivergent employees and creating an inclusive culture, organizations can foster a more diverse and innovative workplace.

Overall, supporting neurodivergent employees in the workplace requires a combination of accommodations, education, support resources, and a culture of inclusivity. By recognizing and valuing the unique strengths and perspectives of neurodivergent individuals, organizations can create a more diverse and innovative work environment and maximize the potential of all employees. This approach naturally leads to the universal design and application of processes, language, and workplace culture that are beneficial for all.

5.5 What Is the Future Opportunity for Government with Respect to Neurodiversity?

The "future organization" will look fundamentally different. To leverage the untapped potential of the neurodivergent population, an important step is for policymakers and advocacy organizations to work to increase awareness and understanding about neurodiversity in the workplace. This can include promoting best practices for hiring and supporting neurodivergent employees, as well as working to remove barriers and stereotypes that prevent neurodivergent individuals from accessing employment opportunities.

In the search for greater efficiencies, organizations are looking to digital transformation as an opportunity. Digital transformation, whereby data and emerging technology will enhance and assist humans with performing various tasks, will become part of the normal routine, with a direct impact on organizational competencies, replacing processing, manual, and transaction-type competencies with creative, problem-solving, and social-type competencies at their core.

As part of this picture, neurodiversity could help organizations bridge the skills gap; there are a range of trending competencies that neurodivergent individuals demonstrate as key strengths—such as focus, creativity and initiative, and analytical thinking and innovation.

However, the traditional organizational approach for neurodiversity is typically focused on challenge remediation. On a skills basis, there is potential to expand this approach to encompass the full neurodivergent profile and the targeting of specific trending workplace skills. This would help with the potential to realize neurodivergent strengths in the workplace and bridge the skills gap.

There is the potential for neurodiversity to create substantial value for government in several ways. For example:

- Increased innovation: Neurodivergent individuals have unique perspectives and approaches to problem-solving that can lead to innovative solutions.
- Improved decision-making: Neurodiverse perspectives can bring different viewpoints to the table, leading to more balanced and informed decision-making.
- Enhanced representation: Neurodiversity can help to ensure that government bodies and policies more accurately reflect the diversity of the population they serve.
- Greater efficiency: By leveraging the strengths of neurodivergent individuals, government agencies may be able to operate more efficiently and effectively.
- Win the war on talent: By driving a "skills-based" approach, government will have a sustainable and scalable talent model.

As you can see, valuing and embracing neurodiversity can help government agencies to better serve their constituents and create a more inclusive and effective society that accelerates the digital transformation journey for government.

While there is still much work to be done to ensure that neurodivergent individuals have the same opportunities and support as their neurotypical peers, there is a growing recognition of the importance of neurodiversity and the unique strengths and abilities of neurodivergent individuals. Overall, addressing the opportunity to leverage neurodiversity towards digital transformation requires a multifaceted approach that involves both employers and policymakers working together to create more inclusive and supportive work environments. By taking these steps, we can create a more diverse and inclusive workforce that benefits everyone.

Reference

National Autistic Society. (2021, February 19). New shocking data highlights the autism employment gap. *autism.org.uk*. Retrieved from www.autism.org.uk/what-we-do/news/new-data-on-the-autism-employment-gap#:~:text=The%20Office%20for%20National%20Statistics,in%20any%20kind%20of%20employment. . . .

Chapter 6

Promoting and Developing Digital Transformation Toward 2030

Hila Axelrad and Sergei Sumkin

Content

6.1 Introduction

Various studies point out the many economic and social advantages of digital progress. Investment in information and communication technology (ICT) carries a positive effect on economic growth, welfare and employees' productivity in both developed and developing countries (Jorgenson & Vu, 2005). While economic growth is

DOI: 10.1201/9781003369783-6

promoted by various ICT components, some of them, such as digital services, ICT infrastructure and electronic governance, are comparatively more beneficial than others (Majeed & Ayub, 2018). Digital technologies contribute to innovation in products and services, as well as in processes, business models and organizational arrangements (OECD, 2017). ICT can reduce poverty by improving poor people's access to education, health, governmental and financial services (Cecchini & Scott, 2003). An increase of 1% in ICT input leads to a 0.408% increase in GDP per capita, when other variables are controlled for, except for market openness (Waqa, 2015). Compared to investments in communication and software, investment in computerization was found to contribute the most to ICT improvement.

A comparison between data from Israel and benchmark countries[1] shows that Israel's public capital inventory of ICT is very low and that there is a large disparity in total ICT investment/GDP ratio, compared to the benchmark countries. Some attempts to close this gap were made through the "Digital Israel" initiative, the Ministry of Communication, the ICT Authority and more. However, a monitored, data-based work plan must be put in place in order to realize the potential of promoting digital transformation in Israel.

In this chapter, we examine the OECD's strategy for promoting digital transformation—the Going Digital initiative—and suggest ways to implement it in Israel. We first analyze the current progress of Israel and then present three ways to set priorities for promoting digital transformation while taking into account the local conditions: (1) a macro model that breaks down the productivity gap (Eckstein et al., 2021), (2) examining the gaps between Israel and the benchmark countries based on the Going Digital indicator (this method allows us to examine the actual situation in Israel compared to other countries and establish priorities for closing gaps in various areas) and (3) examining the road maps for digital transformation in leading countries, and setting priorities in accordance with the various stages implemented by them.

6.2 The Productivity and ICT Investment Gap in Israel

A study conducted at the Aaron Institute examined the causes for gaps in productivity per work hour between Israel and the benchmark countries, focusing on causes that are influenced by government policies. The study showed that Israel was behind in all market production factors (Eckstein et al., 2021). If work productivity in Israel was equal to the benchmark countries, Israel's 2019 GDP would have been higher by 700 billion NIS.[2] Table 6.1 summarizes the results of a macro-economic exogenous factoring that reveals the $25 gap in productivity per work hour between Israel and the benchmark countries.

When comparing the data of production factors, we can see that ICT capital inventory in Israel, which is lower by 19% compared to the benchmark countries, contributes at least[3] 1% to the productivity gap, or $0.30 per work hour. Israel

Table 6.1 Breakdown of the Labor Productivity Gap Between Israel and the Benchmark Countries—Based on GDP per Working Hour, Average for 2016–2019

Human Capital		Private Capital per Worked Hour		Public Capital ICT per Capita		Public Capital per Capita		Total Productivity		Productivity Gap With Benchmark Countries per Work Hour
$6.40	+	$5.30	+	$0.30	+	$7.40	+	$5.80	=	$25.20
26%	+	21%	+	1%	+	29%	+	23%	=	100%

Source: International Monetary Fund, OECD and the Aaron Institute's processing.

This calculation refers only to public administration, while excluding education, health etc.

is also behind in optic fiber infrastructures, as well as hardware and software in both the governmental and the private sector; hence, Israel's gap in ICT investment negatively affects the GDP.

The gap in labor productivity between Israel and leading countries brings into focus the opportunity provided by investing in digital systems—physical infrastructures and transition to online services.

Figure 6.1 presents the level of public capital per capita (ICT and non-ICT) in Israel, in the benchmark countries and in other countries. As can be seen, the level of public capital per capita in Israel is almost the lowest among OECD countries.

A similar picture can be seen when looking at the level of ICT public capital per capita (Figure 6.2), which is also very low in Israel compared to both the OECD average and the average of the benchmark countries.

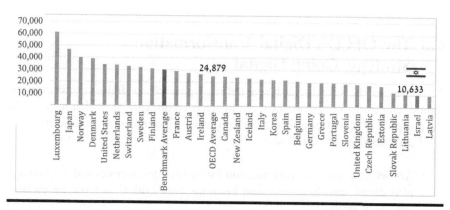

Figure 6.1   Level of public capital per capita, 2017 data in fixed 2011 dollars.

Source: Eckstein et al., 2021.

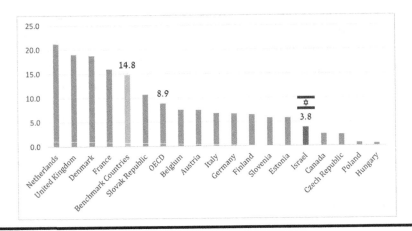

Figure 6.2   Level of ICT public capital per capita, 2017 data in fixed 2011 dollars.
Source: Eckstein et al., 2021.

Under current trends, the gap in the ICT public capital inventory is expected to expand, as the level of per capita investment in Israel is about a third of the per capita investment in the benchmark countries, and the population growth rate in Israel is significantly higher compared to those countries (Eckstein et al., 2019).

As ICT investments are crucial for productivity, growth and quality of life, their rate should be exponentially increased. A calculation that includes the sectors of public administration, health and education suggests that narrowing the gap requires an investment of $18 billion USD. Promoting digital transformation in Israel is of the highest priority as a means of increasing productivity and growth and bringing the Israeli economy to the level of leading countries by 2030.

6.3 The OECD's Digital Transformation Strategy, Going Digital

According to the OECD (2019), a holistic approach to digital transformation should refer to the integration of seven interrelated dimensions, which help realize the potential of digital transformation for the benefit of economy and society.

The dimensions are as follows:

1. **Access**—Access to communication infrastructures, services and data underpins digital transformation and becomes more critical as more people and devices go online.
2. **Use**—The power and potential of digital technologies and data for people, firms and governments depend on their effective use.

3. **Innovation**—Innovation challenges the boundaries of possibilities in the digital age, driving job creation, productivity and sustainable growth. Data-driven innovation, i.e., innovation that includes data collection, analysis and documentation, is essential for digital transformation.
4. **Jobs**—As labor markets evolve, we must ensure that digital transformation generates more and better jobs, facilitating easy and effective transitions between jobs.
5. **Society**—Digital technologies affect society in complex and interrelated ways, and all stakeholders must work together to balance benefits and risks. Furthermore, digital transformation can lead to a prosperous and inclusive society.
6. **Trust**—Trust is essential in digital environments; without it, an important source of economic and social progress will be left unexploited.
7. **Market openness**—Digital technologies change the way firms compete, trade and invest; market openness creates an enabling environment for digital transformation to flourish.

Each dimension includes a number of indicators, out of a total of 45 indicators, that can be used for mapping a country's digital status. According to the OECD, these indicators were created to keep up with frequent changes and allow an ongoing improvement and comparison between countries.

Since each country has its own unique characteristics, the OECD offers some general guidelines for a strategy aimed at realizing the potential of digital transformation. The OECD highlights the need for collaboration between various players in any country and recommends the establishment of a supporting governmental entity. Such entity would be responsible for coordination between ministries, as well as evaluations and supervision over the implementation of the chosen strategy. In addition, the OECD advises countries to include policies regarding all the aforementioned areas at the same time.

Beyond these basic recommendations, each country should establish guidelines according to its own characteristics and existing policies. These guidelines, in turn, dictate priorities and goals. Furthermore, assessment of the current status is required in order to define the right strategy.

6.4 Going Digital Indicators and GDP Per Capita

In the current study, we used ordinary least squares (OLS) regressions to analyze the associations between GDP per capita and the Going Digital model. First, we ran an OLS regression with the log of GDP per capita as the dependent variable and the digital transformation index as an explanatory variable (Figure 6.3). The digital transformation index is an integrated index consisting of six out of the seven Going

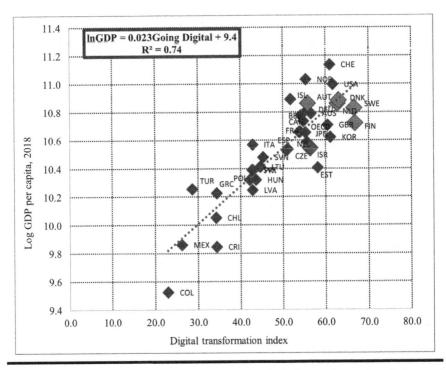

Figure 6.3   Distance to Frontier analysis—the digital transformation index and log GDP per capita.

Source: OECD data processed by the authors.

Digital dimensions (excluding "trust", for which data was not available). Figure 6.3 presents the distance to frontier (DTF), which is the gap between a country's score and the best score in the same dimension. For indicators whose high value indicate a low digital score, DTF is calculated using the following formula:

$$100 \times \frac{maximum\ indicator - indicator\ of\ country\ i}{maximum\ indicator - minimum\ indicator}$$

For indicators whose high value indicate a high digital score, DTF is calculated using the following formula:

$$100 - 100 \times \frac{maximum\ indicator - indicator\ of\ country\ i}{maximum\ indicator - minimum\ indicator}$$

As shown in Figure 6.3, Israel is positioned below the benchmark countries, marked in green, in the promotion of digital transformation and log GDP per capita.

Interestingly, Austria, whose digital transformation level is similar to that of Israel, is ranked higher in GDP per capita. This finding may indicate a more efficient utilization of the achieved level of digital transformation.

Next, we ran an OLS regression using six of the Going Digital dimensions (excluding "trust") as the explanatory variables and log GDP per capita as the dependent variable. As can be seen in Table 6.2, all six dimensions were found to be correlated with 77.7% of the log GDP per capita. We also found a positive and statistically significant relationship between each of the dimensions and the log GDP per capita. The dimensions access, society and jobs were found to have the highest correlation with the log GDP per capita.

We then used OLS regressions to examine the associations between the various indicators of the Going Digital model (explanatory variables) and log GDP per capita (dependent variable). As for the seven indicators under the access dimension, all indicators were found to be correlated with 77% of the log GDP per capita. The indicators "Fixed broadband subscriptions per 100 inhabitants" and "Share of households with broadband connections" were found to have the highest correlation (R^2 of 0.437 and 0.513, respectively).

Table 6.2 OLS Regression Examining Associations Between Six Digitalization Dimensions and Log GDP per Capita

Log GDP Per Capita	1	2	3	4	5	6	7
Access	0.017*** (0.002)						0.008* (0.004)
Use		0.014*** (0.002)					-0.01 (0.003)
Society			0.015*** (0.002)				0.005 (0.03)
Jobs				0.015*** (0.002)			0.004 (0.003)
Innovation					0.013*** (0.003)		0.04 (0.02)
Market openness						0.011** (0.004)	0.001 (0.003)
Intercept	9.596*** (0.118)	9.869*** (0.124)	9.673*** (0.129)	9.832*** (0.123)	10.093*** (0.114)	10.02*** (0.202)	9.458*** (0.136)
Observations	35	35	35	35	35	35	35
R^2	0.687	0.514	0.607	0.540	0.376	0.187	0.777

Source: OECD and Aaron Institute processing.
The seventh dimension was excluded due to lack of data for Israel.
*p < 0.05, **p < 0.01, ***p < 0.001; standard deviation in parentheses.

Under the society dimension, the following indicators were found to have the highest explanatory percentage for log GDP per capita: "E-waste generated kilograms per inhabitant", "Percentage of individuals aged 55–74 using the Internet" and "Percentage of individuals who live in households with income in the lowest quartile who use the Internet". The associations with these three indicators were found to be statistically significant, as well as the indicator "Top-performing 15–16-year-old students in science, mathematics and reading". According to OECD data, Israel's score in this indicator is 29% lower compared to the average score of the benchmark countries.

Under the jobs dimension, the indicator "Workers receiving employment-based training as a percentage of total employment" was found to have the highest correlation with log GDP per capita (0.513). The indicators "Workers receiving employment-based training, as a percentage of total employment" (not necessarily ICT training, assuming that training is an important means to supplement knowledge and skills and is essential for readapting in a digital age) and "ICT task-intensive jobs as a percentage of total employment" were found to be positively and significantly associated with log GDP per capita.

These regressions are a useful tool for screening and mapping the indicators. The findings allow us to examine the specific subindicators according to their associations and significance levels with regard to GDP per capita. However, we should also consider the current gaps between Israel and the benchmark countries. For example, "Percentage of individuals aged 55–74 using the Internet" correlates with 60% of the change in GDP per capita, with a 3% gap compared to the benchmark counties, while "Top-performing 15–16-year-old students in science, mathematics and reading" correlates with 27% of the change in GDP, but with a gap of 16% compared to the benchmark countries.

Unlike other tools for priority setting and strategic plans, the current method reveals gaps compared to leading countries and focuses on specific indicators, which allows us to refer to specific areas, estimate the existing situation and strive to maximize benefits. Hence, this method allows us to allocate budgets intelligently and directly. Furthermore, the inclusion of specific indicators allows control, readjustment when necessary and comparison to other countries.

Beyond measuring the gaps compared to leading countries, we allocated different indicators out of the seven dimensions of Going Digital into the macro model that breaks down the productivity gap (Table 6.1) according to their content (human capital, private capital, public capital etc.). The rationale was to set priorities based on issues that expand the productivity gap, attempting to reduce it and accelerate growth. After allocating and mapping the most impactful indicators, we evaluated their associations with GDP per capita and examined whether the regression supports the priorities created by Table 6.1. Table 6.3 presents the results of the regression that referred to human capital. Following the examination of the indicators, we used a regression where the explanatory variable was "Share of adults proficient at

Table 6.3 OLS Regression Examining the Relationships Between the Human Capital Indicator and Log GDP per Capita

	Per Capita GDP Log
Share of adults proficient at problem-solving in technology-rich environments	0.008*** (0.001)
Intercept	10.1*** (0.068)
Number of observations	24
R²	0.7537

Source: OECD and Aaron Institute processing.
***p < 0.001; standard deviation in parentheses.

problem-solving in technology-rich environments". This indicator alone was found to have a correlation of 75% with GDP per capita. Thus, it supports the notion that the level of human capital is important, and its effect is significant and critical.

Another example refers to investment in private capital. We used a regression to assess the business variables as explanatory variables (Table 6.4). The four presented indicators were found to have a 66% correlation with GDP per capita. We further found that the indicator "Share of businesses making e-commerce sales that sell across borders" and "Share of businesses with a web presence" were statistically

Table 6.4 OLS Regression Analyzing the Relationships Between Business Variables and per Capita GDP Log

	Log GDP per Capita
Score on OECD's digital services trade restrictiveness index	0.001 (0.002)
Share of businesses making e-commerce sales that sell across borders	**0.006*** (0.002)**
Share of businesses purchasing cloud services	0.001 (0.002)
Share of businesses with a web presence	**0.007** (0.002)**
Intercept	9.96*** (0.123)
Number of observations	31
R²	0.6594

Source: OECD and Aaron Institute processing.
**p < 0.01, ***p < 0.001; standard deviation in parentheses.

significant. The conclusion is that promoting digital transformation in and for the business sector is crucial for expanding growth.

It should be noted that the regressions presented here only show correlation between the variables, and not causality. A high R^2 does indicate high correlation, but it is likely to assume that there are other factors involved that are not assessed by the regression, and, therefore, the resulting coefficients are biased. Notwithstanding this caveat, we can safely argue that the regressions show that government investments affect the GDP and are translated to an increase in GDP since we know that ICT and its related growth are connected to government regulation and investment in ICT. We have no intention of using regressions to assess this effect because of the previously mentioned bias. We assume that the overall effect is in accordance with the coefficients of the production function, as analyzed in previous studies (for example, Eckstein et al., 2021). In this chapter, however, we suggest using the priorities derived from the regression analyses to help in setting priorities and choosing areas of investment and development in a digital strategy.

6.5 Building an Overall Strategic Plan for Digital Transformation

Governments have a critical role in promoting digital transformation, which can be divided into four areas:

1. **Investment in digital infrastructure**

   Access to good-quality Internet infrastructure is not a luxury but, rather, a fundamental amenity, like roads or electricity, which carries tremendous social and economic implications. Market failures and infrastructure gaps in small and peripheral towns require government intervention, especially in planning and supervising implementation, as well as sometimes in financing. Such involvement would guarantee access to high-quality infrastructure for the entire population. Further down the line, emphasis should be placed on the usability of infrastructure, for example, through accessible prices. Accessibility is a necessary condition for reducing inequality and providing equal opportunities in terms of services, access to information etc. The top priorities are the speedy promotion of optical fiber coverage, a 5G cellular network and the creation of a cloud services system for the government and the private sector.

2. **Digital transformation of government services**

   A full system of digital government should be established, which requires secure communication and information sharing, as well as the trust of users, to function optimally. This stage should include digitalization of all government ministries and digitalization of business regulation, enabling quick and efficient bureaucratic procedures online, including business registration and import licensing, and promoting a culture of data-based activity in the public sector.

3. **Removing obstacles, solving market failures and reducing bureaucracy and regulation**

The government should act to remove additional obstacles that may cause market failures, particularly those caused by bureaucracy and regulation. Legislation should be adjusted for the purpose of data sharing, digital signatures, digital identification and other issues related to information security and privacy.

4. **Promoting digital literacy**

Promoting digital skills among all population groups and particularly among those who lack them (in Israel: the Arab population, the Ultra-Orthodox Jewish population, and the elderly).

6.6 Summary and Conclusions

Moving a country to a path of digital transformation is a national mission. Without it, economic competitiveness will suffer. This chapter supports the hypothesis derived from the macro model (Eckstein et al., 2021), which argues that digital transformation carries significant macroeconomic effects and that investment in digital transformation affects all industries.

In promoting a strategy of digital transformation in Israel, we must set priorities based on existing conditions. This chapter examines several paths for determining such priorities. The first uses a macro model that breaks down the productivity gap and the priorities set by it, looking at the distribution of Going Digital indicators between its components. Thus, priorities are supported by the results of regressions of indicators with the dependent variable being GDP per capita.

A second way examines the gaps between Israel and the benchmark countries in Going Digital indicators. The full results of this comparison are not presented in this chapter (results are available upon request), but the comparison allows policy makers to examine the actual status of Israel compared to its counterparts around the world and establish priorities for closing gaps or creating a competitive advantage and a lead in chosen fields.

The third way offers an examination of the road maps of leading countries regarding digital transformation and establishment of priorities in accordance with the various stages implemented by these countries. Basic steps may include digital signature, a digital public services web portal for businesses and secure government email systems, after which further development and digital transformation phases will follow. An overview of these steps is not presented here, but a list for further reading is provided in the reference list.

Our recommendation is to combine these methods so that they may support each other. Using these methods, priorities can be established based on the various indicators suggested by the OECD, which could later be used to develop a detailed strategy. Using the different strategic processes, a long-term plan may be developed, divided into different ministries and governmental entities, with the ultimate goal of increasing growth and individual welfare. The next stage could include models for various ministries and an examination of their success and weaknesses. Implementation may require structural changes in government ministries or the government itself or changes in how goals are set and how their achievement is examined. These steps should be taken in an informed way, using ongoing cooperation with all relevant bodies, since these are widescale, cross-ministry processes. Continuous cooperation would allow to identify and solve market failures that may arise during the actual work and implementation.

Notes

1 The benchmark countries are Austria, Denmark, the Netherlands, Finland and Sweden.
2 Using the total market work hours for 2019 and average exchange rate for 2019.
3 There is a trickle-down effect of investment in ICT, which contributes to a more efficient use of all inputs.

References

Cecchini, S., & Scott, C. (2003). Can information and communications technology applications contribute to poverty reduction? Lessons from rural India. *Information Technology for Development*, *10*(2), 73–84.

Eckstein, Z., Lifschitz, A., Menahem-Carmi, S., & Kogot, T. (2019). *Growth strategy 2019*. The Aaron Institute for Economic Policy (Hebrew). Retrieved from www.runi.ac.il/research-institutes/economics/aiep/policy-papers/growth-and-progress/strategy-2019

Eckstein, Z., Menahem-Carmi, S., & Sumkin, S. (2021). *Investment policy strategy and reforms for enhanced productivity and growth*. The Aaron Institute for Economic Policy (Hebrew). Retrieved from www.runi.ac.il/research-institutes/economics/aiep/policy-papers/growth-and-progress/increase-productivity-and-growth/

Jorgenson, D. W., & Vu, K. (2005). Information technology and the world economy. *Scandinavian Journal of Economics*, *107*(4), 631–650.

Majeed, M. T., & Ayub, T. (2018). Information and communication technology (ICT) and economic growth nexus: A comparative global analysis. *Pakistan Journal of Commerce and Social Sciences (PJCSS)*, *12*(2), 443–476.

OECD. (2017). *OECD digital economy outlook 2017*. Paris: OECD Publishing.

OECD. (2019). Going digital: Shaping policies, improving lives, OECD Publishing, Paris, https://doi.org/10.1787/9789264312012-en.

Waqa, J. (2015). *Impact of ICT on GDP per worker: A new approach using confidence in justice system as an instrument. Evidence from 41 European countries 1996–2010.* Master of Science Thesis, Stockholm.

Further Reading

Adhele, T. (2020). *Podcast and blog: Why did Estonia succeed with its digital transformation.* Retrieved from https://ega.ee/blog_post/why-estonia-succeeded-digital-transformation

Agency for Digitization. (2016). *A stronger and more secure digital Denmark: Digital strategy 2016–2020.* Retrieved from https://en.digst.dk/media/14143/ds_singlepage_uk_web.pdf

Datar, M. (2007). Determining priorities of e-Government: A model building approach. In *5th international conference on e-Governance*, Hyderabad.

E-government Suisse. (2020). *2020–2023 e-Government strategy Switzerland.* Retrieved from www.bk.admin.ch/bk/en/home/digitale-transformation-ikt-lenkung/ikt-vorgaben/strategien-teilstrategien/sn001-e-government_strategie_schweiz.html

European Commission. (2016). e-Government in Finland. Retrieved from https://joinup.ec.europa.eu/sites/default/files/inline-files/eGovernmnent%20in%20Finland%20-%20February%202016%20-%2018_00%20-%20v2_00.pdf

European Commission. (2019). *Digital government factsheet 2019 Finland.* Retrieved from https://joinup.ec.europa.eu/sites/default/files/inline-files/Digital_Government_Factsheets_Finland _2019.pdf

OECD. (2019). Digital government review of Sweden: Towards a data-driven public sector. In *OECD digital government studies*. Paris: OECD Publishing. https://doi.org/10.1787/4daf932b-en

RCI—Risalat Consultants International. (2020). *Success story—Estonia's 20 years of digital transformation—The Digital Republic.* Retrieved from https://risalatconsultants.com/success-story-estonia-20-years-digital-transformation.

The Danish Government. (2017). *A solid ICT Foundation, strategy for ICT management in central government.* Retrieved from https://en.digst.dk/media/15367/a-solid-ict-foundation-strategy-for-ict-management-in-central-government.pdf

Chapter 7

Developing Students from All Backgrounds in Data Science for the Government

Rebecca Sharples and Mark Daniel Ward

Content

DOI: 10.1201/9781003369783-7

7.1 Introduction

Our society, across all industries, is experiencing a massive shift in cultural expectations, work–life balance, the way we work, and technological innovation. Of course, the COVID pandemic has impacted many aspects of work modalities, but much more broadly, the massive shift is due to a "changing of the guard" in which millions of baby boomers are retiring and creating a vacuum, with myriad opportunities for younger workers. Simultaneously, a portion of retirement-age workers are deciding to continue working (Sewdas et al., 2017), holding on to jobs that could be shifting to early-career employees. In particular, data science is simultaneously transforming people's lives and workplaces. In addition to the need for new and experienced hires to take data science–related training—either prior to or at the onset of their employment with the government—the current workforce needs to train incoming new workers on the institutional knowledge that they have developed in their professions over the years.

7.2 The Evolving Way We Communicate

People born in Generation X were the last generation who (as a generalization) did not have internet access and often did not have personal computers. Generation X did grow up with pagers but would typically use payphones or landlines to return calls after receiving a page. When cellular phone technology emerged, the devices were hardwired into cars or encased in briefcases and phone bags. As microchip technology and battery power evolved and phones became smaller and more portable, cellular phone technology was more widely adopted. Millennials and Generation Z were introduced to iPhone and Android technology in 2007. During the last 15 years, these technologies have continued to rapidly evolve and can now be considered pervasive. As handheld technology has advanced, so too has other technologies that have resulted in the collection and/or digitization of unfathomable amounts of data to be stored for future use. Furthermore, with the increasing availability of data in most facets of society, decision-making is increasingly data driven, and it is necessary for the government as well as two- and four-year universities and colleges to continue to adapt data science training to meet the needs of the talent pipeline.

7.3 The Need for Data Science Skills across Industries

As communication and computing technologies have transformed our lives, our society, and the way we work, so too have they transformed our opportunity to collect data about every facet of human life. Every aspect of people's lives has been impacted by some form of data collection, data analysis, modeling, and predictive analytics (Hachmeister et al., 2021). This data revolution is constantly evolving and is pervasive, affecting every component of our society, including not only the ways that people live and work, but also the way that the government creates and uses legal frameworks to protect people, companies, industries, scientific development, etc. Industry 4.0 has arisen in tandem with the widespread adoption and integration of data collection and usage (Atharvan et al., 2022). Data-driven decision-making is prevalent and omnipresent, and it cannot be ignored.

Companies, industries, government agencies, scientific organizations, universities, etc. have all collected massive repositories of data. At the same time, data science continues to emerge as a changing, evolving discipline that is increasing the ability of organizations to make intelligent, insightful, reproducible, fair decisions based on data repositories. More recently, streaming data, high-speed networks, edge computing, and other real-time data-driven technologies are revolutionizing the ability of organizations to make decisions. It is imperative that early-career data scientists learn how to analyze data, using available tools, algorithms, devices, and methodologies to capitalize on data repositories and real-time streams of data.

Government and corporate audits are a key example of such data revolutions. As recently as two decades ago, even the largest audit and consultancy firms, such as PwC, KPMG, Deloitte, and EY, were using personal computers and handwritten annotations on printed paper. Physical copies of all aspects of audit cycles were maintained and then stored at offsite locations (for instance, at Iron Mountain), supporting an entire industry of document retention businesses. Once electronic storage became more widely available, data could be synchronized with server-hosted databases, and colleagues would have to communicate to avoid version control issues. Now, however, audit firms and government entities have the ability to conduct audit processes in real time and work directly in the server-hosted database rather than working on biweekly, monthly, or yearly cycles. Current and future undergraduate and graduate students of data science programs, business schools, engineering and technology schools, and medical schools all have a need to implement and adopt technologies that enable audit processes to be performed "live" rather than at regular points in time.

Such innovations and changes are being adopted across all industries, such as manufacturing, agriculture, consumer science, aerospace, retail, automotive, pharmaceuticals, technology, etc. Digitization of scientific journals, medical records, repositories of data from trials, etc. have all accelerated traditional means of scientific discovery in the pharmaceutical industry. Recently, computational drug discovery and genomic analysis are both revolutionizing the speed with which new treatments can be developed and efficiently tested for efficacy. Data-driven advances in the supply chain enable the pharmaceutical industry to further accelerate its ability to translate research and development into practice.

The federal, state, and local governments at all levels have a similar opportunity to adapt to data science innovations. This includes machine learning innovations for aerospace, defense, and the military; analytics and for pharmaceutical development and healthcare systems; the changing face of legal ownership and usage of software, community-developed algorithms and tools, and computational environments; algorithms used by police and judicial branches; data-driven alerts, warning systems, and communications; algorithms that guide ongoing dynamic relationships for global politics and foreign relations; voting systems and districting; and daily administration. Federal, state, and local governments are utilizing citizens' and companies' tax dollars with a responsibility to implement data science innovations in ethical and fair ways to improve efficient and equitable government practices. The government must continue to embrace digital transformation and keep pace with digital innovations in the private sector. For these reasons and many more, the field of data science and the early-career students who create and implement data science innovations are critically important for the growth and success of government at all levels. Government adoption of data science will continue to influence strategic and tactical decisions about every aspect of how its citizens live and work.

7.4 What Should Students Learn That They Are Not Learning Right Now?

One example of a successful program for data science for all is The Data Mine at Purdue University. The Data Mine, currently in its fifth year and experiencing tremendous annual growth, is a foundational data science program within the Office of the Provost, offering fundamental data science experiences to students from all majors throughout Purdue's West Lafayette, Indiana, campus (Hardin et al., 2015). Throughout this chapter, we will reflect on ways that The Data Mine is enabling students to learn and apply data science skills in practice. The Data Mine students are well prepared to address challenges that government organizations (at all levels) face.

This experiential learning program does not use formalized lectures. Instead, The Data Mine provides hands-on projects for students that rely on extremely large data sets for students to learn various data science tools like R, Python, SQL, and bash scripts. In its first year, 2018, the program enrolled approximately 100 students, but it has grown quickly to approximately 1300 undergraduate and graduate students enrolled in fall 2022. The premise of this program is not to make data scientists out of all students but, rather, to enable students from any major to learn data competencies and skills that they can apply in their chosen domain and major area of focus.

A key skill that new graduates will increasingly need, in order to apply data science innovations in government, is the ability to work with massive data sets and/or with data that is streaming in real time. It is also imperative that students have domain expertise and understand the context of the field in which the data science methodologies will be applied. These skills, in tandem, will help students to be better prepared to make data-driven decisions. In particular, recent graduates who choose to work in government need to understand the underlying engineering, legal, medical, scientific, or technical skills so that they are also well positioned to make high-level strategic decisions that might change the focus of an entire organization.

Data science is a field requiring students and professionals to be comfortable working with data that is larger than they can work with locally on their machines. They need to be comfortable working in high-performance computing environments and in cloud-based computing environments. Students and new professionals need to know how to work with data that is stored in remote data warehouses and data lakes or with data that is massively streaming in large quantities and at fast rates. This requires them to have familiarity with working on projects with team members with diverse skill sets. It also requires the individuals to understand how to utilize environments such as JupyterLab. Students do need to be comfortable with data visualizations and dashboards, but it is also increasingly helpful for them to understand how to work on all aspects of application development and full stack development.

Midcareer government employees will continue to have a need for retraining and for expanding their skills. Data science projects at colleges and universities need to be adaptable in working with businesses, corporations, industry, and government at all levels to foster programs for midcareer employees to learn or relearn data-related skills and competencies.

7.5 How Are They Going to Apply Those Skills?

Early-career employees with data science competencies will be well positioned to build new models for government reports or to revisit previous models and expand them to take advantage of data science innovations. Students with skills in both data science and also in organizational behavior and human resources are well prepared to tackle issues such as recruiting, retention, attrition/absence, productivity, changing work environments and work modalities, etc. Political science students who have data science training in cartography and modeling are well prepared to work with government agencies to ensure that voting districts are thoughtfully and fairly specified. Some data science transformations in years to come have not (yet) even been imagined or invented. There are myriad opportunities for early-career employees to be innovative about how data science transformations will impact the government.

7.6 How Do Students Learn to Connect Their Data Science Skills to Applications in a Specific Domain?

Rather than students learning to connect their data science skills to various applications in a specific domain, they will be more dynamic in their fields of choice by starting their career in a job related to their major, and as they build their careers, they realize and explore the need to have more data competency skills. (These data competencies are constantly evolving as well.) Although many students start by choosing a field of study while still in high school, a good percentage of students go into two- and four-year schools not knowing what they want to study, and they instead start with an undecided major in general studies or exploratory study programs (Gordon & Steele, 2015). Programs like exploratory studies allow the students to take a variety of different subjects and explore more to see what they might be interested in pursuing further. Some students know early on what they want to study and can almost immediately begin their major-related classes. As students delve deeper into their concentrations, they may be exposed in some way, through faculty marketing, campus advertising, or offered electives, to the topic of data science. This is the first step in students realizing the extent to which data impacts every aspect of their field and potentially their careers. Early-career data science training enables people to analyze data quickly, effectively, and in a reproducible way—and to set themselves apart from their peers in their fields as they do so.

7.7 Digital Transformation Requires People, and There Are Not Sufficiently Many People Working in the Data Sciences

The government will need to continue to have some emphasis on the targeted recruiting of students with data science competencies. Universities will also need to continue to have emphasis on data science training across all disciplines. The Data Mine at Purdue University is a model for such transformational shifts. The Data Mine has enrolled students from over 100 different majors who work together to solve data-driven issues. The focus of the program is to develop data science skill sets for those students not studying data science as their primary focus or major. Many of these students will seek a data science certificate to supplement their degree, but they are not actually data science majors. These students and early-career professionals will be helpful in furthering the digital transformation for various areas of government that do not pertain specifically to IT. For example, in the CDC, where past testing data could play a critical role in the future of predictive health outcomes if digitized, science professionals with data analytics backgrounds could make a significant impact on the pace at which our government can compete with other governmental agencies around the world.

7.7.1 Chief Data Scientist (a Relatively New Position)

Many companies that have undergone a digital transformation have created a chief data scientist role. This role typically reports to the CEO or another C-suite executive. The person in this leadership position is responsible for ensuring the completeness and accuracy of data and related data analytics activities for an organization. This person serves as a conduit between the technical staff in an organization and the executive-level leadership team. Specifically, this person can take strategic directives and translate them into a tactical plan that makes sense to the technical team. Alternatively, this person can also field technical issues and questions and translate them into business language that can be understood and addressed by executive leadership.

7.8 What Is the Talent Pipeline Like? What Are Universities and Community Colleges in the Data Sciences Doing?

There is currently a shortage of data science and analytics talent in the job market, which includes students coming right out of college from both two- and four-year institutions (Ampil et al., 2017; Gould et al., 2017). More and more universities and colleges, including two-year community colleges, are implementing data science programs into their curricula. Some programs are data science majors, but many are concentrations within mathematics, computer science, or statistics or some type of data science certificate. Graduate programs in data analytics and data science are dramatically on the rise as well (North Carolina State University, 2022).

There is an exploding level of interest in this topic as well, as both students and employers are realizing the importance of data science and the benefit to the business. For example, at Purdue University, The Data Mine is a department under the Office of the Provost that offers a "Data Science for All" program. Students from all majors are able to take fundamental data science courses and apply their skills in research and industry settings. This program recruits students at all levels, including incoming first-year undergraduate students through Ph.D. candidates. Because these courses in The Data Mine are not required as part of any degree program at Purdue, the students are there of their own accord and are driven to succeed. They feel passionate that this material will benefit them in their future careers.

7.9 Looking at the Talent Pipeline for Both New Hires as Well as Experienced Hires Changing the Focus of Their Careers

There is a huge opportunity for government to embrace the digital transformation, not only when recruiting new hires but also when recruiting and/or recruiting experienced hires. By providing annual training or opt-in training, not only will human resources teams be able to ensure the company's workforce will continue to stay relevant in the age of technology, but they are more likely to ensure that their employees are satisfied with what they are learning and what they are contributing in their job functions. This is especially relevant for hires who might not have had data science training opportunities prior to being onboarded. Specifically, many colleges and universities do not yet have data science programs. For those that do have such programs, it is essential to ensure that the program is welcoming and supportive for students from groups that are traditionally underrepresented in the computational and mathematical sciences. As noted in the 2021 National Center for Science and Engineering Statistics Roundtable Report, African American men make up 5.9% of the total U.S. population but take only 3.2% of the share of science and engineering occupation; African American women make up 6.5% of the total U.S. population but only take up 1.8% of science and engineering occupations. Hispanic men make up 9.3% of the U.S. population but only 5.1% of science and engineering occupations, and Hispanic women make up 9.1% of the U.S. population but only 2.4% of science and engineering occupations (NCSES, 2021). These opportunity gaps show what the current talent pipeline looks like for students with data science training but also where there is enormous opportunity to more fully include early-career scientists and engineers in the emerging data science workforce.

7.10 The Importance of Employees with Diversified Skill Sets

Because our culture is so rapidly changing in the way we view and use technology, the way we do our jobs is also changing. This forces us as professionals to be dynamic in what we are able to do on a day-to-day basis. By honing various skill sets, we are able to shift gears abruptly when needed and contribute to a wider range of productive functions at work, thus increasing our value to our employers. This is important because, while roles might become obsolete as technology advances or as workers explore professional development by shifting laterally, these professionals will be able to more quickly shift their focus to other roles that still contribute and add value to the government organization. For example, a college graduate holding a bachelor of science in chemistry might start out as a chemist for the CDC, but after taking some data science training, they may shift into a role doing more chemical analysis or computational drug discovery using machine learning models. Such

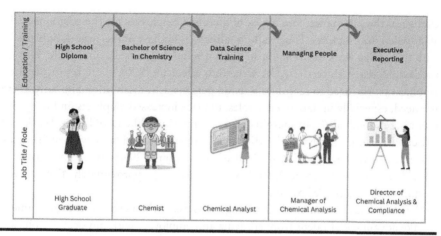

Figure 7.1   Example career progression of a scientist with data analytics training and the opportunities for moving around to different paths within the company.

a person might grow more quickly into a senior manager role with more reporting responsibilities and play a leading role in the federal government, especially when a pandemic arises. See Figure 7.1 for illustration of an example career progression of a scientist with data analytics training and the opportunities for moving around to different paths within a government agency or in an industry role.

7.11 Staff Retention, Promotion, and Midcareer (Re-)training Are More Cost-Effective Than Constantly Rehiring in a Mobile Workforce

Companies that do not spend the energy and resources on maintaining their current employees are likely to lose those employees within five years Craig (2015). With the baby boomer generation leaving the workforce, it will become more and more critical for employers to put in place some kind of mechanism to transfer the knowledge to the younger-generation workers filling the empty spots. Kacmar et al. (2006) note that, when an organization can maintain a stable workforce, the working processes from their employees become more efficient and, essentially, more profitable.

7.12 Accessibility and the Data Sciences

Our culture is shifting significantly, both in what employers expect from their employees but also in what the employees expect for accommodations from their employers. COVID-19 was certainly a catalyst for this shift, but with the recent change in the job market and a lack of qualified employees for the positions available, when an employee is actually qualified, they have more negotiation power with things like work location (onsite/hybrid/remote), hours, flexibility, etc. During the last 32 years (since the ADA went into effect in 1990), there is an increased emphasis on the need to recruit and retain persons with disabilities. Similarly, there is a need, especially in data science roles, to place increased emphasis on hiring and retaining individuals from marginalized communities, like LGBTQA+, Black and African American, Latinx, and Indigenous populations, and more women. The current rate of women in STEM fields after graduation is 29.4% (meaning 29.4% of STEM employees are women), while women make up approximately 47.9% of the workforce overall (NCSES, 2021).

With the advancement of technology, it is easier than ever for the government to take advantage of talent from students and employees with physical disabilities. This is also an opportunity for the government to increase employment of veterans, especially disabled veterans. Data-driven advancements like automation, text to speech, screen readers, edge computing on devices, biomedical devices, etc. all have the potential to improve the lives of Americans who have accessibility needs. Persons with disabilities make up approximately 3.7% of the U.S. overall workforce ages 16+ but only 2.1% of the workforce in science and engineering (NCSES, 2021). Furthermore, the study published by the National Center for Science and Engineering Statistics noted that persons with disabilities were just as likely as those without disabilities to major in science and engineering fields, and the top two disabilities reported were related to the ability to see and hear (NCSES, 2021).

There are also more tools and information widely available for employers to close the gap for their employees needing accommodations. For example, in The Data Mine at Purdue University, our team has a full-time interpreter on staff, and the entire team is enthusiastically learning ASL so that we are better prepared to communicate directly with deaf learners. This mindset also contributes to a sense of community and belonging within the team. A sense of belonging and self-efficacy leads to job satisfaction and adds to the likelihood that an employer will be able to maintain its employees for longer periods of time.

7.13 FAIR and CARE Principles

FAIR and CARE principles govern the use of Indigenous data and should be considered by all organizations in the government when performing data analytics any time Indigenous-related data is used. Specifically, CARE stands for **c**ollective benefit, **a**uthority to control their own data, **r**esponsibility to engage respectfully, and **e**thics (RDAIIDSIG, 2019). The FAIR principles are **f**indability, **a**ccessibility, **i**nteroperability, and **r**eusability. It is important that government at all levels should be mindful of these principles in developing data science initiatives (Wilkinson et al., 2016).

It is especially important to be mindful that data is used ethically and specifically for the benefit of—and in consultation with—Indigenous peoples (RDAIIDSIG, 2019). Moreover, colleges and universities need to develop data science programs and pathways to government careers in such a way that early-career scientists learn about ethical development and usage of data science methodologies and algorithms.

7.14 DEI and Flexible Working Arrangements

Government organizations at all levels—federal, state, and local—should be exemplary leaders in how we want our culture and society to operate, especially with regard to hiring practices and ensuring not only equality but equity across, race, gender, sexual orientation, disability status, etc. By gaining an understanding of the various cultures within our country, not just cis-gender white males, we can more effectively determine how to make sure our employees are working the way they want to work. For example, in a survey conducted by the Slack Think Tank Future Forum, only 3% of Black female employees wanted to return to the office after COVID-19 (Elliott, 2021). Black women are becoming more vocal about this preference after COVID because of the more widely accepted practices of working from home—and they find that it can be exhausting to have to go into work every day and experience and tolerate microaggressions from their colleagues day after day (Williams et al., 2022). Rather than deal with this, talented employees are vocalizing their desire to work from home in what they consider a safe zone environment. By facilitating flexible working arrangements with their employees, government organizations are more effectively fostering an inclusive and cohesive working environment (Elliott, 2021).

In addition, some early-career people may be more open to or interested in working remotely. Especially now that the COVID-19 pandemic has settled into being a part of our everyday life, many people, especially younger generations, are taking advantage of the current market where they can negotiate terms that are more agreeable to their style of living, such as working a hybrid or fully remote schedule.

7.15 Importance of Leveraging Learning about Data Transformations

The topic of data transformation is new for many industries and businesses, as well as government at all levels; however, many companies have already successfully undergone a digital transformation. This may include how they handle their server backups, going from a physical tape system to storing data digitally on the cloud. It could be how a company went from printing and storing all of its work orders in hard copy to having a digital PDF file then converted by software to a digital record or even to using an ERP system to handle the record digitally and store the data in a relational database for easy retrieval. More recently, digital transformations include a substantial conversion to a cloud-based computing environment and a major investment in computational resources for data-driven modeling, prediction, and decision-making.

7.16 Cost-Effective to Foster Internships with Undergraduate Students and How Effective Their Work Can Be

By creating internship opportunities with undergraduate students at all sorts of universities, the government can leverage the talents of students from a variety of backgrounds and with a vast array of skill sets and perspectives. Student-led projects create an opportunity for the student to grow and learn in a safe environment. The employer can foster a relationship with the students that is based on a history of strong work product and work ethic, especially those students who might work on the project for multiple years. Current undergraduate students tend to be more creative and think outside the box, as compared to seasoned professionals, because they bring a fresh view, especially to data-driven problems.

7.17 R&D Types of Projects with Undergraduate Students

Undergraduate students can also work directly with mentors from the government at all levels and also at Federally Funded R&D Centers (see https://www.nsf.gov/statistics/ffrdclist/). Indeed, research can be both more creative and more concrete when students perform the work under the guidance of an instructor or professional in the field (Herrick et al., 2015). Not only does the research improve and reinforce learning outcomes for the students, but also it can lead to strong relationships during the recruitment process for future employment. This type of research prepares the students for graduate school, but it can also be beneficial as they become aware of workforce opportunities in government and ultimately are recruited and retained in such positions (Herrick et al., 2015).

7.18 Gen Z—Has Learned How to Learn

Historically, employees have been trained in a specific job function, and that is the role they focused on until they moved on or received some sort of additional training that would allow them to expand their job function. However, many senior employees, who are now on the cusp of leaving the workforce for retirement, are leaving behind decades of domain expertise in whatever they were experts in. For example, mainframe and COBOL programming is a dying skill set. People trained in those technologies, which were new decades ago but are now so obsolete almost nobody trains in them, are retiring at a pace faster than we are skilling up replacements. The new generation coming into the workforce is more equipped in this dynamic and ever-shifting work environment to learn how to learn. Even though they may not be coming straight out of college as COBOL experts, they may have taken a variety of other programming courses and be equipped to learn the skill quickly and adapt to the needs of the organization. They are not a generation resistant to change but one that embraces change as a gateway to a brighter future.

7.19 Ability for Intergovernmental Agencies to Work Together

Just like universities create partnerships with each other, governmental agencies have the ability to do the same and create synergies across the organizations and departments. Not only could sharing resources (where the nature of the work allows) be more efficient for productivity, but it also could reduce the costs of turnover if employees feel like their skills are dynamic across departments.

7.20 Wanting to Scale Up Digital Transformation, Need to Talk about the Budget

A key component in developing the data science talent pipeline is ensuring there are adequate budgetary dollars allocated towards recruiting and retention for recent graduates with some training in data science. Also, there is opportunity for governmental departments to incorporate data science training into their onboarding process, much like the way big audit firms like PwC or Deloitte send new hires to three weeks of training as soon as they start. Governmental departments could add two or three weeks of heads-down fundamental data science training to almost any position in any agency that might be relevant, setting up their employees to be successful and more effective not only at performing their immediate jobs tactically but also contributing towards more of a strategic departmental effort with their ability to analyze large sets of data relevant to their field.

References

Ampil, C., Cardenas-Navia, L. I., Elzey, K., Fenlon, M., Fitzgerald, B. K., & Hughes, D. (Eds.). (2017). *Investing in America's data science and analytics talent: The case for action* (No. 297803–2017; pp. 1–28). PwC and Business-Higher Education Forum. Retrieved from www.bhef.com/sites/default/files/bhef_2017_investing_in_dsa.pdf

Atharvan, G., Koolikkara Madom Krishnamoorthy, S., Dua, A., & Gupta, S. (2022). A way forward towards a technology-driven development of industry 4.0 using big data analytics in 5G-enabled IIoT. *International Journal of Communication Systems*, *35*(1). https://doi.org/10.1002/dac.5014

Craig, M. (2015). Cost effectiveness of retaining top internal talent in contrast to recruiting top talent. *Competition Forum*, *13*(2), 203–209.

Elliott, B. (2021). Hybrid rules: The emerging playbook for flexible work. *Future Forum*. Retrieved January 28, 2021, from https://futureforum.com/2021/01/28/hybrid-rules-the-emerging-playbook-for-flexible-work/

Gordon, V., & Steele, G. (2015). *The undecided college student: An academic and career advising challenge* (4th. ed.). Springfield, Illinois: Charles C. Thomas, Publisher, Ltd.

Gould, R., Peck, R., Hanson, J., Horton, N., Kotz, B., Kubo, K., Malyn-Smith, J., Rudis, M., Thompson, B., Ward, M. D., & Wong, R. (2017). *The two-year college data science summit* (NSF DUE-1735199; pp. 1–36). National Science Foundation. Retrieved from www.amstat.org/asa/files/pdfs/2018TYCDS-Final-Report.pdf

Hachmeister, N., Wei, K., Thei, J., & Decker, R. (2021). Balancing plurality and educational essence: Higher education between data-competent professionals and data self-empowered citizens. *Data*, *6*(10). https://doi.org/10.3390/data6020010

Hardin, J., Hoerl, R., Nicholas, J., Horton, D., Nolan, B., Baumer, O., Hall-Holt, P., Murrell, R., Peng, P., Roback, D., Lang, T., & Ward, M. D. (2015). Data science in statistics curricula: Preparing students to "think with data". *The American Statistician*, *69*(4), 343–353. https://doi.org/10.1080/00031305.2015.1077729

Herrick, S., Matthias, W., & Nielson, D. (2015). How collaborations with undergraduates improve both learning and research: With examples from international development experiments. *Political Science & Politics*, *48*(1), 48–52. https://doi.org/10.1017/S1049096514001590

Kacmar, K. M., Andrews, M. C., Van Rooy, D. L., Steilberg, R. C., & Cerrone, S. (2006). Sure everyone can be replaced . . . but at what cost? Turnover as a predictor of unit-level performance. *Academy of Management Journal*, *49*(1), 133–144. https://doi.org/10.5465/AMJ.2006.20785670

National Center for Science and Engineering Statistics (NCSES). (2021). *Women, minorities, and persons with disabilities in science and engineering: 2021. Special report NSF 21–321*. Alexandria, VA: National Science Foundation. Retrieved from https://ncses.nsf.gov/wmpd

North Carolina State University. (2022). *Institute for advanced analytics. Graduate degree programs in analytics and data science*. Retrieved from https://analytics.ncsu.edu/?page_id=4184

Research Data Alliance International Indigenous Data Sovereignty Interest Group (RDAI-IDSIG). (2019, September). *CARE principles for Indigenous data governance* (The Global Indigenous Data Alliance). GIDA-global.org.

Sewdas, R., de Wind, A., van der Zwaan, L. G. L., van der Borg, W. E., Steenbeek, R., van der Beek, A. J., & Boot, C. R. L. (2017). Why older workers work beyond the retirement age: A qualitative study. *BMC Public Health*, *17*(1), 672. https://doi.org/10.1186/s12889-017-4675-z

Wilkinson, M. D., et al. (2016). The FAIR guiding principles for scientific data management and stewardship. *Scientific Data*, *3*, 160018.

Williams, J. C., Andrews, O., & Boginsky, M. (2022). Why many women of color don't want to return to the office. Harvard Business Review.

Chapter 8

Data Science Mentoring without Borders

Geanina Watkins

Content

DOI: 10.1201/9781003369783-8

Foreword

Ceri Regan, Programme Manager International Capability

The International Data Science Accelerator Programme is a mentoring project developed and delivered by the Data Science Campus (DSC), Office for National Statistics (ONS), UK. It explores the process, logistics, impact, and possibilities that international mentoring can offer in the field of data science.

The programme is modelled on the UK Data Science Accelerator Programme, which has been run by the DSC since 2017. The programme initially targeted a small number of government analysts who were looking to upskill in data science through a small project with guided mentorship. The programme grew rapidly across the UK due to an increase in demand for data science skills in government at that time, born from the need to work with new data sources for experimental and/or official statistics.

As with most work at the DSC, products are reviewed to see if they can be scaled out internationally to benefit those in other national statistical offices (NSOs). The DSC developed the Data Science Accelerator for international organisations to build their ability to work with new data sources, learning and applying new coding skills and exploring applications of data science tools and techniques.

There were two important elements that played a role in driving forward the international scale-out of this mentoring programme.

1. Through membership of the United Nations Task Team on Training, Competencies, and Capacity Development, the team worked to develop a "UN Big Data Training Curriculum". This had highlighted the need to train analysts globally with big data/data science knowledge and skills. While training courses play their part in developing those skills, the application of learning through hands-on project work was missing.
2. Through the team's regular work and engagement with NSOs (mostly in less developed countries), there was strong awareness of the challenges being faced to recruit data science skills directly into NSOs. This is often not a straightforward process when there is not a large pot of data science graduates to recruit from, or little financial capacity for this type of growth.

Hence a "grow your own" approach, through upskilling of analysts already at the NSO through project work with mentorship, was viewed strongly by the UK DSC as key to supporting the growth of data science capability globally. In early 2021, the team developed plans and agreed on the principles and processes on which the International Data Science Accelerator Programme would be founded. A pilot programme was undertaken during September to December 2021, and the official programme launched in January 2022.

This chapter was drafted after just one full year of the programme being in place. As of September 2021, it has already enriched the learning of 47 analysts at 14 NSOs, and its popularity continues to grow after each successful cohort.

8.1 The International Data Science Accelerator Programme

8.1.1 Introduction

The International Data Science Accelerator Programme is based on the structure of the existing and highly successful UK Data Science Accelerator Programme, which has been delivered by the DSC since 2017.

The UK Data Science Accelerator Programme has been developing the skills of public sector analysts through project-based mentoring since 2015, having been previously run by a different government department. As of September 2021, it has supported over 400 participants from more than 100 UK organisations. In December 2022, it was preparing for its 23rd cohort to be mentored in 2023 and celebrating the end of cohort 22, which brought together 22 mentors and mentees.

This is a capability-building programme that gives analysts from across the UK public sector the opportunity to develop their data science skills. It is supported by the UK ONS and the UK Government Office for Science and Civil Service analytical professions (statistics, economics, operational research, and social research).

The programme's success is not only down to the enthusiasm of participants wanting to learn new skills and help grow their organisation's capacity to make better use of data but also the willingness of experienced data scientists who take time out of their busy schedules to improve the data science skills of the public sector through coaching and mentoring.

The relationship between the mentor and mentee is vital to a successful outcome in an environment where time is limited and there can be challenges to overcome. The key aims of the UK programme are to support the UK National Data Strategy and to increase data science capability across the UK public sector.

Based on the UK programme's foundational elements, the International Data Science Accelerator Programme has been developed with the key aims of building data science capability while also promoting global collaboration and knowledge exchange. The expected impact from the international programme is to

- increase data science capability across global NSOs and
- increase the knowledge, skills, and understanding of the role and application of new data sources for use in experimental or official statistics.

8.1.2 Background

The International Data Science Accelerator mentoring programme is aimed at analysts from NSOs who are looking to improve their data science skills and potentially become data scientists in the future.

There is no cost for mentees in the programme, and mentors don't receive any monetary incentive for sharing their knowledge. It is delivered through the keenness of mentors wanting to share their knowledge and support for others in building big data and data science capability. Hence, as more mentors are attracted to participate in the programme, the programme can expand accordingly. This is an important principle that continues to evolve with each cohort.

8.1.3 The Programme

Created to accelerate existing and new knowledge and to enrich it through practice, the programme is structured around the delivery of a small data science project with mentorship, which can be delivered within a 12-week period. It requires analysts from NSOs across the world to identify a certain challenge or problem within their business area that may be solved using non-traditional data sources or new data science tools and techniques.

The projects are experimental but should result in a prototype that can be implemented at the NSO. Some examples include

- the use of web-scraped data in the development of price indices,
- the development of a reproducible analytical pipeline using an open-source coding tool, and
- the application of machine learning techniques to shipping data to produce estimates of trade or tourism.

It is mandatory that the mentee's project proposal has line management and senior leadership approval at the NSO. It must be agreed that it fits with the NSO's data strategy, and the applicant must be allocated time to do the work by their line manager so that mentees can manage the project work around their current job role.

During the 12-week programme, the mentee spends one day per week working on the data science project and receives remote support from their mentor for two to three hours on their agreed day of the week. If this is not possible, the mentor and mentee agree on a more suitable equivalent to accommodate clashes with schedules, time zones, etc. The mentor and mentee ideally have access to Microsoft Teams or another video conferencing tool to ensure effective communication throughout the cohort.

As the programme brings together professionals from across different time zones, working patterns, and cultures, some flexibility and adaptability have been

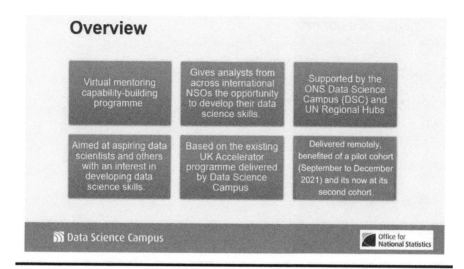

Figure 8.1 High-level overview of the International Data Science Accelerator Programme.

built into the programme. Thus, where mentoring is traditionally done one-to-one, the International Accelerator supports the inclusion of teams of mentees (maximum of three) and teams of mentors (maximum of two).

A high-level overview of the programme is given in Figure 8.1.

The programme brings together mentees (analysts) from NSOs and mentors from other NSOs or established global organisations such as the UN, PARIS21, the International Monetary Fund, and the World Bank.

To ensure progress, the DSC project officer who leads the coordination and administration of this programme has developed a process, framework, and time-line that ensure two cohorts can be run per annum. The framework encompasses the following phases, which will be looked at in more detail in the "How It Works" section:

- promotion and application,
- selection and matching,
- induction,
- cohort check-in 1—short presentations by mentees and mentors,
- cohort check-in 2—short presentations by mentees and mentors,
- cohort check-in 3 and evaluation—short presentations by mentees and mentors,
- graduation—final presentation of project work by mentees, and
- programme evaluation.

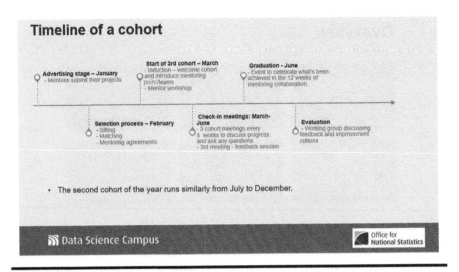

Figure 8.2   Timeline of a cohort.

The associated details and timeline are shown in Figure 8.2.

8.2 The Programme Process

Let's take a look at some of the steps that have been taken to create the International Data Science Accelerator Programme, starting with the programme pilot.

8.2.1 The Pilot

The pilot cohort was designed to test the scaled-out structure of the UK Accelerator Programme process. After a brief promotion phase, it was successful in attracting four pairs of international mentors and mentees from various parts of the world, and the participant countries and associated projects are shared in Table 8.1.

Following a virtual induction held on 13 September 2021, the pilot ran until 3 December 2021. Three cohort check-ins were held during the 12-week period, where the DSC project officer also used meetings to obtain feedback on the programme and to make general observations about the programme. All four teams achieved their initial objectives and reported that the experience was highly enriching and constructive for the development of new data science knowledge and skills.

A formal (virtual) graduation event was held on 14 December 2021, where the UK national statistician was one of several high-profile speakers to offer congratulations to the participants and express support for this exciting initiative.

Table 8.1 Pilot Cohort Participants and Projects

Mentors	Mentees	Project
Ghana	**Zimbabwe**	An analysis of the relationships among unemployment, foreign trade, technology, investment in human capital, and how they influence economic growth in Southern African countries
UN Asia Pacific	**Vietnam**	The system of gold chain and US dollar collection, continuously updated by day and analysed for processing
UAE	**Jordan**	Automate the data coding for (occupation, scientific specialization, economic activity) as classification statistical, using natural language processing and machine learning techniques
Poland	**Vietnam**	Determining the labour demand of employer in the period of COVID-19

A great programme that enforces cross-country networking and emphasised the importance of mentoring teams rather than one mentee, at least at international level. I have enjoyed working with such a great and hardworking team. We have agreed to keep the collaboration moving forward and looking forward to more future projects.

The programme connected us to mentors and colleagues from different countries. Looking forward to working with more regional and international teams."

(H. S.—mentor from the Federal Competitiveness and Statistics Centre, UAE)

Following the pilot, a formal evaluation process was applied and feedback absorbed. Areas for improvement were identified as follows:

■ improved application forms for mentee and mentors that contain shorter and clearer questions,

■ the introduction of an English language knowledge indicator to ensure that the communication between mentors and mentees is possible, and

■ the introduction of a data ethics self-assessment form to be completed by the mentees to ensure a clear understanding of data protection regulations.

8.2.2 *The Launch*

An intensive promotion campaign was used as the programme was launched. Talks were given to an international audience of NSO data science leaders at the EXPO event in Dubai in January 2022. This secured the involvement of the (then) newly established four UN Regional Hubs, which were keen to promote and support the programme across their affiliated regions (Latin America and the Caribbean, Africa, United Arab Emirates [UAE], and Asia and Pacific).

Applications for the first cohort of 2022 were received from five mentors and 45 mentees. Five mentors were matched with nine mentees, and the final project selections are shared in Table 8.2.

Three check-in meetings were held throughout the course of the 12-week period, followed by a graduation event, where participants presented their work and demonstrated their achievements. All pairs/teams delivered on their projects and objectives.

Recognising that international mentees were giving so much of their time to this non-accredited programme, the DSC developed a certificate of completion for all mentees so that they could show evidence from participating in this training. The mentors, without whom this programme could not run, received a personal

Table 8.2 Cohort I—Participants and Projects

Mentors	Mentees	Project
UAE	Sri Lanka NSO	Predict the retail price of top essential import food items of the Sri Lankan food basket
USA/IMF	Czech Republic NSO—team of two	Developing a web application from scratch for life table data using R package Shiny
France/PARIS21	Brazil NSO	Analysis of logs and paradata generated in the test for the 2022 Brazilian population census
Jordan	UAE FCSC—team of two	Web scrapping for ICT Price Index
UK	Malaysia NSO—team of three	Nowcasting Malaysia's gross domestic product (GDP) using machine learning

"Thank you" email from the UK national statistician, although plans are in place to also award a certificate following more recent feedback from mentors.

The success and smoothness of this first cohort meant that the evaluation incurred fewer changes for the following cohorts. However, one crucial area was highlighted as a blocker for further scale out of this programme, and that was the difficulty in recruiting mentors to the programme. This was limiting the number of mentee projects that could be accepted into the programme. Hence, in order to get more interest and to ensure that those interested have enough time to decide on participating, a decision was made to introduce a continuous mentor application stage. This meant that the promotion of the programme plus the recruitment of mentors could be continuous, and potential mentors could choose the cohort timeline that best suited their schedule.

To reinforce the impact of the first cohort, two of the mentors applied to participate in the second cohort.

This programme is better than any course I've been through and seen on Coursera or other platforms out there. By being a mentor, I've learned so much and managed to share knowledge as well. I couldn't recommend it more.

(A. S.—mentor from International Monetary Fund)

To date, including the pilot cohort and two official cohorts, a total of 17 mentors from countries including Ghana, UAE, Poland, USA, France, UK, Netherlands, and Jordan have shared and further developed their data science knowledge with 47 mentees from the NSOs of Malaysia, Sri Lanka, Zimbabwe, Jordan, Czech Republic, Brazil, UAE, Chile, Poland, Indonesia, India, Namibia, Luxembourg, and Vietnam.

8.3 How It Works

8.3.1 Promotion and Application Stage

The promotion and application stage for mentees runs for approximatively six weeks. The promotion of the programme takes advantage of the DSC's well-established international network and uses direct emailing, talks, and presentations to deliver the key messages. Information and links are shared to the application forms for both mentors and mentees.

The mentee submits an application form, detailing a project proposal on which they would like to receive data science mentorship. It must be signed off by line management and senior leadership at the NSO prior to submission.

Mentors are also required to apply to take part in the programme, and they are requested to list their data science knowledge and skills and to obtain line manager sign-off, authorising their time for participation.

8.3.2 Selection and Matching

Once the promotion and application stage has concluded, the submitted mentee applications are sifted by the International Working Group (six or seven members) based on criteria that encompass the following:

- How clear is the project description?
- Is the project approach feasible?
- How well do the skills align to the project approach?
- How viable are the data sources?
- Is the applicant's motivation clear and valid?
- Does the project suit the purpose of the accelerator?
- What would the impact of the project be?

The working group scores each criterion on a scale from 1 to 5 (1 = weakest, 5 = strongest) and a total score is given to each application. Due to the large number of applications, the working group also sets a cut-off score, and only the strongest applications are considered for matching with a mentor.

Mentors' skills and experiences are collected and used to match them to specific mentee projects. In some cases, the match isn't obvious, as mentors may have a wide set of skills that match more than one project. To ensure the mentors are included in the decision-making process, they receive a list of the closest project matches and they select which project they would prefer to provide mentorship for. This ensures that mentees receive the best pairing and mentor for their projects.

All mentor applications are also collated and stored on the DSC's secure mentor database to use for future cohorts, with the mentor's consent.

8.3.3 Induction and Mentoring Support

In order to ensure that both mentees and mentors are clear with what is needed from them during the programme period, key information about the mentor and mentee roles is shared along with the expectations of both. The following agreements are requested before the mentoring commences:

- the programme manager, the mentee, and their line manager sign a memorandum of understanding, and
- the mentor and mentee sign an agreement that states they understand the terms of the collaboration.

Both mentors and mentees receive handbooks with the latest information on mentoring from the UK government website. The handbooks also contain helpful material for virtual mentoring and tips to make the best out of such collaboration.

Being a mentor can be daunting to some, and therefore a mentoring workshop is held to ensure that the necessary support is available to those who require it. The workshop is scheduled to run at the beginning of each cohort, and talks are given by mentors from previous cohorts to share their experiences, give advice, and answer questions.

The induction welcomes the whole cohort and offers the chance for an official virtual introduction to the coordination team, other participants, and senior leaders from the DSC, ONS, and other national or international guest speakers. The induction also incorporates a separate meeting for each team/pair of mentors and mentees to have their initial discussion. During this meeting, the team/pair of mentors and mentees makes an agreement about when to meet each week, the mentoring approach, objectives, timeline, and preferred language.

A Slack channel is set up for the whole cohort as a common platform to network and collaborate across during the duration of the programme.

8.3.4 Periodical Check-In Meetings

Throughout the 12-week programme, the DSC project officer meets every four weeks with the whole cohort to discuss progress, be informed of any challenges, answer any further questions, and provide any updates. The third and last check-in meeting also involves a 30-minute programme evaluation and feedback session. The information received is vital for the evaluation session undertaken after every cohort.

8.3.4.1 Graduation

The graduation event brings the cohort together to celebrate the progress achieved within the 12 weeks of mentoring. High-level speakers, such as the UK national statistician or director general of the DSC, are invited to thank and praise all participants and to hear the results from the project work.

Line managers and other senior leaders from the mentored NSOs are also invited to witness the results.

After the graduation, mentees receive a certificate of completion signed by the DSC programme manager for international capability, the mentor, and the director general of the DSC. The mentors receive a thank you email from the UK national statistician.

8.4 Demonstrating the Power of Mentoring

8.4.1 Examples of Projects

The first cohort brought together mentees from Malaysia, Sri Lanka, Czech Republic, UAE, and Brazil and mentors from France, USA, UK, UAE, and Jordan.

The following examples have been chosen due to their level of challenge and the impact of their collaboration at the personal and organisational levels.

The first project outlined was a particularly challenging one for the mentee from Sri Lanka due to the electricity curfew that was being imposed in the country at the time. Despite this, the mentee succeeded in learning R-shiny and finalised their project, without any previous experience in R programming and with full support being provided by the UAE mentor.

> **Project Title:** Retail Price Forecast of Top Essential Food Items of the Sri Lankan Food Basket (a Web App Using R-shiny)
>
> **Mentor:** Preeti Ranadive Pandhu: Statistics Centre, Abu Dhabi
>
> **Mentee:** Thejan Sri Rathnayake: Department of Census and Statistics, Sri Lanka (DCSSL)

8.4.1.1 Overview of the Project by Thejan Sri Rathnayake

The project looked at developing a comprehensive automated web application to collect, prepare, store, visualize, and accurately predict retail prices of each selected food item from the Sri Lankan food basket.

The changes in the price level of essential goods, especially the essential food items required for day-to-day living of consumers, is an essential element to be considered in the dynamic changing economic environment. The essential food items in the food basket of Sri Lanka consist of locally produced items, as well as imported items. The purchasing price of those items is determined by several factors related to each item. An accurate prediction of the retail prices of these items is vital for many reasons but challenging due to the uncertainty linked to the related factors. Trying to tackle this challenge was the main motivator for the project.

The project used secondary data collected by government agencies such as the DCSSL, Sri Lanka Customs, Department of Agriculture, and Consumer Affairs Authority. First, we classified the top essential items into two categories (imported and locally produced), and then we identified the price determinant factors of the items in both categories (import cost, applicable taxes for the items in the import category, and production cost for locally produced items). Finally, we contacted the particular agencies that collect the data for each category.

The main goals were:

- to collect and integrate related data to determine future prices of food items into a MySQL database;
- to develop an interactive Shiny dashboard to visualize main features (historical price movements; week-on-week, month-on-month, and year-on-year change; and the latest week price);

- to determine historical behaviours of the retail price and related other variables; and
- to create an automated system to clean and prepare the data, select an optimum linear or dynamic regression model with highest predicting accuracy, perform error handling, and forecast the prices of every item for the next 12 months.

The main challenges were as follows:

- difficulty in the collection-of-data process required for the analysis due to the nature of the data,
- the frequency of data—different agencies collect data at different frequencies (Sri Lanka customs keeps import-related records on a daily and shipment basis; DCS collects retail prices of the items on a weekly basis; and local production, farmgate price data are collected every month), and
- finding the necessary time to complete the frontend and backend work for the project (data collection, database management system, and visualization and prediction using reactive programming techniques) while tackling other work and family priorities.

The main learning outcome from the project is the effective and powerful use of reactive programming techniques in R-shiny combined with MySQL. Additionally, the experience gained as a mentee of an international mentoring programme is noteworthy throughout my career.

Since finishing the project and coming up with the application, it was found useful not only by the DCSSL (Sri Lanka's own NSO) but also by several other companies and agencies that deal with price statistics. Making assumptions and business decisions through outputs from a reliable, timely, and accurate dynamic system such as the one developed through this project is what was needed for the last few years, according to the stakeholders we collaborate with.

Additionally, it has also been discovered that the cost-of-living decisions of the country are made more evident using this system.

8.4.1.2 The Mentor's Thought

This project has achieved several objectives:

- storing the data in much more robust way with the MySQL database, which made it easy to pull the data whenever required from the previous method of storing data;
- visualizing and making interactive dashboards to allow the user to select and focus on the items of their choice; and
- predicting the prices for the upcoming time period to help decision makers.

8.4.1.3 Conclusion

All of the set objectives were met and will serve the desired purpose and beyond, as proven by the most recent development of the application.

The system has also the potential to be further automated by adding web scraping techniques for data collection and advanced machine learning (ML) techniques for more accurate predictions.

The second example demonstrates a successful collaboration in which a UK mentor supported a team of three mentees from Malaysia on a complex and ambitious project.

Project title: Nowcasting Malaysia's GDP using ML
Mentor: Will Malpass: Data Science Campus UK
Mentee team: Veronica S. Jamilat, Fatin Ezzati Mohd Aris, and Siti Khadijah Jasni: Department of Statistics Malaysia

8.4.1.4 Overview of the Project by the Mentee Team

Our project aimed to identify a new and potential approach in nowcasting Malaysia's GDP. The current practice of estimating GDP advanced estimates was using the conventional method that requires many resources. In contrast, this project used ML to nowcast GDP to reduce the burden faced by current practice and at the same time strengthen the capacity within the organization.

There is an urgent need to strengthen the capacity specifically on producing timely advance estimates (nowcasting) of GDP (and other economic indicators) in an efficient manner. The conventional way requires tremendous effort from limited resources. The current literature has proven that ML methods produce promising nowcasting economic indicators.

The datasets for this project were obtained from various sources, i.e., published data from the Department of Statistics Malaysia and Bank Negara Malaysia and public data from websites. Datasets used in this project are in monthly and quarterly aggregated data.

The main goal of our project was to identify a new potential approach in nowcasting Malaysia's GDP using ML models.

The main challenge was exploring new techniques and tools in handling data modelling using ML and other models in a short period of time.

We enjoyed learning so many techniques in nowcasting GDP (and other economic indicators as well) and using GitHub to share our work. We've been introduced to many approaches of ML in nowcasting in 12 weeks. Through this programme, we also sharpened our analytical and Python skills.

As a result, this collaboration has increased the awareness of utilizing a modern approach, specifically in estimating advance estimate of GDP, which offers almost similar results with the use of minimal resources. The approach we used for this project has the potential to be replicated and expanded to other economic indicators such as labour statistics advanced estimates production.

8.4.1.5 The Mentor's Thought

The International Data Science Accelerator is a very satisfying programme to take part in as a mentor. It was fantastic to see how the mentees progressed in their practical skills and knowledge of nowcasting over the allocated 12 weeks. The mentees would often run into new and difficult challenges surrounding this topic, and so the focus needed to shift from week to week—so working on this project felt far from stale. Squeezing such ambitious projects into this window is a very good challenge for those used to a longer time horizon.

It's amazing to hear the positive feedback the team has had throughout their project, and what's especially exciting to me is the potential that this now has to benefit other areas in their organisation outside of GDP estimation.

Our chosen format of weekly updates worked well (between mentor and mentees), and the accelerator-wide updates throughout the program provided a good opportunity to consolidate the findings and next steps of our project. The collaboration felt largely seamless—the sharing of code/material was straightforward, and the team were very open to new ways of working (e.g., use of GitHub), and fortunately there were no headaches from our time zone difference! Readily available support and guidance from the organisers throughout the program was very much appreciated.

This type of collaboration provides a boost to our international reputation, and it was interesting to observe all the other organisations working in the same space as us (data science in the public domain) throughout this program.

In terms of impact, there are clear benefits to the mentees' personal development in terms of technical upskilling as well as the aforementioned benefits of the project to their organisation. This collaboration also provides the mentor a valuable opportunity to work on novel problems outside of their usual day-to-day tasks, as well as the personal satisfaction associated with helping develop and advise on a meaningful project.

8.4.1.6 Conclusion

Overall, mentoring enabled our team to achieve our goals. It has increased the awareness of using a modern approach within the organisation which offers promising results with utilizing resources in an efficient way. The International Accelerator provides support needed to keep the momentum, and the setup is easy to follow provided both mentor and mentee have a clear understanding on achievable goals within the given time.

8.4.2 *Impact*

Preparing and encouraging mentees to eventually become mentors is part of the International Accelerator expected impact. This intention depends, partially, on the experience as a mentee in the programme. To ensure the collaboration is as fruitful and inspiring as possible, both mentors and mentees are briefed accordingly with regard to their roles and expectations. As a result of this approach, one of the pilot mentees became a mentor during the first official cohort.

Some of the participants and projects submitted aim to solve an organisational challenge or prove to be essential in raising more interest from senior leaders with regard to the power of data science. In one particular case, being part of this programme has achieved such impact and that the organisation is willing to invest more into data science.

8.5 Taking the Programme Further

8.5.1 *Findings*

The International Data Science Accelerator Programme is ending its second cohort and preparing for a third. There are various avenues the programme could consider for improvement or for broadening the international scale outwards.

In order to establish what works best for all parties involved in such a programme, the evaluation sessions organised at the end of each cohort are vital. These meetings bring together the working group, which analyses the feedback from the last cohort and makes decisions to improve the programme before the next cohort.

Based on the current intake and flow of the process, the next evaluation looks at the potential of placing a cap on the number of participants in any one cohort. This would ensure that the programme can grow optimally while ensuring it can be effectively managed within the available resources, without overwhelming or overcrowding the programme.

Constant monitoring of the programme, how it runs, and what impact it has on participants, organisations, the coordination team, and DSC form the main aspects to look at during the evaluation sessions and also ensure the programme continues to be relevant, needed, and viable.

8.5.2 *Potential Development*

Exploring potential ways that the programme could be further developed is an exercise being undertaken to unlock ideas while also reassuring that it already achieves the desired outcome and needs no major change in its current form and context. The areas currently being explored are as follows:

- increasing the coordination team to allow the programme to accept an ever-increasing number of participants and bigger cohorts;
- considering expanding the 12 weeks so that larger projects could be included and having only one cohort per year;
- considering reducing the length so that the mentorship runs for 10 weeks but allows three cohorts per year;
- considering other topics that could benefit from mentoring, such as cohorts on data visualization, which could alternate with data science;
- considering greater involvement of the UN Regional Hubs for Big Data and Data Science to consider more bespoke regional offerings.

The possibilities are numerous; however, they're always dependent on the capacity and resources available for organising and running such a programme.

8.5.3 Spreading the Word

This is a programme that depends on the willingness to share knowledge and the desire to further develop the data science capability of others. It relies on the number of data science professionals who want to give a bit of their time and impart their knowledge and skills to others who need them. It equally needs a generous intake of project proposals from NSOs interested in developing in this field.

Without mentors and mentees putting in their applications and expressions of interest, the programme would not exist. Therefore, a thorough and strong communication plan is essential to ensure NSOs and other organisations around the world know of the existence of this programme and are encouraged to participate.

Because most of the communication and advertising of the programme is done virtually, there is no guarantee that the message reaches the audience. Thus, the participation details and application stage advertisements are sent out to many contacts procured through DSC and ONS international networks.

Every opportunity is taken to promote the programme at international senior level meetings and international conferences and events whenever possible. Figure 8.3 shows the information usually used in presentations to advertise the call for mentors.

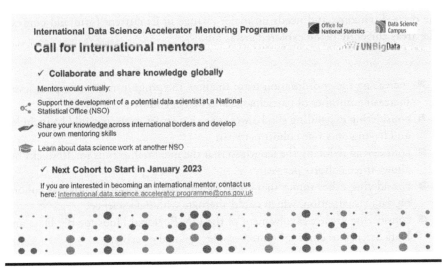

Figure 8.3 Call for international mentors information.

8.6 Conclusion

There is no doubt that the International Data Science Accelerator Programme has a positive impact on the data science worldwide stage. Whether it achieves sharing new techniques, imparting knowledge, inspiring other NSOs to participate or create their own programme, creating an international network of data scientists, or showing the importance of data science for the public good, the programme has managed to reach many in its first year.

Due to the success and impact, the initiative is strongly supported by the DSC's and ONS's most senior leaders. The UK national statistician has given his time to speak at the induction and graduation events, thanking mentors and mentees for their time and work and sharing his international mentoring experiences and their rewards:

"It's always a real pleasure to witness such passing of knowledge between people, so that we can really move techniques forward and across the world. Also, to be able to allow the opportunity for all to use the same tools and techniques. I spent much of the 1980s and 1990s, and to a lesser extent the 2000s, helping in workshops around the world, many organised by the UN or the World Health Organisation, or United States Agency for International Development, all under the idea of getting people from across different parts of the world together, to be able to explore new ways of analysis and to be able to support and improve the quality of the analysis that was taking place in particular countries.

Many of the things I did were in sub-Saharan Africa, so it's great to see not only mentees from Zimbabwe, but also mentors from Ghana carrying along the flags of data science support. The Levantine/Middle East, Asian, European, South American presence in this programme is also so important in ensuring we're connecting as much of the world as we can.

As a mentor, aside of the actual time spent with the mentees, which was incredibly rewarding, the main thrill came years later when I got to see people publishing work or getting research grants which were using the kind of learning and techniques shared with them. I'll always encourage anyone to be ambitious, to be bold and use these opportunities and collaborations.

Statisticians and data scientists have an amazing chance to make such a difference through using the data available nowadays, compared to what was available 45, 35 or even 25 years ago. The possibilities are numerous, to take data science into a new place, on the public stage, for the public good."

Acknowledgement

Reviewed and edited by Ceri Regan, Programme Manager International Capability, Data Science Campus, Office for National Statistics UK.

Chapter 9

Data Science and Technology Trends for Official Statistics

Opportunities and Challenges

Saeid Molladavoudi and Marie-Eve Bedard

Content

DOI: 10.1201/9781003369783-9

9.1 Introduction

Big data surrounds us! It can be found on the phones we use every day, the gadgets we wear, and the cars we ride. It even has an impact on how we think, communicate, learn, make decisions, and live. The term "big data" refers to the extremely large volumes of digital information produced and shared every day at an unprecedented rate and comprises everything from social media posts and internet searches to sensor data, satellite images, and high-frequency market transactions. Businesses, governments, and other organizations gather and analyze this data to better understand human behavior and make more effective decisions. Retailers, for example, utilize big data to analyze our purchasing behavior and target us with advertisements. Big data is becoming increasingly popular as a way for businesses and organizations to improve their services and products, and this is especially true for official statistics.

Official statistics are statistical data produced by national statistical offices (NSOs) to measure societal issues, such as economic activities, population, and environmental concerns. Official statistics are utilized to make important decisions, from national economic policies to municipal traffic restrictions, as well as to evaluate social, welfare, or reintegration programs' effectiveness. Traditionally, data has been manually obtained by experienced specialists who may require hours for collection, classification, labeling, and even traveling to gather a large enough probabilistic sample to use for analyses. However, technologies and digital platforms are increasingly producing and collecting data automatically with the help of state-of-the-art techniques, such as online tracking, image capturing, and web scraping. These datasets, which are frequently too large and complicated to process with conventional approaches, have several potential advantages to leverage, including the opportunity to obtain a more accurate picture of what is transpiring in the economy, society, and environment, as well as the ability to recognize patterns more rapidly. NSOs already use big data to produce official statistics more efficiently and precisely (Runningen Larsson & Zhang, 2022). Big data is also utilized to learn about the patterns and correlations among various datasets (Yang et al., 2021), to enhance the accuracy of predictions and forecasts, to aid in the development of new data analysis methods, and to increase the efficiency of statistical processes (Statistics Canada, 2020).

However, there exist valid concerns regarding the use of big data in official statistics. One major risk is that the data may not be representative of the entire target population, which is because it is frequently created and revolves around a certain number of entities. For example, data obtained over the internet confines the information to persons who utilize such technology, leaving out a whole population that does not. For certain analyses, particularly those that obtain data through online scraping or similar methods, it may significantly bias the direction of the results. Privacy and confidentiality concerns also need to be considered under various regulatory frameworks.

Despite these challenges, there are significant opportunities to employ big data in official statistics, and with the correct methodology and further research on the models used, it can help enhance the quality of statistical products (Canadian Statistics Advisory Council, 2022). The advantages of employing big data are non-negligible, and the use of big data in official statistics is becoming more prevalent and is something that is here to stay (Erman et al., 2022)!

9.1.1 An Ever-Changing Data Landscape

The new data ecosystem, which is composed of a complex network of interconnected systems, technologies, and processes, is a rapidly evolving landscape that is changing the collection, storage, processing, and dissemination of information. In recent years, the big data revolution combined with the proliferation of connected devices and digital technologies has transformed our perception of data and its role in society. Indeed, data is nowadays vital for the developing new products and services, improving existing ones, and driving business decisions. Moreover, not only has the content of data changed, especially the volume, frequency, and diversity, but so has the context. The data ecosystem has evolved considerably, and new players, relationships, technology, and restrictions have emerged. This new and ever-changing data ecosystem can be characterized by several key properties, such as its scale, complexity, and interactions.

The sheer volume of data created on a continuous basis is one of the distinguishing aspects of the new data ecosystem. While the exponential growth of data provides opportunities for organizations to gain valuable insights and drive innovation, the tools and infrastructure required to manage and analyze such massive amounts of data, while ensuring its security and privacy, can be prohibitively expensive and resource-intensive, not considering the level of skillset required of the employees managing this data and infrastructure. The dynamic nature of the data that is being generated in real time or near real time raises new difficulties that may necessitate greater computing resources and technologies to enable real-time analyses and decision-making capabilities to maximize the value of data. Furthermore, the emerging technologies, such as distributed systems, can be complex and require significant investment, and organizations must carefully manage and monitor their data and infrastructure to ensure they can maintain adequate levels of performance and scalability while adhering to laws. Simultaneously, these agencies and departments must ensure continuous training and development of their employees in order to use, safeguard, and model this data.

Another important feature of the new data environment is its complexity. Previously, companies and individual customers generated the majority of data. However, data is now generated in an unstructured way by a number of sources, including social media, sensors, gadgets, and machines, making it difficult to evaluate and handle using traditional approaches. This data frequently contains a significant amount of noise and irregularities, making it difficult to extract relevant insights, not counting that they often come from multiple platforms or systems. Therefore, organizations are increasingly relying on sophisticated analytics, such as machine learning (ML) and artificial intelligence (AI) techniques, to uncover patterns and trends in data to allow more effective decision-making.

Traditional data collection might be restrictive in comparison to such data collection approaches that can accumulate easily available data, particularly for governments that have layers of security and confidentiality over each of these data sources or types. More often than not, additional bureaucratic processes and steps must be completed in order to maintain the anonymity of the individuals through various screening instruments and procedures. Several of these processes can be eliminated with the use of ML and advanced approaches, resulting in relevant analyses that are quicker and more accurate, with the possibility of incorporating models that can aid in risk assessment, e.g., agent-based models. These approaches, however, need specialized skills and experience, and entities must invest in the appropriate resources and training to apply them successfully. Training requirements for future hires and new graduates may include, for example, further development of readily available resources onsite, online learning platforms (e.g., Coursera), and organization-wide learning seminars in data science or data engineering laboratories.

The need for robust and resilient data management processes and governance frameworks is another implication of the new data ecosystem. Data is no longer isolated to a single place or organization but is increasingly shared and traded across different systems and domains, constantly forming new connections and relationships. This implies that enterprises and organizations must have policies and processes in place to ensure data quality and consistency, as well as security, interoperability, accessibility, and compliance with relevant legislative restrictions. Fortunately, this important facet of governance and transparency, which is also one of the main pillars of the concept of responsible AI (see subsection 9.2.2), is currently under strong work towards horizontal guidelines and ethics.

There are various data technologies offered by different market players. Cloud databases, data warehouses, and data lakes are examples of data-storage technologies that are widely used at the organizational level, as they provide flexible options to eliminate data copies by enabling data transactional tiers. Additionally, data-processing technologies aid in the cleaning, transformation, and analysis of data, including platforms for ML and data pipelines, as well as data visualizations. Cybersecurity technologies protect the data against misuse and unauthorized access, as well as the integrity of the system, providing greater security for the organizational cyber environment. Access control, encryption, and activity monitoring are among these technological features that are becoming more critical with the advent of new attack vectors and malicious behaviors.

In an ever-changing data ecosystem, national data stewards, or NSOs, must reevaluate their business processes to address the increasing expectations put on them by society in order to generate more accurate representations of society in a timely manner. A variety of stakeholders, including policymakers, organizations, and the general public who need more disaggregated data on specific issues and subjects, are driving the need for better, quicker, and more relevant statistical information.

9.2 Data Science Trends and Opportunities

Although the topic of data science is not new, an increasing number of organizations are adopting it to gain an advantage over competitors or simply to remain competitive. In fact, the adoption of data science and ML-based solutions and products has grown significantly across all sectors over the last several years (McKinsey Global Survey on AI, 2022). They have been used in official statistics as a result of the recent exponential growth in alternative data sources and the availability of data analysis tools (Yang et al., 2021). In reality, NSOs face new possibilities and difficulties as a result of changes in the substance of big data, as well as the context around it in this new data ecosystem, including the creation of new data and sophisticated analytical products.

Data science and survey methodologies, as well as subject matter areas within NSOs, have special and deeply ingrained interactions. The effectiveness of adoption of data science and modern methods in official statistics depends on these interactions and collaborations. Traditionally, NSOs would gather data over the course of months or years, process and analyze it, and then finally report the results with significant delays. Since the data was frequently outdated when it was published, this approach left the knowledge of the decision-makers and citizens with considerable gaps. Because of modern methods and emerging technologies, NSOs can now collect and analyze data much more rapidly, allowing for quick and accurate analysis or displaying a time-sensitive scenario that is significant for decision-makers who must respond to increasing political demands. Previously, NSOs would publish datasets that were difficult for nonexperts to understand, accompanied by long and complicated analyses that deterred the broader audience from consuming them. Data science methods and tools can now influence how NSOs disseminate their findings. Combined with storytelling, these tools can enable NSOs to create new ways for displaying data that are more accessible to a larger audience, which makes it easier for NSOs to convey their results to the broader public, thereby increasing their transparency and accountability.

The goal here is not to cover every aspect of data science and ML that can be used in the production of official statistics but, rather, to focus on a few subareas with potential, even though at different maturity levels, that can be integrated into various components of statistical programs, such as collection, transformation, integration, analysis, and dissemination. For example, this chapter does not include applications of popular ML disciplines such as natural language processing, computer vision, reinforcement learning, and time series analysis.

9.2.1 Automated Pipelines

Open-source software and resources have evolved significantly in recent years, making the creation of robust and efficient automated statistical pipelines a possibility. An automated statistical pipeline is a collection of software and tools that automatically receive data from numerous sources, combine them into a format that can be used to create statistics, and then evaluate the outputs. Various methods can be used to reduce manual labour for data collection, such as application programming interfaces (APIs), as well as automated quality checks, metadata management, and formatting of certain preprocessing steps. These automated processes can be used to discover errors in data entry, validation, and processing as well as to locate missing or erroneous data and spot outliers. A wide range of technologies, including open-source options and commercial offerings from businesses, is available for automated data collection and quality checks.

Furthermore, in the realm of ML, there has been an increase in new tools and platforms that provide different types of automation throughout an end-to-end ML pipeline, such as feature engineering, model selection, and parameter tuning. This type of automation, also known as AutoML, is envisioned as a set of configurations managed by a human expert (as a controller) to optimize some of the time- and compute-expensive elements of the development process that do not need domain expertise (Waring et al., 2020). Another advantage of utilizing AutoML is that it can search for more possibilities for parameter setups than human trial-and-error search techniques. Many open-source libraries and cloud vendors provide services aimed at automating certain procedures that, when applied correctly and under the supervision of a human expert, can provide efficiency in development cycles and improve the performance of statistical programs in NSOs that use ML models. Such tools are beneficial in a government setting, as they enable the employees to focus on more meaningful and less repetitive tasks as well as accelerate the development process and increase the quality of the outcomes.

9.2.2 Interpretable and Explainable ML

Interpretable ML deals with the creation of algorithms that can be understood by human subject matter experts (Molnar, 2022), intending to construct models that are both accurate and intelligible to people while enabling them to be used in high-stakes decision-making processes without entailing a blackbox model. Interpretability can help to increase decision-making transparency, which is vital in domains such as official statistics. Furthermore, understanding the internal mechanisms of a model might assist the subject matter expert in fine-tuning for improved performance and help users and developers to create confidence and quality assessments. Despite the benefits of interpretability, it is not without drawbacks. The absence of a common definition of interpretability across all disciplines, as well as the domain knowledge required to assess and interpret what the model has learned from the observational data, is undoubtedly a challenge. Another drawback is that tradeoffs between accuracy and interpretability are sometimes required; it is often not trivial to have both in equal proportion (although recent advances in ML methods are closing this gap). In general, interpretable ML is still an active area of study, with considerable work to be done before it can be widely used in applications.

On the other hand, explainability in ML is the process of understanding how and why a sophisticated and blackbox ML model makes specific predictions using secondary interpretable models (Rudin, 2019). A variety of methods can be used to describe blackbox models to ascertain which input features are most crucial in generating the predictions, e.g., by examining the weights of the model or performing a sensitivity analysis that examines how the model's predictions vary when individual inputs are changed. Another possibility is to utilize a local interpretable model that offers a more complete description of the model's behavior, which is particularly useful when the model makes complex predictions such as those involving nonlinear relationships.

As increasingly complex and blackbox models are used in NSOs for different purposes, for example, in data collection, transformation, integration, and processing, contextualization seems necessary to map the ML model's properties to system requirements based on various business objectives within NSOs. For instance, it is typically argued that explainable ML models are most useful in situations where data are complex and unstructured while increasing the complexity of the model itself for predictive purposes. The context requirements, such as the business goals, user demands, and success criteria, will then define if model explainability is required or whether prediction performance is the goal, even if it means sacrificing transparency or further explainable modelling to make complicated models human intelligible (Murdoch et al., 2019).

9.2.3 Causal ML

Causal ML is an area of ML that focuses on identifying and discovering cause-and-effect correlations by attempting to discover the elements that impact the results of a certain event to uncover causal linkages and provide answers to "why" questions (Pearl, 2019). For example, a causal ML algorithm may be used to forecast the effects of a new medicine on an illness or determine the origins of a disease. Statistical approaches such as regression analysis are frequently used in causal analysis, even though more modern systems based on deep learning have been developed recently. Simplistically, regression analysis would reveal the relationships among variables; however, a causal model would typically rely on a hypothesis that might be the cause or the latent relationship by means of classification, i.e., confirmatory analysis. It may also be used to understand how changes in one variable may affect the others.

If a government agency is attempting to forecast the impact of a new policy on a target population, a causal discovery algorithm might assist in identifying the elements that are most likely to influence the policy's results. Furthermore, causal ML can be used to create models that better anticipate outcomes based on historical data. For instance, this could result in more precise estimations of economic indicator forecasting. Finally, employing causal ML in official statistics can help enhance decision-making by offering more insights into cause-and-effect relationships; for example, if an NSO attempts to determine the causes of an increase in unemployment, a causal ML algorithm might assist it in discovering the socioeconomic elements most likely to be related to the phenomenon.

9.2.4 Synthetic Data and Data Access Facilitation

Synthetic data is data that is created artificially, such as computer-generated data that does not exist in the real world. Synthetic data can be generated using a variety of methods, including the use of generative models. It may be created from scratch or constructed from existing data sources and has a wide range of applications, including in ML and highly regulated areas where privacy and confidentiality regulations limit data access, such as health and finance. For instance, it may be used to train ML models when real-world data is unavailable or costly and may be generated under controlled conditions, allowing more accurate algorithm testing and debugging (i.e., increased data utility) while protecting data privacy and confidentiality by hiding sensitive information. Hospitals, for instance, may want to use synthetic patient health data to build prediction models for disease outbreaks but are prevented by privacy laws. Synthetic data may be used in NSOs to make data available to external researchers and communities interested in conducting research utilizing existing survey data (High Level Group on the Modernization of Official Statistics (HLG-MOS) Synthetic Data Project, 2022). Indeed, ensuring the anonymity of individuals and businesses is crucial for NSOs, who operate under strict statutory regulations, and synthetic data generation may be a viable method for sharing data while protecting its value without risking the confidentiality of the data subjects.

9.2.5 Generative AI

An emerging class of large language and text-vision models is paving the way to creating content, such as marketing materials, code, and drawings, from existing data at the human level. The capacity of this branch of AI, known as generative AI, to produce faster and inexpensive creative outputs, such as pictures, text, or music, with minimum intellect and knowledge work, is gaining ground. By decreasing the costs of knowledge production, generative AI has the potential to greatly boost labour productivity and economic value. Potential applications for generative AI in general would include some intriguing applications, such as creating fresh data samples, in which generative AI may be used to generate customized data samples with human prompts. Other applications include the generation of synthetic data, such as product descriptions, job descriptions, and chats, for training ML models. This is advantageous for datasets that are either extremely small or difficult to obtain.

Aside from automating and expediting some human cognitive processes, generative AI models may be used in conjunction with causal ML to generate simulation scenarios, improve survey designs, and test and validate statistical models. For example, generative AI models can be used to generate synthetic versions of survey data to test and evaluate survey designs by identifying survey questions that are most effective at collecting the desired information and can assist in identifying potential biases or confounding factors that may affect the response rates and, hence, the reliability of the survey results.

9.3 Emerging Technologies

In this section, we will list some of the new technologies, tools, and platforms that can be utilized within NSOs and statistical programs for a variety of purposes, spanning from collection and integration to processing and dissemination.

9.3.1 Cloud Computing

The adoption of cloud services can assist NSOs in becoming nimbler and more responsive to changing user demands, improving operational efficiency and lowering costs. Additional possible benefits of using cloud computing in official statistics include lowering the cost of data collection and processing, making it easier to interchange data internally within NSOs and externally with stakeholders, collaborating on projects, and avoiding data duplication. All of these benefits are critical for an NSO to reduce the need for a storage environment through a cloud provider, but it also implies that a data centre may no longer be required, saving physical space (e.g., no server area) and potentially cost savings.

9.3.2 Data Collection Tools

The term "data collection tools" may refer to a variety of ways for gathering data for statistical purposes. New data collection techniques and technologies can be used as part of the evolution of official statistics into a system known as trusted smart statistics to aid NSOs in transforming from active data collection to more automated, passive, and consented collection (Ricciato et al., 2019). These solutions, such as applications or online surveys on mobile devices, allow for more accurate and timely data collection, which may then be leveraged to offer reliable and relevant information while simultaneously reducing human labour. This type of data collection is growing more popular, as it is easier for people to reply to surveys or submit information using their mobile devices. Of course, employing these tools can also have restrictions, as the sample would contain only the segment of the population who use mobile devices.

Another automated data collection method is online scraping, also known as web scraping, which captures data from websites and converts it into a structured format. NSOs can use online scraping to acquire data for a variety of purposes, including market research, sales price monitoring, economic activity tracking, and data compilation for statistical analysis. It may also be used to automatically create web apps and databases or to acquire data that would otherwise be difficult or impossible to get, such as websites that do not have an API or that include information that is difficult to obtain directly. It may also be used to collect data quickly and efficiently from a range of sources, including social networks, news agencies, and online stores, while complying with their policies and terms of use. Web scraping, for example, may be used to collect data to investigate public opinion on a variety of socioeconomic topics and track trends from platforms such as Twitter and Facebook. These are only a few examples of newly accessible data-collection technologies that can be utilized by NSOs worldwide.

9.3.3 Privacy-Enhancing Technologies

Even though cybersecurity protocols for data protection at rest, e.g., symmetric key encryption, and in transit, such as transport layer security, have been standardized and widely adopted, mechanisms to protect data while being processed have received little attention until recently. Privacy-enhancing technologies (PETs) have evolved in recent years to provide data protection while allowing data processing (Van Blarkom et al., 2003). The term "PETs" refers to a variety of methods that claim to secure data at every stage of its life cycle, including collection, processing, and dissemination of the findings. These cutting-edge techniques include distributed ML (such as federated learning), trusted execution environments, differential privacy, homomorphic encryption, secure multiparty computation, and zero-knowledge proofs.

The power of data may be unleashed with the help of PETs without compromising privacy or confidentiality. For example, privacy-preserving delegated analysis and multiparty computation can provide opportunities to draw conclusions from distributed and inaccessible data. NSOs can use PETs to address the privacy preservation needs of their sensitive data to fulfil their mandates. A few examples include remote neural network classifier training on the cloud in a privacy-preserving manner (Zanussi et al., 2021), privacy-preserving record linkage, and privacy-preserving crowdsourcing by leveraging federated learning.

It is important to emphasize that PETs simply provide risk reduction, which can make the difference between a statistical project being approved or rejected. PETs do not resolve the crucial tradeoff between security and privacy on the one hand and data usage on the other. In fact, some PETs are built to solve the issue of input privacy, i.e., to protect the privacy of data entered into a joint function, such as a statistical algorithm by one or more collaborating parties, while others are more focused on the topic of output privacy, which often relies on sensitivity analysis or aggregation, such as conventional statistical disclosure restrictions. Typically, NSOs have years of expertise utilizing the latter to ensure that no sensitive personal or microdata is disclosed throughout their activities, which is compliant with the relevant statutory frameworks. Using these strategies in the context of an NSO might save hours of manual screening for every data request or publication released.

9.3.4 Blockchain

A distributed database called a blockchain enables the safe, open, and unchangeable storage of data (Leible et al., 2019), where the cryptographic hash of the preceding block, timestamp, and transaction information are included in each block of the chain. A network of nodes that independently verify and log transactions maintains the blockchain. Blockchain has the potential to transform official statistics by offering a transparent and secure platform for collecting and verifying data, supporting accuracy and integrity with outfacing statistical procedures. It can help NSOs to shift the public sentiment from 'trust' to 'proof' by utilizing a verifiable and immutable record-keeping approach for their data and processes. Additionally, smart contracts may be used to automate several common statistical production activities, such as data collection, processing, and publication. It has the potential to track asset ownership and movement, confirm identities, and prevent fraudulent activities. Since blockchain is a distributed database, it can boost data flow across organizations, including NSOs, in the same or other nations while reducing the risk of data breaches.

9.3.5 Digital Twins

A digital twin is a digital clone or replica of a physical system or item that is intended to match reality (Holopainen et al., 2022). Digital twins can be used to simulate system behaviour and track and observe their physical counterparts in the real world. It is an interactive simulation of systems that enables prediction or intervention. In fact, the continuous link between a digital twin and its real twin distinguishes it from other digital models, such as simulation studies. Access to enormous volumes of transactional and sensor data is a game-changing requirement for establishing and building digital twins, which can be built with different goals in mind or in different sizes.

Digital twins can be applied to official statistics in a variety of ways. For example, they may be used to track and monitor social and economic indicators, such as unemployment rate or inflation, as well as environmental factors, such as air pollution and water quality. By enabling improved decision-making, a digital twin built on data from the physical system unlocks values and enables a constructive feedback loop into the physical twin. To model the effects of policy changes on economic and social indices, NSOs can employ digital twins to enhance their portfolio of analytical products. This increase in the variety of statistical information offered by NSOs can enable experts and decision-makers to create "what-if" scenarios and test their hypotheses. NSOs have the capacity to unleash the power of digital twins to enhance the operation, maintenance, and delivery of local and national assets, systems, and services.

9.3.6 Quantum Computers

Quantum computers utilize the ideas of quantum physics to store and process information (Rietsche et al., 2022). One of the essential notions behind quantum computing is that quantum computers can leverage this feature to perform specific tasks far more quickly than classical computers because a quantum bit (qubit) can simultaneously represent zero and one, or quantum superposition. One possible use of quantum computing in official statistics could be in the field of quantum ML and hierarchical text classifications, which are frequently employed in statistical programs to create standardized and consistent product taxonomies. Examples include the automatic classification of retail products and services to produce different product statistics. These widely used coding schemes are organized into tiers, with each level becoming increasingly comprehensive as one moves up the hierarchy. The hierarchical structure of the data, however, is typically not taken into consideration by existing ML-based methods in these classification challenges, as some classes may be semantically closer within the hierarchy than others, even to distinct subcategories. The open question is whether using this symmetry in data in ML text classification will increase the accuracy of statistical outputs and whether doing so would benefit from the use of quantum computers.

9.4 Challenges

National averages on economic, sociological, and environmental issues are no longer sufficient as increased societal pressure is placed on timely, disaggregated, and high-quality data outputs. Many NSOs have already begun to produce disaggregated insights by utilizing alternative data sources, modern methods, and data science tools and approaches. However, the path ahead for NSOs is not straightforward and without challenges, as there are several problems related to big data, human resources, emerging technology, and current and upcoming regulations. In the following, we take a closer look at each one and explain what they signify for NSOs' operations.

9.4.1 Data Marketplace

In recent decades, data markets have developed in shape and form in conjunction with the exponential growth of information. Businesses may utilize data markets to buy and sell datasets, allowing them to monetize their data assets and improve their revenue. These data marketplaces can provide real-time or historical data categorized by industry, region, or even data type. They have grown in popularity as a platform for monetizing vast volumes of data for numerous reasons, such as the increased value of data, profitable sell of data assets, and limitations of dataset size and type, based on what is needed operationally. As data markets grow in popularity due to the wide range of customizable options they provide, NSOs must learn to coexist alongside organizations and corporations whose objective is to monetize their data assets as main players in this fast-changing market. Data marketplaces, for example, can enable access to high-quality information that would otherwise be unavailable and assist NSOs in lowering the expenses of large-scale, active data collection efforts. Additionally, it can also enable statistical agencies, for example, through the use of PETs, to more actively participate in this market and offer their data to research institutes and other nongovernmental organizations for other uses, generating harvestable benefits that would support the infrastructures without compromising the privacy and confidentiality of the data, as per their statutory regulations.

9.4.2 Data Governance

A data governance framework is often made up of a combination of rules, procedures, roles/responsibilities, and technologies that work together to guarantee that the organization's data is correct, consistent, and in compliance with applicable legislation. NSOs must collect, evaluate, and disseminate data that is critical to decision-making. Even though the steps required to make NSOs' data governance frameworks robust will vary depending on the organization, its needs, and regulatory requirements, some general approaches will still be common to achieve that goal, such as defining clear policies and procedures for how data should be collected, managed, and used by the organization, including the principles of necessity and proportionality; setting up roles/responsibilities; and assigning them within the data governance framework.

9.4.3 Implementation of Responsible ML

In subsection 9.2.2, explainable AI methods were mentioned as potential opportunities for NSOs to leverage the power of sophisticated blackbox models in the development of novel and disaggregated statistical outputs. Recall that both explainable and interpretable AI fall under the umbrella of responsible or trustworthy ML (or AI), which encompasses other areas, such as ethics, procedural fairness, bias, and robustness. To guarantee a consistent approach to ML operationalization, proper ML adoption demands a thorough and dynamic risk management framework, as well as organizational support. Contextualization, or the exercise of mapping ML model traits to system properties or requirements, appears to be essential as more ML-based solutions are used in NSOs for a range of purposes, including data collection, integration, editing, processing, and dissemination.

It is worth noting that NSOs already have data quality frameworks and standards in place to ensure the development of high-quality statistical outputs (Statistics Canada, 2017) and (United Nations, 2019). Another important aspect of implementing responsible ML principles is to avoid utilizing biased data (e.g., data that is not representative of the target population) while training ML models, which may result in false inferences about a finite-sized population. Model explainability may be required for contextualization, in the sense that certain ML models must be explainable by subject matter experts to be held accountable. Explainability and interpretability are critical characteristics for ensuring that ML models are used successfully and that the consequences of these complex models on outcomes are understood. What is important is to develop a suitable monitoring and feedback mechanisms to aid in the detection and resolution of issues regarding ML models, such as model and concept drifts.

To enable responsible AI-based system implementation while adhering to the principles of necessity and proportionality (Statistics Canada, 2022), NSOs must collaborate with other stakeholders such as policymakers, regulators, and the general public. This collaboration can assist in guaranteeing that AI is correctly created and employed inside the NSO's statistical systems but also that the current gaps between social and legal licenses are bridged. It will also contribute to public confidence and trust in data science, AI methodologies, and technologies that are being utilized in government settings.

The European Union's (EU's) General Data Protection Regulation (European Commission, 2018) is a major legal framework that governs data use and offers safeguards for protecting personal data and individuals' rights. In addition, the EU AI Act (European Commission, 2021) is a proposed rule that establishes a legal framework for the use of AI in the EU around the development, deployment, and application of AI systems. The AI and Data Act in Canada is a bill submitted to the Canadian House of Commons, which would regulate the use of AI-based technologies and data with enforcement on consent before collecting or sharing data through a new regulatory body, the Canadian AI Regulatory Authority. In the United States, the federal government has unveiled an AI strategy (US White House Office of Science and Technology Policy, 2022) to guarantee that the country remains a worldwide leader in AI research and development, while simultaneously ensuring that AI technologies are produced responsibly and ethically. Compliance to these new and upcoming regulations, standards, and frameworks will become essential for corporations and even government agencies, including NSOs, to embrace AI-based solutions, especially in high-stakes applications.

9.4.4 Alternative Quality Indicators

Quantifying the uncertainty and validity of model predictions is a specific challenge when implementing sophisticated and blackbox ML-based solutions in mainstream statistical tasks. As previously stated in subsection 9.2.2, typically, a lack of access to the internal workings of these models would necessitate the development of secondary and more explainable models to offer insight into the factors that a model may consider when performing predictions. When working with real-world data, missing values or incorrect and noisy labels are common, which may affect the ML model training and, hence, the quality of the predictions made by the model. It is crucial to be aware of these difficulties when attempting to quantify uncertainty, as they can introduce additional sources of error. Managing different types of uncertainties within a single model is a more prevalent challenge; for example, aleatoric uncertainty denotes data randomness, whereas epistemic uncertainty denotes ignorance of the true generating process behind the data. Coping with the uncertainty can be challenging, and case-specific methods may be required. This is especially important in the context of official statistics, where a measure of statistical uncertainty is necessary to conform to its fundamental principles (United Nations, 2014).

Although uncertainty quantification in ML modelling is indeed more difficult because the majority of complex and nonparametric ML models only provide point predictions, a few approaches can be used to quantify uncertainty and potentially mitigate the risk. Use of Bayesian methods to characterize uncertainties at the inference time in deep neural networks (Gal & Ghahramani, 2016) or conformal prediction (Vovk et al., 2005), which is another example of distribution-free uncertainty quantification to generate prediction sets around any type of model's predictions with predictive coverage guarantees, are a few examples. When employed in official statistics, other methodologies such as selective abstention and confidence calibration can also be utilized as uncertainty quantification methods to build confidence or prediction ranges around model predictions.

9.4.5 New Partnerships

The data ecosystem is in a constant state of flux, which can be especially challenging for NSOs. With the advent of big data, NSOs are under pressure to not only produce more data but also to do so faster and at a more granular level. Additionally, public response rates are declining as people become less willing to participate in traditional surveys (Australian Bureau of Statistics, 2022). To meet these challenges, NSOs need to build new partnerships with other organizations, such as those in data marketplaces that have access to alternative sources of data. These partners often include private sector entities or academic institutions that may provide information that would otherwise be unavailable to NSOs. Building such relationships will help NSOs to tap into additional sources of information so that they can continue fulfilling their mandates despite the increasing demands from the society.

9.4.6 *Talent Management*

Talent management may include anything from recruiting and hiring to performance management and career progression plans and programs. Depending on their maturity level, NSOs may need to modify their workforce in order to acquire, evaluate, and disseminate products and services based on big data quantities, new technologies, or infrastructure. This may entail significant investments in acquiring new personnel or training current employees with new skill sets, such as data science and AI, big data analytics, and computer science. Hiring and retaining excellent data scientists remains one of the most challenging issues, which is due to a global shortage of individuals with certain skill sets that boosts competition for talent across numerous industries. Furthermore, the lack of a defined career path as well as a recruiting and development strategy will increase the difficulty of attracting and retaining competent employees.

9.5 Closing Remarks

As NSOs continue to modernize, they will have an increasing number of tools, modern methods, resources, and platforms at their disposal to improve their products and services to their stakeholders. However, similar to any other technology adoption, it comprises a combination of technological, legal, and social concerns that must be handled in tandem to guarantee that NSOs continue to execute their mandates successfully while producing better, faster, and more disaggregated statistical products. Building trust, committing to innovation, adhering to high-quality statistical information and services, and growing collaborative efforts are among the aspects that may assist NSOs in increasing their data science capabilities in concert with their modernization activities.

Acknowledgement

The authors would like to thank Caroline Mimeault and Christos Sarakinos for their valuable feedback.

Disclaimer

The content of this article represents the position of the authors and may not necessarily represent that of Statistics Canada.

Bibliography

Australian Bureau of Statistics. (2022). *Raising survey response rates by using machine learning to predict gold providers.* Retrieved from www.abs.gov.au/statistics/research/raising-survey-response-rates-using-machine-learning-predict-gold-providers

Canadian Statistics Advisory Council. (2022). *Canadian statistics advisory council 2022 annual report—trust, governance and data flows in the national statistical system.* Retrieved from www.statcan.gc.ca/en/about/relevant/CSAC/report/annual2022

Erman, S., Rancourt, E., Beaucage, Y., & Loranger, A. (2022). The use of data science in a national statistical office. *Harvard Data Science Review, 4*(4). https://doi.org/10.116 2/99608f92.13e1d60e

European Commission. (2018). *2018 reform of EU data protection rules.* Retrieved from https://ec.europa.eu/commission/sites/beta-political/files/data-protection-factsheet-changes_en.pdf

European Commission. (2021). *Artificial Intelligence Act.* Retrieved from Proposal for a regulation of the European Parliament and the Council laying down harmonised rules on Artificial Intelligence (Artificial Intelligence Act) and amending certain Union legislative acts. https://eur-lex.europa.eu/legal-content/EN/ TXT/?uri=CELLAR:e0649735-a372-11eb-9585-01aa75ed71a1

Gal, Y., & Ghahramani, Z. (2016). Dropout as a Bayesian approximation: Representing model uncertainty in deep learning. In *Proceedings of the 33rd international conference on machine learning* (pp. 1050–1059). New York: Proceedings of Machine Learning Research (PMLR).

High Level Group on the Modernization of Official Statistics (HLG-MOS) Synthetic Data Project. (2022). *Synthetic data for official statistics: A starter guide.* Retrieved from https://github.com/usnistgov/HLG-MOS_Synthetic_Data_Test_Drive/raw/nist-pages/guide/Synthetic%20Data%20for%20NSOs%20A%20starter%20guide.pdf

Holopainen, M., Saunila, M., Rantala, T., & Ukko, J. (2022). Digital twins' implications for innovation. *Technology Analysis & Strategic Management* Pages: 1 – 13. https://doi. org/10.1080/09537325.2022.2115881

Leible, S., Schlager, S., Schubotz, M., & Gipp, B. (2019). A review on blockchain technology and blockchain projects fostering open science. *Frontiers in Blockchain, 2.* https://doi.org/10.3389/fbloc.2019.00016

McKinsey Global Survey on AI. (2022). *The state of AI in 2022—and a half decade in review.* Retrieved from www.mckinsey.com/capabilities/quantumblack/our-insights/the-state-of-ai-in-2022-and-a-half-decade-in-review

Molnar, C. (2022). *Interpretable machine learning: A guide for making black box models explainable* (2nd ed.). Retrieved from https://christophm.github.io/interpretable-ml-book/

Murdoch, W., Singh, C., Kumbier, K., Abbasi-Asl, R., & Yu, B. (2019). Definitions, methods, and applications in interpretable machine learning. *Proceedings of the National Academy of Sciences, 116,* 22071–22080.

Pearl, J. (2019, March). The seven tools of causal inference, with reflections on machine learning. *Communications of the ACM, 62*(3), 54–60.

Ricciato, F., Wirthmann, A., Giannakouris, K., Reis, F., & Skaliotis, M. (2019). Trusted smart statistics: Motivations and principles. *Statistical Journal of the IAOS,* 589–603. https://doi.org/10.3233/SJI-190584

Rietsche, R., Dremel, C., Bosch, S., Steinacker, L., Meckel, M., & Leimeister, J.-M. (2022). Quantum computing. *Electronic Markets, 32,* 2525–2536. https://doi.org/10.1007/ s12525-022-00570-y

Rudin, C. (2019). Stop explaining black box machine learning models for high stakes decisions and use interpretable models instead. *Nature Machine Intelligence, 1,* 206–215. https://doi.org/10.1038/s42256-019-0048-x

Runningen Larsson, M., & Zhang, L. (2022, August 23–24). *Using non-survey big data to improve the quality*. Retrieved from www.nsm2022.is/process-and-analyze

Statistics Canada. (2017). *Quality assurance framework*. Retrieved from https://www150. statcan.gc.ca/n1/pub/12-586-x/12-586-x2017001-eng.htm

Statistics Canada. (2020). *An integrated crop yield model using remote sensing, agroclimatic data and crop insurance data*. Retrieved from www.statcan.gc.ca/en/statistical-programs/document/3401_D2_V1

Statistics Canada. (2022). *Principles of necessity and proportionality*. Retrieved from www. statcan.gc.ca/en/trust/address

United Nations. (2014). *Fundamental principles of official statistics*. Retrieved from https:// unstats.un.org/unsd/dnss/hb/E-fundamental%20principles_A4-WEB.pdf

United Nations. (2019). *National Quality Assurance Frameworks Manual for Official Statistics*. Retrieved from https://unstats.un.org/unsd/methodology/dataquality/un-nqaf-manual/

US White House Office of Science and Technology Policy. (2022). *Blueprint for an AI bill of rights*. Retrieved from www.whitehouse.gov/wp-content/uploads/2022/10/ Blueprint-for-an-AI-Bill-of-Rights.pdf

Van Blarkom, G., Borking, J., & Olk, J. (2003). *Handbook of privacy and privacy-enhancing technologies (the case of intelligent software agents)*. The Hague: College Bescherming Persoonsgegevens.

Vovk, V., Gammerman, A., & Shafer, G. (2005). *Algorithmic learning in a random world*. Berlin; Heidelberg: Springer-Verlag.

Waring, J., Lindvall, C., & Umeton, R. (2020). Automated machine learning: Review of the state-of-the-art and opportunities for healthcare. *Artificial Intelligence in Medicine, 104*, 101822. https://doi.org/10.1016/j.artmed.2020.101822

Yang, S., Kim, J., & Hwang, Y. (2021). Integration of data from probability surveys and big found data for finite population inference using mass imputation. *Survey Methodology, Statistics Canada, 47*(1). Retrieved from www.statcan.gc.ca/pub/12-001-x/2021001/article/00004-eng.htm

Zanussi, Z., Santos, B., & Molladavoudi, S. (2021). Supervised text classification with leveled homomorphic encryption. In *Proceedings of the 63rd ISI world statistics congress. Virtual*. Retrieved from www.isi-web.org/files/docs/papers-and-abstracts/87-day2-cps027-supervised-text-classification.pdf

Chapter 10

Challenges Posed by the Digital Transformation Paths of the Online Access Act in Germany

Implementation and the Need to Raise Awareness

Esther Ruiz Ben and Margit Christa Scholl

Content

DOI: 10.1201/9781003369783-10

10.1 Introduction

The Act to Improve Online Access to Administrative Services otherwise known as
the Online Access Act (OAA)—which came into force in 2017, obliges the federal
and state governments to also offer their administrative services electronically via
administrative portals by the end of 2022.[1] Specifically, this includes two tasks: digitization and networking. On the one hand, administrative services at the federal,
state, and municipal levels must be digitized. On the other, an IT infrastructure
must be created that enables every user to access the administrative services with
just a few clicks. User orientation has top priority in OAA implementation. This
means that all digitization processes are geared to the needs of users.[2] The OAA
attempts to boost the digital transformation of public services that was initiated
in Germany two decades ago but has met a series of delays.[3] Germany is a federal state with a federal government and administration as well as 16 independent
state governments and administrations, in addition to municipalities, which also
have a municipal sovereign right of self-determination. The OAA is situated in a
complex multilevel German public sector and a highly fragmented digital landscape (Fleischer & Carstens, 2022). The foundations for the digital transformation
paths in the German public administration were conceived as early as 2000 in
the German e-government initiative BundOnline 2005 (Wittkemper & Kleindiek,
2003). The legal basis for the development of e-government in Germany was established later as a set of public rules and norms to follow in the implementation of
digital tools in public sector areas (see e-government laws). The problems that chal-
lenged the public sector were connected to pressures coming from the private sector
and citizens to increase the efficiency of public sector service delivery (see OECD,
2015). These pressures include citizens' expectations of innovative and digital public services that support their day-to-day lives in a globalized world that is more and
more interconnected through digital technologies and confronted with increasing
complexity and information technology (IT) vulnerabilities that are impossible to
take stock of and fully understand. Citizens' and public servants' expectations and
awareness of digital vulnerabilities, however, were not sufficiently acknowledged in
the digital transformation path of public services for a long time. In Germany, the
implementation challenges of e-government have been conceived and confronted
from a top-down perspective—i.e., from the federal government down to the states
and, from there, to the municipalities—and this also applies to the development of
the OAA (Rackwitz et al., 2021). Moreover, from its first implementation phases,
e-government has frequently been reduced to a functional innovative solution
for the problems challenging the public sector and has not involved deep social
consultation.

From the inception of the e-government strategy, publications in Germany
made mention of citizen interests and participation, but it was not possible for this
to be put into practice in the long term.[4] This lack of inclusion of citizens' perspectives and demands in e-government innovations and the complex multilevel

legal and stakeholder framework in Germany has deep consequences. In comparison to its neighboring countries in Europe, such as Finland, Estonia, Malta, and the Netherlands, Germany performs very poorly in e-government indicators. However, it must be remembered that the comparisons also rely on dissimilar factors such as size, structure, and population figures. In the last Digital Economy and Society Index 2022 published by the EU Commission, Germany ranks only 25th above Italy, Bulgaria, and Romania in terms of e-government users interacting online with public authorities over the Internet in the last 12 months.[5] Even if the OAA sets out a clear objective for the digitization of administrative services—a process that is to be completed by the end of 2022, with all German administrations currently working on the fulfillment of this goal—in practice, most OAA projects concentrate purely on the legally required digital application and disregard the underlying process of handling administrative services (Deutscher Bundestag, 2022). So again, although there is an ongoing conversation about digitizing administrative services in relation to the OAA, most OAA projects are purely focused on the digital submission of applications as required by law and disregard the underlying process of handling administrative services (see Schmidt et al., 2021; Rackwitz, 2021; Deutscher Bundestag, 2022a and 2022b for a critical overview of the OAA implementation).

In this chapter, we explain the main challenges posed by the OAA digital transformation paths in Germany. We emphasize the need to raise awareness of both the needs of citizens and the situation in the public administrations in terms of digitization and the challenges involved, along with the opportunities and risks it entails.

The chapter is organized in five parts. First, we provide a brief contextual overview of the OAA in Germany's e-government innovation path. Second, we explain the specific design and development of the OAA in Germany. In the third section, we discuss the particular acceptance and adoption barriers of online government services in Germany. These barriers are not limited to citizens' lack of awareness about the implementation of digital public services. The barriers to adopting digital public service delivery are also present in the daily practice of employees in public organizations with a constantly growing range of tasks, fewer staff, and increased stress. In particular, both citizens and public servants are required to take responsibility for data protection and information security, including IT security and cybersecurity, often without having the necessary knowledge, skills, or experience.

After examining the barriers for confronting the challenges posed by the digital transformation of the OAA, we focus in the fourth section of our chapter on the security barriers and suggest some methods for raising security awareness in the development of online services. In the fifth section, we look at some examples of how these awareness methods are applied and conclude the chapter with a discussion of the challenges facing successful implementation of the OAA and solutions to the problems involved, accompanied by an outlook on future research.

10.2 Digital e-Government Innovations in Public Service in Germany

Electronic government (e-government) constitutes a regulatory framework for the definition of innovative organizational standards and requirements for a far-reaching reform of the public administration. This reform, which is characterized by extensive design, the implementation of existing ideas about the digitization of the public sector, and the use of digital technologies, seeks to remodel the traditional bureaucratic—mostly paper- and staff-based—administrative processes. As Beck (2021) emphasizes, digital innovations in e-government are not only technological in nature but also include deep organizational, constitutional, social, and infrastructural changes. Previous structures and workflows are not simply transferred into the digital systems. New organizational forms are introduced and redefined in a digitization process that is tied into the overall structure of public and private legal democratic norms.

In the case of Germany, from the perspective of the internal organization of the administrative bodies, a reform of constitutional and administrative law has been necessary to implement e-government innovations. From a constitutional point of view, the digital infrastructures and the networks that connect the 16 federal states and the federal government needed coordination. Digital documents and declarations of intent had to be legally acknowledged as well (Beck, 2021)—for example, the supplementation of Germany's Basic Law (GG) to include Art. 91 c GG.

Infrastructural innovations needed for the implementation of e-government include the hardware facilities and cloud services necessary for telecommunication services that enable cooperation within an administrative organization and across administrative levels (i.e., electronic mail room, seal, stamps, etc.). Another group of basic innovations in e-government are the special digital applications such as business registration and social assistance, as well as those still in the planning phase such as the issuing of driving licenses (Beck, 2021). These applications require active citizen involvement in the process in order to make the administrative processes paperless and accepted in the long term. This intention is definitely included in theoretical terms in the five goals of the German National E-Government Strategy (NEGS) and its current updated version. The federal and state governments undertake the alignment of their actions with the following guiding principles:[6]

- Benefits for citizens, companies, and administration: Citizens and companies can finally deal with as many of their concerns as possible in a variety of ways, regardless of location and time, at bundled contact points; access is barrier-free, and operation is user-friendly.
- Profitability, efficiency, and performance: Authorities work together quickly, in a network and across levels, in order to minimize the administrative burden on citizens, companies, and the administration itself; the processes are customer oriented and digitized throughout.

- Information security and data protection: Citizens and companies can see which public bodies are processing their personal data, the protective measures are reliable, and data protection is guaranteed.
- Transparency and social participation: Citizens use electronic media to actively participate in the formation of political will and opinions and in the design of public task fulfillment; open data and freedom of information are promoted.
- Future viability and sustainability: The federal, state, and local governments support innovations and the willingness to change; services and applications can be bundled and reused; e-government contributes to ecological sustainability.

However, the practical implementation of these goals has clearly been difficult. Jakobi (2019, p. 198) gives an overview of the initiatives—both successive and parallel—driving e-government innovations at different governmental levels. E-government implementation in Germany was not driven by a uniform strategy until at least 2010. Overall, e-government in Germany has been part of the EU's competitive strategy right from the beginning of e-government implementation. However, German federalism and the departmental principle have helped fragment the representation of German e-government interests in Brussels (Jakobi, 2019).[7] Jakobi (2019) points out that e-government in Germany suffers from a high level of institutional and organizational inertia—resulting from administrative federalism, the departmental principle, and the requirement for written forms. The institutional inertia has been significantly reduced by two amendments to the Basic Law.

The approbation of the IT State Treaty that came into force on April 1, 2010, which primarily regulated the establishment of an IT Planning Council, also helped decrease the institutional inertia of German e-government. The treaty was intended to place federal state cooperation on a binding and permanent footing. Moreover, the IT Planning Council began to coordinate e-government implementation and established a national e-government strategy (NEGS) in the same year. The orientation toward the EU is clear in this NEGS milestone in Germany. However, as some scholars remark, the question of how a broader use of e-government offers can be generated has been neglected (Wentzel, 2010; Jakobi, 2019). Today, the IT Planning Council is supported by the newly founded organization Federal IT Cooperation (FITKO), which, as the central coordination and networking point for digitization projects in public administration in Germany, is intended to bundle together all competencies and resources.[8]

The extensive organizational inertia in German e-government is likely to persist due to the highly complex structures established during the last decades, including fragmented political institutions and very different private and public organizations and interests (see also Jakobi, 2019). In addition, an assumed cognitive resistance among citizens has also helped delay the e-government dynamic in Germany.

This citizens' attitudes towards the e-government innovations are nevertheless well funded (Jakobi, 2019). Citizens were discursively but not *directly* included and consulted in the numerous German e-government initiatives (see Jakobi, 2019, p. 198) and governance networks. One example of this lack of citizen consultation and top-down decision making by governmental actors at different governance levels and in various IT companies involved in the German e-government innovation path is the introduction of De-Mail for communication with the public administration (Roßnagel, 2013).[9] We will explain more about this topic in section 9.3 of this chapter.

In 2013, the e-government law was approved and adopted. With the second change in the constitutional text in 2017 (Schliesky & Hoffmann, 2018), the federal states and the state gave sole competence for the regulation of digital access to federal and state public services and the implementation of these services in line with the OAA (Jakobi, 2019). In addition, the compromise of offering all public services online by the end of 2022 was established. In the next section, we explain the implementation process involved in the digitization of public services within the framework of the OAA.

10.3 Implementation of Online Government Services in Germany: Online Access Act

The OAA has been understood and implemented in different ways in the EU and in its member states, although COVID-19 has been an important catalyst for the digitization of public services in the EU (Schmidt & Krimmer, 2022). Germany has retained its predominantly top-down digitization procedure. Decisions about which services should primarily be offered online or about how to inform citizens about the digitization of prioritized public services have been taken by the government without large-scale citizen consultations. This is reflected, for example, in the last EU e-government benchmark of 2021 showing that users are only informed on 61 percent of the public authority portals about whether and what personal data is used by the administration.[10]

As recent research by Rackwitz et al. (2021) reveals, a "purely legal approach" for the digitization of public services is not enough to guarantee successful implementation. Even if there is a shift toward more collaborative leadership styles in German public administration among different administrative authorities and organizations and in terms of direct citizen participation oriented toward new public management, this approach is still an exception (Rackwitz et al., 2021). An example of this intention to move toward more collaborative leadership governance forms and more balanced digital sovereignty between the state and citizens is the organization of user-oriented and interdisciplinary digital labs to develop ideas, prototypes, and implementation concepts for digital public services (Fleischer & Carstens, 2022). It is not known how these labs resonate among the wider German population or how they impact the adoption and acceptance of online public service. In the past two years, the implementation of the OAA has been fueled by the dramatic need for social services and the shortcomings made evident by the pandemic crisis.

In any case, German public administrations are obliged under the OAA to provide citizens with an electronic ID (eID) that enables them to submit applications and sign them online. In addition, the digitization program of the OAA includes the development of a joint online portal and the digitization of public services for enterprises and for citizens within the EU. This German joint online portal must be connected to the Single Digital Gateway (SDG) accessible all over the EU, creating synergies between federal, state, and local governments.[11]

Under the OAA, the 575 public services bundles comprising over 6,000 administrative services at the federal, state, and local levels in Germany must be digitized by the end of 2022.[12] State and local authorities are responsible for delivering 460 of these services, and 115 are delivered by the federal government (BMI, 2019). The public services have been grouped into 14 major subject areas, bundling 35 life scenarios and 17 company situations and differing in the number of services they comprise (BMI, 2020). Each of these life areas is supervised by a federal ministry together with a ministry of the German states and on a voluntary basis supported by further federal ministries, states, and local municipalities (BMI, 2018). The OAA thus constitutes the first opportunity in the digitization path of German public administrations to engage federal, state, and local authorities in identifying, designing, and defining solutions for the implementation of digital public services. Four major areas of cooperation between the administration levels enabled after the amendment of the Basic Law, Art. 91c GG, are security and data transfer, network structure, standardization (interoperability, secure data transport), and principles of cooperation between state and federal governments (Beck, 2021). The subsequent usage of the services is voluntary even if all digital public services are available at every administrative level. The IT Planning Council coordinates and formulates standards for cooperation between organizations and the state, federal, and local authorities.[13] In each legislature, decisions must be taken about digitization milestones and constitutional designs that are compliant with data protection laws. These decisions must align with basic constitutional principles such as federalism, popular sovereignty, and the autonomy of certain administrative institutions.

As Beck (2021) points out, particularly important in a competently differentiated multilevel system is the strengthening of digitization through specific laws—for example, through federal and state e-government laws, freedom of information, information access, and information-processing laws—as an expression of the OAA. Important steps toward a cross-level digitization of administrative services include electronic identification and the realization of electronic administrative procedures embedded in continuous processes. These processes need to be identified and classified by the technical designers and developers of the digital systems in the implementation of the OAA.

Important actors in the OAA implementation and in the e-government landscape are thus the IT service providers that are responsible for "translating" the administrative procedures and work processes into the digital governance and public service solutions. IT service providers focus on ensuring that the digitized services are in demand through tenders during the political legislatures. This measure for maintaining the demand of digitized public services is only indirectly connected to the users' perspectives and needs. Citizens' acceptance of the digitized public services within the framework of the OAA is nevertheless now an important part of the IT service providers' business model.[14] Public administrations in Germany do not have the expertise and resources to confront digitization acceptance problems, which they also need to solve for themselves within their organizations. Since the OAA does not include any specific parameters, the EU Commission's maturity model is applied as a criterion for determining whether a public service has been successfully digitized. A public service is regarded as digitized once the corresponding application and all supporting documents can be processed online. In 2020, only 5 percent of all public services (27 services) met this digitization requirement (BMI, 2019; Fleischer & Carstens, 2022).

In order to achieve the goal of OAA in Germany, three principles are currently being followed. The first principle, "One for All" (EfA), means that one state, possibly in association with others and the federal government, is responsible for the digitization of a service, and the result is shared with the other states.[15] EfA is seen as the key to fast, nationwide administrative digitization and is therefore an important instrument for those implementing the OAA at the federal, state, and local levels. The second principle relates to the specialist applications and is called the "F module."[16] In the "F module project," the *F* stands for specialized procedures. A platform with preprogrammed modules is being developed: these can be combined to generate the desired specialist processes—software applications that support the digital processing of administrative tasks in the background. From 2023, the first prioritized modules from the pilot process should be reusable throughout Germany. The third principle is called "Federal Information Management (FIM)."[17] FIM is intended to reduce the effort required to implement legal requirements and to provide easily understandable information for citizens about administrative services, uniform data fields for form systems, and standardized process specifications for administrative enforcement.

Despite all these efforts, it is clear that currently, at the end of 2022, this ambitious OAA plan will not be achieved. At the beginning of September 2022, only 143 of the targeted 575 administrative services were available online. At that time, 49 OAA services (around 8.5 percent) could be processed completely digitally—including all supporting documents and notifications.[18] Bearing in mind the institutional and legal characteristics of the digitization path in German public services, how accessible are digital public services in Germany? How do citizens adopt the already digitized public services? In the next section, we explain these aspects of the digital transformation path of German public services.

10.4 Acceptance of and Adoption Barriers to Online Government Services in Germany

As the OAA does not explicitly define the accessibility of digitized public services, the EU model is applied as a basis for regulating this.[19] According to this model, the digitization status of the public services is classified in four maturity levels.[20] At the first level, there is just a description of the service that citizens can print. At the second level, an online application is basically possible, but the data transfer cannot be checked online. Once the third maturity level has been achieved, the online public service is considered to be completely digitalized. This includes the application process, authentication, and proof of transmission. At level four, proof of transmission is not necessary. This is already available in the administration. According to the "Once-Only Principle (OOP)," data that is already available in the administration should not be collected again from users but instead reused in other administrative procedures with the consent of users.[21]

This information—as well as access to the OAA implementation plan and a wealth of other information about the digitization of public services in Germany—is spread through the very different online portals of the 16 federal states and through the OAA website.[22] There is no lack of information available for citizens about the plans and legal background of the OAA. On the contrary, there are many different government websites offering this basic information or infographics. However, the acceptance of digital public services in Germany is very low. According to the latest results of the annual eGovernment Monitor conducted by the D21, the satisfaction among citizens in Germany with the online services currently available in their city or municipality fell back to 47 percent in 2021[23]—a 15-percentage-point drop in comparison with the previous year. The most striking declines relate to the reliability of the systems, ease of use, currency of the offerings, and the ability to find the required information. In addition, adoption barriers, including services that are not offered online and a lack of consistency in the offerings, are common causes of dissatisfaction from the public's perspective.

In accordance with the German top-down approach of implementing the OAA, decisions about which services should be primarily offered online and about how to inform citizens about the digitization of the prioritized public services have been taken by the government without major citizen consultations. Citizen participation in the digitization of public services usually comes into play in the final phases when decisions about design and usability priorities have already been made. One consequence of this approach is that citizens do not adopt the public services that are available online because they lack usability, even if this is a crucial principle already included in the OAA.[24]

Many public services and digital transactions require citizens to identify themselves unambiguously. For online public administrative transactions, citizens can use the online function of the personal identity card (electronic identification or eID).[25] The last D21 eGovernment Monitor also reveals that 35 percent of respondents in Germany with a valid ID card have activated eID—but only 9 percent have used it so far. Citizen registration with digital credentials is crucial for the implementation of the OAA and particularly for accessing the German joint online portal that is to be connected to the SDG accessible all over the EU. Underlying the SDG, the OOP outlines that citizens and businesses need provide data only once in their transactions with public administrations (Schmidt et al., 2021). The OOP specially applies for the use of online public services in every federal state and municipality. To access the public services online, citizens can register a user account.[26] For this, citizens can use the online ID function (covering the national identity card, electronic residence permit, or eID card for EU citizens), an electronic identification and trust services (eIDAS)-compliant eID from an EU country of origin, an ELSTER (Electronic Tax Return Service) certificate, or a username and password.[27] The request for one of these digital credentials depends on the confidentiality level of the data that needs to be exchanged with the public administrations in order to use the public service. After setting up the user account, the required personal data is transferred from the user account under the OOP. In Germany, the EU's eIDAS regulation is based on eID. This regulation, which was approved in 2014 and completely implemented in 2018, establishes the standard framework for the cross-border use of electronic means of identification applying to the eID function.[28]

The D21 eGovernment Monitor reveals that the acceptance of these credentials over the years has not progressed very much. Particularly in the case of eID usage, the low acceptance is partly because there have been major hurdles, such as the requirement for special devices and the scarcity of application options. A recent review of research on the acceptance of eID shows that its public acceptance constitutes a multifaceted phenomenon influenced by a wide range of variables with a different degree of impact (Tsap et al., 2019). Tsap et al. (2019) have summarized 12 categories that influence the acceptance of eID: awareness, trust, privacy concerns, security, complexity, ease of use, functionality, control and empowerment, cultural and historical factors, path dependency, transparency, and other.

Awareness refers to understanding the system, the reasons for it, and the purpose behind it and knowing how the system works and how to use it. This last aspect is not limited to controlling the technical aspects of usage. The control of technical functionality does not guarantee the acceptance of eID. This must be connected to the awareness aspect of understanding and seeing the purpose of eID. *Trust* is the most prevalent category in the research of Tsap et al. This category connects two aspects together: trust in the public institutions offering eID and trust in eID itself. *Privacy* refers to risks, fears, and threats to citizens' rights in relation to their digital identities, and *security* refers to the reliability, trustworthiness, and safety of the software and hardware provided by the state for using eID.

In Germany, these awareness and privacy and security aspects[29] relating to the acceptance of eID have also affected the perception and usage of the electronic credentials. As the D21 eGovernment Monitor shows, the most important barrier affecting the acceptance of eID is that citizens are not aware of this digital registration credential. The D21 eGovernment Monitor also reveals that to improve the acceptance of eID, it is important not only to consider a general explanation of how eID functions but also to clearly show the concrete application possibilities that represent added value for citizens. Another possible indicator of the lack of awareness and acceptance of digital public services is the existence of a marketplace of private companies offering to carry out the application of official certificates, for example.[30] In addition, security and privacy fears are related to the adoption practices of digital public services that also reveal a generational digital divide. The D21 eGovernment Monitor shows that 48 percent of citizens are interested in enabling the use of eID with their smartphones. The highest interest in this group is among citizens under 30 years of age, those who have already used online government services, and people with a university education. For people over 60 years old, personal contact and the easy accessibility of local authorities play the most important role. Other barriers are only of secondary importance for this age group. With increasing age, there is a marked tendency to trust in personal contact, while the concrete presentation of the alternatives offered online is looked on less favorably. For those under 50, personal contact is not a critical factor. In the younger age groups, functionality problems are the biggest hurdle, followed by the lack of consistency (D21 eGovernment Monitor, 2022).

In summary, the main challenges preventing citizen acceptance of online public services in Germany are the lack of awareness of existing online services coupled with usability problems and the lack of trust in data privacy and security. In addition, the adoption of online public services is characterized by a generational digital divide. This raises the question of whether a multichannel provision of public services preserving analogue solutions would be a better digitization path in order to reach every citizen. The fragmentation of the offerings and information—particularly in relation to the registration forms for using online public services via user accounts in a very complex institutional federal system (each German federal state offers a user account portal in parallel to the federal user account and the administration portals of the online public services in the state)—also contributes to stagnation in the acceptance of digital public services in Germany. In the next section, we concentrate on the awareness aspects related to data privacy and security in the use of digital public services. We explain some approaches to raising awareness among both citizens and administrative staff.

10.5 Raising Awareness of the Need for More Security When Developing Online Services

To raise awareness of digital public services and their implications for privacy and security online, it is necessary to understand how users perceive and understand the requirements of online services with regard to data exchange. This includes public servants interacting with citizens through digital public services as well as citizens using digital public services in new risk situations, such as home offices. Cybersecurity is the backbone of the successful digitization of society, and having an awareness of cyber situations is an essential aspect of managing them (Andreasson et al., 2020). The COVID-19 pandemic has accelerated digitization in all countries. Research by Andreasson et al. (2020) in Swedish government agencies shows that employee communications at the beginning of the pandemic focused more on first-order risks, such as videoconferencing and teleworking, than on second-order risks, such as invoice fraud and social engineering. Andreasson et al. (2020) also note that nearly two-thirds of government agencies have not yet implemented their cybersecurity policies but only initiated or documented them. Statistics clearly show how working from home (WFH) has changed the cybersecurity landscape for businesses and created new risks (Eiza et al., 2021). Is this why German authorities are cautious?

WFH has become a very real experience for a large part of the population. At the same time, practice shows that the legal basis for it has been poorly prepared, even though the German Federal Ministry of Labor and Social Affairs is planning to create a legal entitlement to WFH (Barrein, 2022). Germany is below the EU average in terms of the proportion of people with home offices, with mainly well-qualified, full-time workers interested in WFH (Brenke, 2016). If employers in Germany were to change their thinking, the proportion of homeworkers could rise to over 30 percent (Brenke, 2016). It is interesting to note that the widest gap between employees' wishes for WFH and the opportunities offered by employers can be found in the financial sector and in public administration (Brenke, 2016). So, what does WFH have to do with online public services? We assume that people transfer their expectations from their own experiences to the use of other services, creating a visible gap in their sense of fulfillment. For example, messaging solutions are evidently becoming increasingly popular in the environment of (federal) administration and are in use in many government agencies (BSI, 2022, p. 66). However, many users stick to traditional (mobile) telephony for formal communication with companies, government agencies, doctors, and other nonprivate addressees and organizations because of its better accessibility (Bundesnetzagentur für Elektrizität, Gas, Telekommunikation, Post und Eisenbahnen, 2021, p. 48). Köhler (2022) makes it clear that in the public sector environment, messaging apps belong to the "shadow IT" category because of their considerable weaknesses in terms of data protection and information security, administration and integration, and support—their use thus requires a number of things: General Data Protection Regulation (GDPR) compliance, useful functionalities, intuitive usability, the smooth exchange of information and interaction across all offices and subject areas, centralized administration, and outsourced hosting in order to be able to use a decoupled channel in crisis and emergency situations (Köhler, 2022). One wonders, therefore, why the government administration's online services seem to pay scant attention to its own principles.

Škiljić (2020) and Nyikes (2021) see a clear responsibility on the part of governments and public authorities to ensure the cybersecurity of citizens as Internet users by obliging ICT service providers to offer fundamentally secure services (possibly at extra cost). "Security awareness and digital literacy" on the part of users are important, but according to Nyikes (2021), ICT must guarantee IT security and relieve users of the burdens associated with this. The question is whether service providers can produce such a guarantee. After all, don't users themselves also need to be made more aware of security issues? We assume that in addition to technical cybersecurity solutions from institutions, individuals will also have to become more aware of the risks and how to use digital tools. This is a learning process on both sides. With regard to online public services, it means that citizens, public servants, and the digital public service designers share the responsibility for data protection and security. This is a lesson that needs to be learned in the realms of OAA implementation and in the Digital Transformation Path of public services in Germany.

Another way to raise awareness of the need for more security when developing online services is to implement data privacy notice instruments within the user accounts for accessing digital public services. In our research study of the project "Instruments for active and safe consumer participation in Online Public Services (IVTOPS)," we examine how information about data privacy and security in the process of registering user accounts for access to digital public services affects citizen acceptance.[31] In this section, we present some results of this study relating to how citizens perceive and understand the requirements for accessing and using their accounts. We rely on a combination of qualitative and quantitative materials collected with the aim of elaborating usable security instruments for online public service accounts.

The research began with an analysis of documents about the implementation of the OAA and the digital service accounts followed by interviews conducted with professional experts (N = 4). In a second step, the interviews were conducted with six citizens living in the states of Berlin and Brandenburg. The individuals who participated in these interviews were recruited through personal contacts, two of them having had no previous experience with digital public services. The questionnaire was administered and disseminated online through a snowball principle and also included associations in Berlin/Brandenburg dedicated to people with disabilities, the elderly, and single parents. The final sample included 32 participants.

The interview guides for the professional experts and citizens included questions about access to and the need for digital public services, knowledge about existing online offerings, and the perceived requirements for usage. The interviews with the citizens included a "walk" through the service account of Berlin and Brandenburg. In a third step, the citizens were confronted with several visual additions to the websites, including the logos of eIDAS, the certificate of the German Federal Security Institute (BSI), use case graphics for the service accounts, a chatbot, a video, and links to the GDPR text.

The online survey questionnaire included three parts. In the first part, participants were asked for a self-assessment of their digital competences and confidence and about their knowledge and usage of digital public services and possible barriers for not using them. In the second part, the participants were required to access the service account of Berlin or Brandenburg and go through the registration steps without completing it. In the third step, the participants went back to the questionnaire website and responded to questions about the perceived sensitivity of the data required for registering the service accounts and about their recollection of data protection. Moreover, the participants were asked again for a self-assessment of their digital competences and about their trust in the online service accounts as well as their intention of using the account in future and the more salient factors influencing their decision. The online survey instrument also included three items about digital sovereignty.

The analysis of all these qualitative and quantitative materials serves as the basis for designing usable security instruments together with citizens. In this chapter, we concentrate on the analysis of the questions connected to the topic of digital sovereignty. In concrete terms, these questions are the three items included in the survey:

- ▪ "When registering at the online service account, I can decide at any time about the transfer of my private data."
- ▪ "I understand all the information in the service account about data privacy and security."
- ▪ "Access to online public services is very easy for me."

Both the qualitative and quantitative materials collected in this study confirm the lack of citizens' digital sovereignty in the usage of online public services: this relates to their perceptions of deciding for themselves about the transfer of data and their understanding of data privacy and security information. The results of the IVTOPS project cannot be regarded as representative because of the small size of the samples. Nevertheless, they give a concrete and up-to-date insight into how online public services are faring in German society.

On the one hand, citizens are unaware of the existing implementation of the OAA and feel insecure about data privacy risks. On the other, they do not read data privacy protocols provided in the online service accounts, which is also a usability problem in the design of service accounts.[32] The promise of social inclusion through the implementation of the OAA does not seem to be close to fulfillment. The OAA is intended to advance social justice, but the lack of support for citizens' digitization awareness and digital sovereignty, both affected by an implementation focused on enterprises, acts against it by further widening the digital divide. This short study exemplary shows that the acceptance challenges posed by the digital transformation paths of the OAA in Germany seem far from being successfully resolved or even effectively confronted.

In the next section, we comment on more examples of participatory approaches in the implementation of the OAA.

10.6 Examples of More Participatory Approaches in the Implementation of the Online Access Act

Participatory approaches in the implementation of the OAA relate to different interconnected aspects of citizens' knowledge, usability, awareness,[33] and trust in the digital public service delivery systems and the government's delivery of public services online. The lack of citizen knowledge in Germany about available digital public services requires an effort from the federal governments to inform all citizens effectively and transparently about the implementation of the OAA. This means covering the wide diversity of digital competences with an eye on persistent digital divides exacerbated in Germany by the COVID-19 pandemic, for example.[34] In the specific case of Germany, the provision of information has not been effective, considering citizens' lack of knowledge of digital public services (D21 eGovernment Monitor, 2022). Some good examples of supporting citizen participation through information can be observed in neighboring EU member states. Countries such as Malta, Estonia, Finland, and Denmark perform better in terms of transparency and user-centricity than Germany, according to a recent e-government benchmarking.[35] Transparency and user-centricity can help enhance citizen trust and participation in the implementation of the OAA, supporting a more engaged and conscious usage of digital public services. The participation of citizens in the implementation of the OAA also relates to the knowledge of key enablers of access to these services such as eID. In Germany, citizen awareness about the different registration modes for accessing online public services (see section 9.4) is low. The most effective and secure of the common key enablers for identifying and authenticating the use of digital public services is eID. However, as a recent e-government benchmarking reveals, only 67 percent of online public services in the EU can be accessed with eID. Good practices relating to the widespread usage of eID can be seen in EU countries such as Denmark, Estonia, and Finland, where more than 90 percent of the online services can be accessed with eID.[36] Enabling access to online public services with eID is a good example of supporting citizen participation in the implementation of the OAA.

Another example of enhancing participation in the implementation of the OAA is the improvements to the usability of public service websites.[37] The exploration of them begins at a particular website showing the public services offered online or with user accounts, where citizens can register to access the services provided online. Using eID, citizens can register just once to have access to every online public service in Germany. On the websites where citizens start their online journey, they must exchange data with the public administrations. Thus, how citizens' awareness of data privacy is supported on these websites is very important for establishing sustainable participation in the implementation of the OAA. To improve the viability of user accounts with regard to data privacy, it is helpful to consider the concept of usable privacy. This concept refers to the user-centricity of data privacy information. Data privacy is understood as the citizens' right to control and manage their personal data, ensuring user self-determination at any time as defined by the GDPR. In line with the concept of usable privacy, data privacy information should be transparent and understandable for every citizen. Moreover, on the websites where the online public services are initially accessed, the request for personal data should be maintained at a minimum, while always following the GDPR and, in Germany's case, §8 of the OAA. Usable privacy is an example of a participatory approach to implementing the OAA. It includes several instruments such as privacy-enhancing technologies (PETs) as well as the direct participation of users—in our case, we focus on citizens—in the design of all data privacy aspects. PETs constitute a system of IT measures for supporting data privacy through the elimination or reduction of personal data requirements or the prevention of unnecessary processing of personal data. In particular, the concept of data protection by design, which calls for the inclusion of data privacy protection measures and PETs in the IT design, is directly supported by the GDPR.[38] Data privacy by design as well as the usage of PETs for the improvement of data privacy information provision in digital public services are further examples of participatory approaches in the implementation of the OAA. Data privacy by design and PETs could also help enhance the general usability of online public service websites, which is one of the most neglected aspects of the digitization of public services from the perspective of citizens (European Commission Directorate-General for Communications Networks, Content and Technology, 2022). In any case, PETs should be adapted to the particular context of user accounts to enable single registration to access digital public services. The outputs of our ongoing IVTOPS research, which also considers the pitfalls of PETs (see Schaub et al., 2015), will deliver some possible implementation solutions.

In summary, examples of more participatory approaches in the implementation of the OAA include *transparency* in creating digital public services and planning access to them and the application of *awareness methods* such as data privacy by design, the application of PETs, the usable privacy evaluation of digital public service portals, and collaborative redesign undertaken together with citizens. Moreover, *usability* improvements applying design thinking methods (see Plattner et al., 2011) in the development of digital public services should be connected to the knowledge of these services. For example, the Federal Government Commissioner for Information Technology's *Nine-Point Plan for a Digital Germany* includes the usability of digital platforms for public services as a priority.[39] Labs for designing these platforms also exist within the framework of the OAA implementation, although citizens are unaware of the work being done there.[40] Thus, the implementation of the OAA would take better advantage of these usability efforts if they were reinforced by transparency—i.e., the broad dissemination of information with a proactive approach and wider involvement of citizens.

10.7 Summary, Conclusions, and Outlook for Future Research

In this chapter, we have examined the challenges that the digital transformation paths of the OAA pose in Germany. Owing to the highly complex structures established during the last decades, including fragmented political institutions and very different private and public organizations and interests, e-government innovation suffers from a persistent organizational inertia (Jakobi, 2019). The resistance to the adoption of digital public services among citizens, which is exacerbated by the lack of consultation and inclusion (Roßnagel, 2013) in German e-government initiatives, also contributes to the delay in the e-government dynamic in Germany. Situated in this digital transformation path, the OAA has been implemented following a top-down approach (Rackwitz et al., 2021), which has been more exposed during the pandemic crisis, evidencing the dramatic need for digital social services. Citizens' lack of trust and awareness of digital public services (D21 eGovernment Monitor, 2022) as well as data privacy aspects and usability problems are associated with the top-down approach in the digitization path of public services in Germany as well as the fragmentation of their offerings and of information about the digitization of public services. In addition, the adoption of online public services is characterized by a generational digital divide. Preserving analogue solutions could be a better digitization path to reach every citizen. In summary, including more participatory approaches in the implementation of the OAA, such as *transparency* in creating and making digital public services accessible, introducing *awareness methods* to data privacy in the design process, and applying design thinking to *usability* improvements, are some of the possible solutions to the challenges posed by the OAA-related digital transformation paths in Germany commented upon in this chapter. Table 10.1 summarizes our conclusions as applied to the concrete case of digital citizens' accounts for single registration.

If we look at our reflections on German online public services in the course of the OAA in the larger context of the digital transformation path of public services, namely that of the dynamic development of smart cities, our results will be further confirmed. Cortés-Cediel et al. (2020), for example, examine the European Smart Cities initiatives and their three dimensions—technological (TEC), institutional (INS), and human (HUM)—as proposed by Nam and Pardo (2011). The results from Cortés-Cediel et al. (2020) make it clear that the top-ranked smart cities have initiatives in all three dimensions. It is crucial that the smart cities clearly place people at the center of their initiatives and, at the same time, take both technological and institutional aspects into account. For the HUM dimension, following Cortés-Cediel et al. (2020), the most prevalent factors are social inclusion, technology, social learning, and creative and community-based networks, followed by innovation environments, services for migrants, and family and child support. For the TEC dimension, technological and physical infrastructures as well as smart computing and digital technologies are the main goals Cortés-Cediel et al. (2020). Finally, relevant to the INS dimension are citizen participation in decision making; bottom-up processes; complaints and suggestions; and social awareness, action, and activism, followed by the connection of public administration to other services, coupled with integration and interoperability Cortés-Cediel et al. (2020). In our opinion, this means that for individual digital public services, their implementation should be approached in a much more integrative manner: the users are of central importance, supported by institutional participation processes and secure technology.

For future research, it is important to analyze which forms of awareness raising are particularly effective and sustainable for the specific case of single registration. With regard to data privacy awareness, as Schaub et al. (2015) show, notice complexity, lack of choices (take it or leave it), notice fatigue, and decouple notices are the main hurdles with data privacy notices. These aspects should be considered in the development of usable privacy measures (see Table 10.1). Another important topic for future research is the consideration of multichannel solutions in the implementation of the OAA. An unresolved question related to this is the extent to which usability and transparency can resolve the challenges of the generational digital divide and help establish trust in the digitization of public services. Further research could also focus on the question of how transparency can support more inclusive and participatory digitization paths in public services. What aspects of digital public service design and what granularity

Table 10.1 Summary of Challenges and Possible Solutions in the Digitization Path of Public Services

	Digital Public Services Portals and Citizens' Accounts	*eID (eIDAS)*	*Digital Public Services*
Knowledge	Transparency	Transparency	Transparency
Data privacy awareness	Usable privacy	Usable privacy	Data privacy by design, PETs, evaluation, and redesign
Usability	Heuristics[41]	Standard for accessing digital public services (citizens' accounts)	Design thinking, heuristics, evaluation, and redesign
Generational digital divide	Multichannel solutions	Usability	Multichannel solutions

and timing should be provided and how? How should the processing of citizens' personal data be effectively communicated? These questions should be considered in the digital transformation of public services and the implementation of participatory paths.

Acknowledgments

We would like to thank the Federal Ministry for the Environment, Nature Conservation, Nuclear Safety, and Consumer Protection (BMUV) for funding the project "Instruments for active and safe consumer participation on Online Public Services (IVTOPS)" under grant number 28V1403A20. We would like to acknowledge the anonymous reviewers for their helpful critical comments. Many thanks, too, to Simon Cowper for his detailed and professional proofreading of the text.

Notes

1 www.onlinezugangsgesetz.de/Webs/OZG/DE/grundlagen/info-ozg/info-ozg-node. html;jsessionid=F29BE22E9012ABB3ACEF9A35948ACD89.2_cid322 (accessed November 8, 2022).

2 Ibid.

3 www.onlinezugangsgesetz.de/Webs/OZG/EN/home/home-node.html (accessed December 10, 2021).

4 www.it-planungsrat.de/der-it-planungsrat/nationale-e-government-strategie (accessed November 2, 2022).

5 https://digital-strategy.ec.europa.eu/en/policies/desi-digital-public-services (accessed September 23, 2022).

6 www.it-planungsrat.de/der-it-planungsrat/nationale-e-government-strategie (accessed September 18, 2022).

7 According to the constitutional departmental principle (*Ressortprinzip*), each minister is responsible for his or her own area of responsibility. The chancellor is not allowed to "rein in" the powers of his or her ministers, and, in turn, each minister must take care to make decisions within the political framework set by the chancellor. www.bundeskanzler.de/bk-de/aktuelles/das-bundeskabinett-346746 (accessed September 2, 2022).

8 www.fitko.de/ (accessed November 1, 2022).

9 See www.bundestag.de/resource/blob/874860/e28d62c4a0822b538eb037157ddbc340/WD-3-192-21-pdf-data.pdf (p. 5) (accessed November 28, 2022).

10 www.kommune21.de/meldung_37462_B%C3%BCrger+profitieren+von+Digitalisierungsschub.html (accessed October 17, 2022).

11 www.onlinezugangsgesetz.de/Webs/OZG/EN/home/home-node.html;jsessionid=B8E64E97603083719507285148954EB0.1_cid340 (accessed November 7, 2022).

12 www.it-planungsrat.de/en/federal-cooperation/implementing-the-online-access-act (accessed September 26, 2022).

13 www.it-planungsrat.de/Projekte/Koordinierungsprojekt (accessed September 28, 2022).

14 See, e.g., https://kommune-digital-app.de (accessed September 29, 2022).

15 www.onlinezugangsgesetz.de (accessed October 8, 2022).

16 www.onlinezugangsgesetz.de/Webs/OZG/DE/themen/foederale-architektur/modul-f/modul-f-node.html#doc18042520bodyText1 (accessed October 8, 2022).

17 https://fimportal.de/ (accessed October 8, 2022).

18 https://dashboard.ozg-umsetzung.de/ (accessed September 15, 2022).

19 https://digital-strategy.ec.europa.eu/en/policies/web-accessibility (accessed October 4, 2022).

20 https://leitfaden.ozg-umsetzung.de/display/OZG/2.2+Digitale+Services+im+Sinne+des+OZG (accessed October 2, 2022).

21 https://toop.eu/once-only (accessed October 1, 2022).

22 For example, https://www.onlinezugangsgesetz.de (German version) and https://www.onlinezugangsgesetz.de/Webs/OZG/EN/home/home-node.html English version) (accessed May 1, 2023).

23 https://initiatived21.de/egovernment-monitor-2021-pm/ (accessed October 2, 2022).

24 www.onlinezugangsgesetz.de/Webs/OZG/EN/home/home-node.html (accessed October 10, 2022).

25 www.personalausweisportal.de (accessed October 10, 2022).

26 For example, in the so-called "BUND service account": https://id.bund.de/en/ (accessed May 1, 2023).

27 www.elster.de/eportal/start; https://joinup.ec.europa.eu/collection/egovernment/document/elster-electronic-tax-return-system-elster (accessed September 20, 2022).

28 www.personalausweisportal.de/Webs/PA/EN/government/eIDAS_Regulation/eIDAS-regulation-node.html (accessed October 3, 2022).

29 According to the International Association of Privacy Professionals, "Data privacy is focused on the use and governance of personal data—things like putting policies in place to ensure that consumers' personal information is being collected, shared and used in appropriate ways. Security focuses more on protecting data from malicious attacks and the exploitation of stolen data for profit. While security is necessary for protecting data, it's not sufficient for addressing privacy." https://iapp.org/about/what-is-privacy/ (accessed October 16, 2022).

30 www.antrag24.de/ (accessed October 1, 2022).

31 https://ivtops.wildau.biz/en.html (accessed November 6, 2022).

32 This is a well-known phenomenon (see, for example, Cranor, 2012).

33 This is conceptualized as understanding, seeing reasons/purpose, and knowing how the system works and how to use it (see pages 156–157 of this article).

34 www.bertelsmann-stiftung.de/en/topics/latest-news/2021-1/november/-digital-divide-in-society-is-widening (accessed October 17, 2022).

35 "1. User Centricity—To what extent are services provided online? How mobile friendly are they? And what online support and feedback mechanisms are in place? 2. Transparency—Are public administrations providing clear, openly communicated information about how their services are delivered? Are they transparent about policy making and digital service design processes, as well as about the way people's personal data is being processed?" (European Commission Directorate-General for Communications Networks, Content and Technology, July 2022, p. 7). https://op.europa.eu/en/publication-detail/-/publication/a7d80ca2-3895-11ed-9c68-01aa75ed71a1 (accessed November 28, 2022).

36 https://op.europa.eu/en/publication-detail/-/publication/a7d80ca2-3895-11ed-9c68-01aa75ed71a1 (accessed November 28, 2022).

37 See, for example, Nielsen's 10 usability heuristics: www.nngroup.com/articles/ten-usability-heuristics/ (accessed October 24, 2022).

38 See Art. 25, 28, 29, and 78. https://eur-lex.europa.eu/legal-content/EN/TXT/HTML/?uri=CELEX:32016R0679&from=EN (accessed October 13, 2022).

39 Under the *Nine-Point Plan for a Digital Germany* published by the Federal Government Commissioner for Information Technology, the usability of the digital public services is addressed in point four: "Set up user-friendly digital platforms to make services accessible more quickly and easily and to facilitate communication with public authorities: The federal portal and user account for businesses will go into operation in 2020." www.onlinezugangsgesetz.de/SharedDocs/downloads/Webs/OZG/EN/9-point-plan.pdf?__blob=publicationFile&v=2 (accessed October 24, 2022).

40 See, for example, www.digilabs20.eu (accessed October 24, 2022).

41 www.nngroup.com/articles/ten-usability-heuristics/ (accessed October 24, 2022).

References

Andreasson, A., Artman, H., Brynielsson, J., & Franke, U. (2020, December). A census of Swedish government administrative authority employee communications on cybersecurity during the COVID-19 pandemic. In *2020 IEEE/ACM international conference on advances in social networks analysis and mining (ASONAM)* (pp. 727–733). New York: IEEE.

Barrein, A. (2022). *Das Recht auf Home-Office. Duncker & Humblot*. Dissertation, Universität Hannover.

Beck, W. (2021). Aktuelle e-government Regelungen in Deutschland, Österreich und der Schweiz. In J. Stember, W. Eixelsberger, A. Spichiger, A. Neuroni, F.-R. Habbel, & M. Wundara (Eds.), *Aktuelle Entwicklungen zum e-government. Neue Impulse und Orientierungen in der digitalen Transformation der öffentlichen Verwaltung* (pp. 3–29). Springer.

BMI (Bundesministerium des Innern, für Bau und Heimat). (2018). *Digitale Verwaltung. Nutzerorientiert und modern. Digitalisierungsprogramm zur Umsetzung des OZG: Blaupausen für die Verwaltungsdigitalisierung*. Berlin.

BMI (Bundesministerium des Innern, für Bau und Heimat). (2019). *Leitfaden Zum Digitalisierungsprogramm Des It-Planungsrates*. Berlin.

BMI (Bundesministerium des Innern, für Bau und Heimat). (2020). *OZG-Informationsplattform*. Berlin.

Brenke, K. (2016). Home Office: Möglichkeiten werden bei weitem nicht ausgeschöpft. *Diw Wochenbericht, 83*(5), 95–105.

BSI—Federal Office for Information Security (Ed.): Die Lage der IT-Sicherheit in Deutschland (2022). Retrieved October 27, 2022, from www.bsi.bund.de/SharedDocs/Downloads/DE/BSI/Publikationen/Lageberichte/Lagebericht2022.html?nn=129410

Bundesnetzagentur für Elektrizität, Gas, Telekommunikation, Post und Eisenbahnen: Nutzung von ONline-Kommunikationsdiensten in Deutschland—Ergebnisse der Verbraucherbefragung (2021, January 2022). Retrieved October 30, 2022, from www.bundesnetzagentur.de/SharedDocs/Downloads/DE/Sachgebiete/Digitales/OnlineKom/befragung_lang21.pdf?__blob=publicationFile&v=3

Cortés-Cediel, M. E., Cantador Gutiérrez, I., & Rodríguez Bolívar, M. P. (2020, July). Technological and human development of smart cities: An empirical characterization of EUROCITIES case studies. In *Proceedings of the 53rd Hawaii international conference on system sciences*. AIS (Association for Information Systems). Retrieved May 1, 2023, from http://hdl.handle.net/10125/64022

Cranor, L. F. (2012). Necessary but not sufficient: Standardized mechanisms for privacy notice and choice. *Journal on Telecommunications and High Technology Law, 10,* 273.

D21 eGovernment Monitor. (2022). Retrieved October 2, 2022, from https://initiatived21.de/egovernment-monitor-2021-pm/

Deutscher Bundestag. (2022a). Digitale Verwaltung – Stand und Zukunft des Onlinezugangsgesetzes einschließlich eID-Verfahren, Standards, Open Source, Nachvollziehbarkeit und Transparenz. Retrieved May 1, 2023, from https://dserver.bundestag.de/btd/20/031/2003140.pdf

Deutscher Bundestag. (2022b). Mehr Tempo bei digitaler Verwaltung – Onlinezugangsgesetz fortführen, Nutzungslücken schließen, Rechtsanspruch einführen. Retrieved May 1, 2023, from https://dserver.bundestag.de/btd/20/043/2004313.pdf

Eiza, M., Okeke, R. I., Dempsey, J., & Ta, V. T. (2021). Keep calm and carry on with cybersecurity@ home: A framework for securing homeworking IT environment. *International Journal on Cyber Situational Awareness, 5*(1), 1–25.

European Commission Directorate-General for Communications Networks, Content and Technology. (2022, July). *eGovernment benchmark 2022. Synchronising digital governments*. Retrieved April 26, 2023, from https://digital-strategy.ec.europa.eu/en/library/egovernment-benchmark-2022

Fleischer, J., & Carstens, N. (2022). Policy labs as arenas for boundary spanning: Inside the digital transformation in Germany. *Public Management Review, 24*(8), 1208–1225, DOI: 10.1080/14719037.2021.1893803.

Grünwied, G. (2017). *Usability von Produkten und Anleitungen im digitalen Zeitalter.* Erlangen: Publicis Pixelpark.

IT-Planungsrat. *Digitalisierungslabor.* Retrieved April 26, 2023, from https://www.onlinezu-gangsgesetz.de/Webs/OZG/DE/grundlagen/agile-methoden/digitalisierungslabore/digitalisierungslabore-node.html

IT-Planungsrat. *Digitalisierungsprogramm des IT-Planungsrats (Phase II): Start in die Verwaltungsdigitalisierung.* Retrieved May 1, 2023, from https://www.onlinezugangsgesetz.de/Webs/OZG/DE/themen/digitalisierungsprogramm-bund/bund-node.html

Jakobi, T. (2019). e-government in Deutschland. In A. Busch, Y. Breindl, & T. Jakobi (Eds.), *Netzpolitik.* Wiesbaden: Springer VS. https://doi.org/10.1007/978-3-658-02033-0_9

Köhler, J. (2022, September 13). Behörden-Messender für die interne Kommunikation. *eGovernment Computing.* Retrieved October 30, 2022, from www.egovernment-computing.de/behoerden-messenger-fuer-die-interne-kommunikation-a-04a1a340eedb205eb544462de2e8891f/?print

Nam, T., & Pardo T. A. (2011). Conceptualizing smart city with dimensions of technology, people, and institutions. In *Proceedings of the 12th annual international digital government research conference: digital government innovation in challenging times* (pp. 282–291). Retrieved May 1, 2023, from https://doi.org/10.1145/2037556.2037602

Nyikes, Z. (2021). The cybersecurity challenges of COVID-19. *IPSI Transactions on Advanced Research, 17*(2), 57–62.

OECD. (2015). *Draft digital government toolkit.* Paris: OECD. Retrieved November 28, 2022, from https://one.oecd.org/document/GOV/PGC/EGOV(2015)2/en/pdf

Plattner, H., Meinel, C., & Leifer, L. (Eds.). (2011). *Design thinking: Understand—improve—apply.* Berlin; Heidelberg: Springer-Verlag.

Rackwitz, M., Hustedt, T., & Hammerschmid, G. (2021). Digital transformation: From hierarchy to network-based collaboration? The case of the German "Online Access Act". *dms—der moderne staat—Zeitschrift für Public Policy, Recht und Management,* (1), 101–120.

Roßnagel, A. (2013). Auf dem Weg zur elektronischen Verwaltung—Das e-government-Gesetz. *Neue Juristische Wochenschrift, 66*(37), 2710–2717.

Schaub, F., Balebako, R., Durity, A. L., & Cranor, L. F. (2015, July). A design space for effective privacy notices. In *Eleventh symposium on usable privacy and security. Symposium on Usable Privacy and Security (SOUPS) 2015, July 22–24, Ottawa, Canada* (pp. 1–17). Retrieved May 1, 2023, from https://dl.acm.org/doi/10.5555/3235866.3235868

Schliesky, U., & Hoffmann, C. (2018). Die Digitalisierung des Föderalismus. *Die öffentliche Verwaltung, 71*(5), 193–198.

Schmidt, C., & Krimmer, R. (2022). How to implement the European digital single market: Identifying the catalyst for digital transformation. *Journal of European Integration, 44*(1), 59–80. https://doi.org/10.1080/07036337.2021.2011267

Schmidt, C., Krimmer, R., & Lampoltshammer, T. J. (2021). "When need becomes necessity"—the single digital gateway regulation and the once-only principle from a European point of view. In H. Roßnagel, C. H. Schunck, & S. Mödersheim (Hrsg.),

Open Identity Summit 2021, Lecture Notes in Informatics (LNI) (pp. 223–229). Bonn: Gesellschaft für Informatik.

Škiljić, A. (2020). Cybersecurity and remote working: Croatia's (non-) response to increased cyber threats. *International Cybersecurity Law Review, 1*(1), 51–61.

Tsap, V., Pappel, I., & Draheim, D. (2019). Factors affecting e-ID public acceptance: A literature review. In: *Electronic Government and the Information Systems Perspective: 8th International Conference, EGOVIS 2019,* Linz, Austria, August 26–29, 2019, Proceedings Aug 2019 (pp. 176–188) https://doi.org/10.1007/978-3-030-27523-5_13

Wentzel, J. (2010). Die Nationale e-government-Strategie: Ein Schritt vor, zwei zurück? *VM Verwaltung und Management, 16*(6), 283–292.

Wittkemper, G., & Kleindiek, R. (2003). BundOnline 2005: The e-government initiative of the German Federal Administration. *Journal of Political Marketing, 2*(3–4), 107–126. https://doi.org/10.1300/J199v02n03_07

Chapter 11

The Future of Work in Federal Government Requires Telework

Eric Egan

Content

DOI: 10.1201/9781003369783-11

11.1 Introduction

Before switching to my current position researching digital government and technology policy, I spent nearly seven years working as a public sector consultant, where I helped state and local governments with their digital transformation journeys. At times, my job required me to embark on up to four flights per week so that I would be on the client site Monday through Thursday. As these projects often included rolling out complex, large-scale software solutions costing millions of taxpayer dollars, our government clients understandably preferred that our team be present in person to address any issues that would inevitably crop up across the months and often years required to complete such initiatives. In March 2020, however, the COVID-19 pandemic flipped the consulting model completely on its head.

For white-collar jobs like mine, the teleworking model—defined broadly as work performed from a remote location typically using telecommunications and information technology (IT)—moved from uncommon to necessary in a matter of months. Federal agencies in the United States were no exception to this situation. The pandemic forced the federal government to adapt quickly, and many agencies were not prepared to do so. Even though teleworking and the technologies that support it extend back nearly 50 years, the federal government struggled to keep pace with the private sector in adopting and investing in telework over the last few decades. However, the benefits of telework revealed during the pandemic made it clear that remote and hybrid environments should play a critical role in the future of work across all industries, including the federal government. Telework certainly presents unique challenges for government moving forward, particularly in cybersecurity, but evidence largely suggests that remote and hybrid work contribute to employee welfare, promote productivity, offer resiliency during crises, and allow federal agencies to recruit and retain talent who demand telework.

And yet there are some in Washington who remain unconvinced in continuing, let alone expanding, telework for federal employees. However, these politicians are working against an inexorable reality about the workplace: telework is here to stay. Remote and hybrid options not only improve the work experience for federal employees but also align with broader federal digital transformation priorities—from cloud migration and data analytics to IT modernization and enhanced customer experience. The future of work and federal IT requires telework, and federal agencies need bipartisan support from elected officials to get this critical work done.

11.2 A Brief History of Telework

Conceptualized to address personnel challenges that continue today, such as work-life balance and traffic congestion, the idea of teleworking has been around for several decades. While the private sector generally accepted and adopted teleworking practices over the years, the U.S. federal government struggled to do the same over the same period. This had consequences not only in how federal agencies responded to the COVID-19 pandemic but also in determining the federal government's relatively poor positioning for the future of work.

11.2.1 The Private Sector Invests

Telework, remote work, work from home, mobile work, distance work. The concept has many names, and while it is often considered a 21st-century notion, the idea of teleworking has been around for nearly five decades. Jack Nilles, a physicist and NASA engineer now considered the "father" of telework, coined the term "tele-commuting" as early as 1973. Living in Los Angeles, Nilles was sensitive to issues around traffic congestion and high gas prices—sound familiar?—and begin to think through alternative arrangements to bypass these problems. As he lived in a time prior to the proliferation of the personal computer (PC), Nilles's approach focused more on the use of satellite offices to shorten commute times (Newport, 2020). This model may not have been the ultimate method adopted for telework, but the overall concept stuck, and by the early 1980s, companies with the technical infrastructure to support telework—particularly those who could leverage existing call center models, such as IBM—employed thousands of employees who could work from home (Butler, 2018).

Over the next 20 years and through the 1990s when PC prices dropped, mobile phones emerged, and internet use became more common, many businesses moved portions of their workforce out of their cubicles through teleworking initiatives. AT&T, for example, had around 22,500 U.S. employees telecommuting at least once per month in 1994, with 7,500 of these employees effectively fully remote (Johnson, 1994). AT&T even celebrated its first "Employee Telecommuting Day" that year (Newport, 2020). Obviously, there were—and continue to be—restrictions on the type of work that could be performed remotely, but many businesses clearly saw value in this type of work model.

The beginning of the 21st century brought better, faster internet services and new platforms that extended the experience of telework from phone and email to video and real-time direct messaging. Companies, such as Skype in 2006, began rolling out scalable video conferencing (VC) technology (Newport, 2020). Today, there is a full variety of commercial platforms for interactive VC, from big names like Zoom and Webex to lesser-known companies like Whereby and Dialpad. Even prior to the pandemic, companies were utilizing end-to-end digital workspaces like Microsoft Teams and Slack that not only allowed their employees to communicate with one another quickly and easily but also to co-edit and collaborate in real time on documents and work products. In March 2020, Microsoft Teams already had 32 million active users (Kent, 2020).

Though the adoption of organization-wide telework received some pushback from commercial leaders in the 2010s—perhaps as fallout from the 2008 financial crisis, where concerns around productivity resulted in overwork and micromanagement in places like Silicon Valley—commercial organizations clearly saw investing in the infrastructure of telework as critical for the future of work. Because of this investment, the private sector was able to adapt much faster to the remote environments that the pandemic necessitated, particularly compared to federal agencies. Moving forward, many companies have embraced teleworking as part of their "new normal" operating models. According to one survey, most industries support telework flexibility, with over half of employees participating in some remote work. These findings include industries that have traditionally found teleworking models more difficult to implement, such as healthcare, where 45 percent of staff participate in remote work (Dua et al., 2022). Similarly, the Bureau of Labor Statistics found that, among organizations that increased telework due to the pandemic, over 60 percent expect the increase in telework to continue after the pandemic ends (Bureau of Labor Statistics, 2022). As the next subsection demonstrates, the federal government's teleworking story is quite different.

11.2.2 The Federal Government Lags

In terms of awareness and planning over the years, the federal government was not too far behind the private sector in exploring the potential benefits of teleworking, but investment in and adoption of teleworking was slower and more erratic. Around the time Nilles introduced "tele-commuting" to the English vocabulary, the federal government was defining what would become its flexible work arrangement policy. The Federal Employees Flexible and Compressed Work Schedules Act of 1978 introduced alternative methods for how federal employees could work and opened the door for opportunities like telework.

The General Services Administration's (GSA's) Office of Governmentwide Policy published a report titled "The Evolution of Telework in the Federal Government" in February 2000 that provides an early history of federal telework, notably detailing several efforts across multiple agencies that attempted to pilot or ignite broader adoption of telework within the federal government but met with little success (Joice, 2000). Many agencies had instituted informal teleworking activities in the 1980s, but these were primarily as-needed, case-by-case arrangements, and it was not until the 1990s that federal governments really began to explore the governmentwide benefits of teleworking in earnest. The report does highlight one prescient example in which the Environmental Protection Agency (EPA) successfully leveraged telework as an emergency response to the 1989 Loma Prieta earthquake, after which the "EPA conducted several studies of this experience [and] learned quite a bit about the feasibility and utility of Flexiplace [a term used at the time for federal teleworking] as both a general workplace strategy as well as an emergency response strategy" (Joice, 2000).

The Clinton administration's National Telecommuting Initiative, released in 1996, represents the federal government's first substantive commitment to adopt teleworking. As a joint effort between the Department of Transportation and GSA, the program set ambitious goals, such as having 60,000 federal teleworkers by 1998 and 160,000 by 2002. These goals were unmet—according to a 2002 report from the Congressional Research Service, there were only 74,487 federal teleworkers at that time—and the initiative fizzled out. However, the federal government continued developing policy and soft commitments to telework throughout the 2000s, such as the following:

- **The Department of Transportation and Related Agencies Appropriations Act of 2001:** Required federal agencies to establish telecommuting policies and encourage employee participation.
- **National Institute of Standards and Technology (NIST) security guidelines:** Broad recommendations for securing technology used by teleworkers, such as the use of firewalls for home internet and secure web browser and operating system configuration (Georgetown University Law Center, 2009).
- **Telework.gov:** An Office of Personnel Management (OPM) website launched in the early 2000s that provides information regarding the federal government's telework policy (Telework.gov, n.d.).
- **The Telework Enhancement Act of 2010:** Expanded requirements for federal agencies' telecommunicating policies, such as designating a telework managing officer, developing telework training, and incorporating telework into agency operation plans.

Ironically, this period also saw the federal government plan for a hypothetical influenza pandemic, which included an underdeveloped teleworking strategy as an emergency response (Georgetown University Law Center, 2009).

After the Telework Enhancement Act, however, there was little change in federal teleworking policy and no major efforts to increase adoption until the COVID-19 pandemic nearly 10 years later. In 2012, only 29 percent of eligible federal workers participated in teleworking. This increased substantially during the pandemic, with peaks of nearly 90 percent of eligible employees and 45 percent of all federal employees teleworking (Office of Personnel Management, 2021b). After years of planning and unsuccessful pilots, the pandemic provided a much-needed use case highlighting the benefits of telework in the federal government—from enhanced performance and productivity to improved work-life balance and talent retention—and convinced many policymakers to take a more deliberate approach in long-term adoption.

11.3 The Modern Politics of Federal Telework

Even though the federal government has been aware of the benefits of telework for decades, adoption has been sluggish despite the practice becoming increasingly common across nearly all other industries. As the prior section demonstrated,

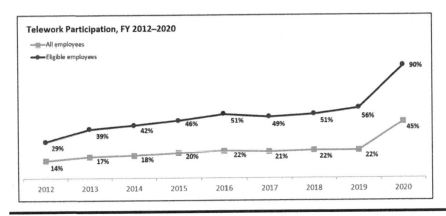

Figure 11.1   Federal telework participation, percentage of all employees versus eligible employees, FY 2012–2020 (Office of Personnel Management, 2021b).

there were efforts to expand federal teleworking even before the pandemic, but the pandemic accelerated adoption and reignited the debate. Circumstances made teleworking a short-term necessity for all, a long-term priority for some, and an apparent no-go option for others.

11.3.1 Those in Favor

At the beginning of the pandemic, the Trump administration sent mixed messages regarding its plan for federal teleworking. With over two million active federal employees, there were a lot of questions regarding how to minimize health risks while continuing employment and operations of critical services. Telework offered a clear solution, but the Trump administration was consistently averse to the approach—though ultimately there was bipartisan consensus to accept telework as a necessary response to the emergency (Naylor, 2020). The approach under the Biden administration was more receptive to leveraging telework during the pandemic. Notably, OPM updated its decade-old federal telework guidance in November 2021. Though this effort was clearly driven by pandemic circumstances, it also presents a clear message that the long-term future of work in federal government should prioritize telework. After all, the subtitle is not pandemic-specific but, rather, the broadly encompassing "Leveraging Telework and Remote Work in the Federal Government to Better Meet Our Human Capital Needs and Improve Mission Delivery." In a new addition, the OPM guidance distinguishes teleworkers from "remote" workers, the latter of which are not expected to visit their agency's office regularly and thus have geographical flexibility (Office of Personnel Management, 2021a).

Recent messaging from federal leaders of the Biden administration also reflects this priority to expand federal telework. In a July 2022 memo, OMB director

Shalanda Young directed agencies "to reimagine their workplace approach informed by lessons from the COVID-19 pandemic, as well as nationwide workforce and workplace trends (e.g., hybrid work inclusive of onsite work, telework, alternative work schedules, online collaboration, and remote work policies and practices)" (Young, 2022a). Similarly, OPM director Kiran Ahuja stated in the same month that telework and workplace flexibility are necessary to recruit and retain top talent in a post-COVID world and that workplace flexibilities "promote resilience of federal government operations in the face of disruptions, enhance productivity, and improve employee morale" (Mitchell, 2022).

The President's Management Agenda, an executive roadmap for management priorities across federal agencies, also includes plans for telework given its future role in nationwide workplace and workforce trends (Office of Management and Budget, n.d.). Additionally, Congress took steps this year to solidify teleworking policies adopted during the pandemic. The Telework Metrics and Cost Savings Act of 2022 focuses on gathering data and exploring impacts on cost savings from pandemic-level teleworking activities with the ultimate goal of providing evidence that teleworking is good for federal government. As one of the bill's sponsors, Rep. Gerry Connolly (D-VA), explained, enhanced need and demand for telework among federal employees and the national workforce should and will persevere. . . . Telework saves money, helps recruit top talent, makes environmental sense, and it ensures a continuity of operations at agencies that families, businesses, and veterans can rely on each day. (Wagner, 2022)

Despite the evidence in favor of telework, however, some politicians have recently criticized the Biden administration's telework policies and stubbornly oppose its expansion.

11.3.2 Those Opposed

In a December 2021 letter to OPM, House Minority Leader Kevin McCarthy (R-CA) wrote that "the Biden Administration's 'maximum telework' edict is not working for the American people, many of whom are struggling to secure in-person services from their federal government" (Alms, 2021). Rep. Jody Hice (R-GA), the ranking member of the House Committee on Oversight and Reform, stated in a July 2022 hearing that the Biden administration's efforts to make the federal government a "model employer" by offering greater workplace flexibility like that of the private sector is really just "a catchphrase for treating federal workers like a privileged, protected class" (House Committee on Oversight and Reform, 2022; Thibodeau, 2022).

While these concerns are valid regarding the federal workforce generally, these politicians are conflating other problems facing the federal government with teleworking. It is true that customer satisfaction with federal agencies is at historically low levels due in part to poor service delivery, but federal customers want more digital interactions rather than in-person services (Egan, 2022). With millions of employees working for the federal government, there are, no doubt, individuals who fall into the "bad apple" category in taking advantage of teleworking environments. While civil service rules do make it harder to fire federal employees for performance compared to the private sector, a good employee does not become a bad one simply because they are working from home (Katz, 2015). In fact, they are more appreciative and more likely to stick around (Campo et al., 2021).

Ultimately, these politicians' concerns really have nothing to do with telework but, rather, issues around customer service and performance management broadly in the federal government (as well as long-running perceptions that telework is too expensive to roll out and that teleworkers are less productive). However, federal agencies can expand telework, improve customer experience, and reform federal personnel rules at the same time, all while increasing productivity. Opposition to expanding telework in the federal government works against best practices and national trends across practically all industries. As the next section demonstrates, there are legitimate challenges around teleworking, but it is ultimately critical for the future of work in the federal government.

11.4 Benefits and Challenges of Federal Telework

Expanding federal telework is not without its challenges—particularly in cybersecurity—but the benefits clearly outweigh the risks. Simply put, the evidence supports prioritizing telework as a central component in the future of work in the federal government. Current federal employees prefer—and potential employees expect—the flexibility telework provides and are arguably more productive as remote or hybrid workers. However, perhaps most importantly, a digital workforce aligns with the federal government's broader digital transformation goals.

11.4.1 Employee Preference

Federal employee preference is clear regarding telework. A July 2022 report from Cisco found that 58 percent of government employees are currently working from home five days per week, and the majority are satisfied with this arrangement. Only 7 percent of respondents stated they would prefer to fully return to the office in the future (Moffett, 2022). Another survey found that nearly two-thirds of the federal workforce is satisfied with their current work situation regarding hybrid work, with one respondent stating, "we've been fully remote for over two years. . . . The mission has been accomplished with no interruption, so why the requirement to be in the office?" (Friedman, 2022).

The federal government's own research into employee satisfaction with telework has reached the same conclusions. OPM's 2021 Federal Employee Viewpoint Survey reported that "employees who work for an organization that offers telework are more engaged than employees that work for organizations where telework is not available" and that teleworkers "experience a greater sense of organizational commitment" (Office of Personnel Management, 2021b). Pre-pandemic findings from OPM under the Trump administration likewise found that teleworking options "increased the desire to stay at current agency" for 76 percent of respondents and "improved morale" for 83 percent of respondents (Office of Personnel Management, 2018).

From the employee perspective, these results are not surprising. In general, different studies have found that telework

- reduces commute time and, as such, environmental impact;
- reduces costs, such as savings from childcare, food, gas, and public transit;
- reduces stress;
- allows for more time with family and supports work-life balance;
- provides greater flexibility in work location; and
- improves job satisfaction (Loubier, 2017; Indeed, 2021).

The benefits of teleworking are particularly pronounced when organizations afford employees different options, such as hybrid models, that allow them to maintain a presence in the office and interact with colleagues in person. For perhaps the clearest signal in broad worker preference for teleworking options, over 60 percent of employee respondents from a survey said they would take a pay cut to continue teleworking (Bero, 2021). Job satisfaction is an important part of productivity, and right now the data suggests that workers appreciate teleworking options.

11.4.2 Productivity Is More Than Where One Works

Broadly speaking, the evidence suggests that telework does not inhibit productivity and may in fact boost productivity. In the private sector, 83 percent of employers report that the shift to remote work has been successful for their company, with more reporting greater increases in productivity overall rather than decreases (Caglar et al., 2021; Ozimek, 2020). Mercer, an HR and workplace benefits consulting firm, surveyed 800 employers, and 94 percent stated that work productivity was the same or higher since employees started working from home during the pandemic (Maurer, 2020). Some of the productivity benefits are quickly apparent, such as less commute time and fewer office distractions, but many organizations began reworking business processes in a digital environment, including reducing wasteful or unnecessary meetings and leveraging project management software.

The results referenced from the private sector above extend to the federal government, debunking notions from some politicians that teleworkers are not productive. About half of the over 50,000 Department of Defense employees surveyed in 2021 believe their productivity had increased while teleworking (Inspector General, 2021). Similarly, over half of supervisors surveyed in a 2018 OPM survey responded that "telework supports [their] employees' ability to perform" (Office of Personnel

Management, 2018). In fact, as teleworking continues to expand in the federal space, agencies will have to monitor whether employees are overperforming rather than underperforming. In a February 2022 report, the Government Accountability Office (GAO) found overwork or "hidden overtime" to be an identified challenge amongst federal agencies, an important finding that demonstrates the importance of designing controls and leveraging performance data to ensure workers remain satisfied with teleworking environments rather than exploited by them (GAO, 2022).

Policymakers' concerns around telework lowering productivity are overblown and more likely a symptom of organizational distrust, poor management practices, and institutional barriers, such as the government's slow adoption of technology that supports remote work. For example, meeting engagement on virtual platforms presents challenges, but given that organizations expect most meetings to have at least one remote participant, this is more a matter of learning curves and adopting new practices to ensure meetings are inclusive and successful in hybrid environments. Online meeting platforms like Zoom are already evolving to support these environments, including integrating functionality to remove background noise. As the federal government broadly invests in IT modernization efforts while continuing to expand telework, it can expect to see even greater productivity measures.

11.4.3 Policymakers Should Be Talking about Security

The real challenge surrounding telework is not one of worker productivity but, rather, a technical challenge, particularly security. As mentioned in this chapter, the federal agency NIST develops security guidance around telework in the federal government, such as protecting wireless internet networks through virtual private networks and keeping software updated, but the breadth and complexity of a remote workforce presents unique challenges (Greene, 2020). The previously referenced February 2022 GAO report highlights some of these challenges, claiming that agencies are struggling to manage the increased IT infrastructure required to support telework (GAO, 2022). A growing number of remote workers means a greatly distributed network with a huge number of potential access points for malicious actors, including physically unsecured devices at homes that can access government networks and government devices on home networks. Government endpoints are already complicated and widespread because, in addition to millions of computer users, they include operational technology like power plants and building systems. In short, teleworking introduces unique and changing cybersecurity risks, and federal agencies need to adapt accordingly.

Fortunately, the federal government is already prioritizing initiatives that work to mitigate these security concerns, such as building out zero-trust architecture across federal IT systems (Young, 2022b). Zero trust is an approach to cybersecurity that aims to eliminate implicit trust and validate every digital interaction, including using multifactor authentication (MFA), which requires users to present two or more pieces of identifying evidence before accessing a website, device, or application. With so many access points in remote and hybrid environments, MFA is an essential security component in the proliferation of telework in the federal government.

Federal agencies' ongoing cloud migration efforts are also critical to telework adoption, as quality cloud solutions can offer greater security than on-premise environments. Since many cybersecurity threats come through external phishing or emailing as opposed to the server environment, the segmented network that a cloud solution offers means users are not sitting on the agency's network where the data is stored. Furthermore, most cloud solutions come with data encryption capabilities out of the box, preventing data from being exposed to bad actors (Montgomery, 2020). Accelerating cloud adoption is important given the amount of sensitive data the federal government collects, uses, and stores every day. As such, the Federal Risk and Authorization Management Program (FedRAMP), the standardized approach to assessing cloud services for use by federal agencies, plays an important role in expanding federal telework. The FedRAMP certification process is critical in ensuring that particular cloud solutions support secure federal teleworking, but it can also do this while better accelerating federal cloud adoption overall (McLaughlin, 2020).

However, ultimately, cybersecurity is about the user. Nearly 90 percent of cybersecurity breaches arise from human error, and that is true whether they are using a desktop computer in a federal office, a laptop at home, or their smartphone at a coffeeshop (MeriTalk, 2022). Similar to mitigating productivity and organizational deficiencies, training and change management can go a long way in avoiding security-related issues in an environment of remotely distributed users. Training for federal employees should include how to mitigate the telework-specific cybersecurity threats discussed in this section. Finally, federal agencies could use savings from telework—such as lower travel costs, lower property and utility costs, and fewer sick days—to invest in better home networks and change management activities to improve collaboration and operational outcomes. Investing in users—in this case, a large federal workforce—is vital from both a security and talent retention perspective.

11.4.4 Talent Matters

The Partnership for Public Service, a nonprofit, nonpartisan organization that focuses on various issues surrounding the federal government, recently released a report titled "Retention Strategies for Generation X and Generation Z Federal Employees" that explores current perspectives from this workforce of the future. The report's findings are clear: both Gen X and Gen Z expect flexibility through teleworking. For Gen X, these workers are comfortable with technology, currently moving into management roles, and having families, which is why "flexibility regarding where and when they work to support their overall well-being" is greatly valued. For Gen Z, also known as Zoomers, many of these employees entered the workforce during the pandemic and have come to expect remote environments as part of their work life. One Gen Z respondent shared that "while there might be some benefits to going into the office—like being able to talk to and know your team on a more personal and in-depth level—work can still be done effectively at home" (Hyman et al., 2022).

This quote also highlights the value of investing in culture, team-building interactions, and camaraderie in teleworking environments. Though the Pew Research Center found "Zoom fatigue" not to be widespread, teleworkers have expressed feeling less connected with their colleagues (Igielnik, 2022). Employees with more work experience and strong networks may not need the same kind of high-touch interactions as less experienced staff members just starting their careers. Pew also found that some workers do not feel as productive working from home as they do in the office (Horowitz et al., 2022). These considerations are important as federal agencies plan out long-term remote and hybrid environments, particularly as they are competing for this talent and continue to contend with skills gaps in critical areas like cybersecurity.

In this talent competition, private companies are further along in telework adoption, offering flexibility regarding when and where to work, and federal employee engagement continues to be lower than in the private sector. Based on survey data, federal employee satisfaction "showed the largest year-over-year decline in satisfaction scores, based in part on federal employees being required to return to the office for at least part of the workweek" (Heckman, 2022). Furthermore, not everyone lives in or wants to live in Washington, D.C., or the numerous other locations federal agencies are based. Telework allows the federal government to access talent from across the country and beyond. Lastly, federal agencies are also competing with one another for talent. As this report points out, workers expect remote and hybrid environments, and those federal agencies resistant to or that are prevented from implementing teleworking policies will struggle with both talent acquisition and retention. As the federal government continues to expand its digital infrastructure and services, hiring and keeping skilled talent is as crucial as ever—and these days, this talent wants the flexibility teleworking offers.

11.4.5 Federal Telework Aligns with Digital Transformation

One brief, final point that ties this chapter with the overarching theme of this book: much of the technology that supports a robust teleworking infrastructure, such as cloud migration, digital case management, and secure networks, also supports broader federal digital transformation goals. Digital transformation in the federal government means shifting away from paperwork and improving customer experience, enhancing cybersecurity, upgrading digital infrastructure and replacing legacy systems, and leveraging the full potential of data. Like digital transformation broadly, teleworking does more than make things easier or more efficient; it also provides an opportunity to improve a variety of social and economic markers in the country, such as

- reducing carbon emissions;
- helping to close the digital divide and provide broader access to better internet services;

- alleviating challenges around regional inequalities, including housing and cost of living; and
- and improving worker well-being and mental health.

In short, teleworking and digital transformation build on one another, working together to pivot the federal government from an outdated, analog model and transform it into a digital organization that serves the customers and employees already living in a digital world.

11.5 Conclusion

Historically, the federal government has not kept pace with telework expansion, and this slow adoption has had consequences both in resiliency under emergency circumstances—as was the case during the pandemic—and in meeting the needs of a workforce that increasingly expects remote and hybrid options. While some policymakers have recently pushed for expanding telework across the federal government, others remain resistant, with one congresswoman asking, "Why would we make something permanent that we haven't even checked into for its effectiveness?" (Wagner, 2022). There's nothing wrong with monitoring the performance in federal employees—most taxpayers expect it—but naysayers in Washington should look at the existing evidence. Though not without its challenges, telework improves employee morale and aligns with worker preference, supports adaptability in service delivery, contributes to productivity, and helps recruit and retain critical talent. Lastly, digital transformation is one of the few issues with bipartisan consensus in the federal government, and teleworking is a critical piece of this transformation. The federal government cannot afford to hesitate in expanding remote and hybrid work when it needs to incorporate telework principles into major, ongoing IT modernization initiatives. You cannot separate one from the other.

References

Alms, N. (2021, December 10). Top House Republican pushes back on government telework. *FCW*. Retrieved from https://fcw.com/workforce/2021/12/top-house-republican-pushes-back-on-government-telework/259302/

Bero, T. (2021, September 27). Employees are accepting pay cuts to keep working from home. They shouldn't. *The Guardian*. Retrieved from www.theguardian.com/commentisfree/2021/sep/27/employee-pay-cuts-work-from-home

Bureau of Labor Statistics. (2022, October 21). Over one-third of private-sector establishments increased telework during the COVID-19 pandemic. *TED: The Economics Daily*. Retrieved from www.bls.gov/opub/ted/2022/over-one-third-of-private-sector-establishments-increased-telework-during-the-covid-19-pandemic.htm

Butler, H. (2018). The history of remote work: How it became what we know today. *Crossover*. Retrieved from www.crossover.com/perspective/the-history-of-remote-work

Caglar, D., Couto, V., Sethi, B., & Faccio, E. (2021, January 12). It's time to reimagine where and how work will get done. *PwC*. Retrieved from www.pwc.com/us/en/services/consulting/business-transformation/library/covid-19-us-remote-work-survey.html

Campo, A. M. D. V., Avolio, B., & Carlier, S. I. (2021). The relationship between telework, job performance, work—life balance and family supportive supervisor behaviours in the context of COVID-19. *Global Business Review, 0*(0). https://doi.org/10.1177/09721509211049918

Congressional Research Service. (2002). Telework in the Federal Government: Background, policy, and oversight. *Congressional Research Service, Library of Congress.* Retrieved from www.everycrsreport.com/files/20020403_RL30863_110dea024df5a dee8891d2a4fc4056bdd41a2be0.pdf

Department of Transportation and Related Agencies Appropriations Act. (2001). Pub. L. 106–346 114 Stat. 1356. Retrieved from www.congress.gov/bill/106th-congress/house-bill/4475/text

Dua, A., Ellingrud, K., Kirschner, P., Kwok, A., Luby, R., Palter, R., & Pemberton, S. (2022, June 23). Americans are embracing flexible work—and they want more of it. *McKinsey & Company*. Retrieved from www.mckinsey.com/industries/real-estate/our-insights/americans-are-embracing-flexible-work-and-they-want-more-of-it

Egan, E. (2022, October 24). With customer satisfaction at a new low, federal agencies still fail to measure it well or provide enough digital services. *ITIF*. Retrieved from https://itif.org/publications/2022/10/24/federal-hisp-digital-customer-experience/

Federal Employees Flexible and Compressed Work Schedules Act. (2018). Pub. L. No. 97–221 96 Stat. 227. Retrieved from www.congress.gov/bill/95th-congress/house-bill/10518/text

Friedman, D. (2022, November 1). Survey: As agencies turn to hybrid work, many feds want more remote options. *Federal News Network*. Retrieved from https://federalnewsnetwork.com/workforce/2022/11/survey-as-agencies-turn-to-hybrid-work-many-feds-want-more-remote-options/

Georgetown University Law Center. (2009). *Telework in the Federal Government: The overview memo.* Georgetown University. Retrieved from https://scholarship.law.georgetown.edu/cgi/viewcontent.cgi?article=1015&context=legal

Government Accountability Office. (2022). *Federal telework increased during the pandemic, but more reliable data are needed to support oversight* (GAO-22–104282). Retrieved from www.gao.gov/products/gao-22-104282

Greene, J. (2020, March 19). Telework security basics. *Cybersecurity Insights, a NIST Blog.* Retrieved from www.nist.gov/blogs/cybersecurity-insights/telework-security-basics

Heckman, J. (2022, July 21). OPM says federal employees 'agency-hopping' to telework-friendly offices. *Federal News Network*. Retrieved from https://federalnewsnetwork.com/hiring-retention/2022/07/opm-says-federal-employees-agency-hopping-to-telework-friendly-offices/

Horowitz, J. M., Minkin, R., & Parker, K. (2022, February 16). COVID-19 pandemic continues to reshape work in America. *Pew Research Center*. Retrieved from www.pewresearch.org/social-trends/2022/02/16/covid-19-pandemic-continues-to-reshape-work-in-america/

House Committee on Oversight and Reform. (2022, July 21). *Hice: The federal workforce exists to serve the American people* [Press release]. Retrieved from https://republicans-oversight.house.gov/release/hice-the-federal-workforce-exists-to-serve-the-american-people/

Hyman, M., Powder, M., & Pietsch, P. (2022, November 15). Retaining my generation: Retention strategies for generation X and generation Z federal employees. *Partnership for Public Service*. Retrieved from https://ourpublicservice.org/publications/retaining-my-generation-retention-strategies-for-generation-x-and-generation-z-federal-employees/

Igielnik, R. (2022, May 4). As telework continues for many U.S. workers, no sign of widespread 'Zoom fatigue'. *Pew Research Center*. Retrieved from www.pewresearch.org/fact-tank/2022/05/04/as-telework-continues-for-many-u-s-workers-no-sign-of-widespread-zoom-fatigue/

Indeed. (2021, February 23). *Telecommuting benefits for employees and employers*. Retrieved from www.indeed.com/career-advice/career-development/telecommuting-benefits

Inspector General. (2021). Evaluation of access to department of defense information technology and communications during the coronavirus disease-2019 pandemic. *Department of Defense*. Retrieved from https://media.defense.gov/2021/Apr/01/2002612366/-1/-1/1/DODIG-2021-065.PDF

Johnson, G. (1994, September 21). AT&T; home work: Telecommute day reaches O.C. *Los Angeles Times*. Retrieved from www.latimes.com/archives/la-xpm-1994-09-21-fi-41318-story.html

Joice, W. (2000). The evolution of telework in the Federal Government. *Office of Governmentwide Policy, US General Services Administration*. Retrieved from http://passages-pro.fr/wp-content/uploads/2020/06/JOYCE-these-doctorale-History-telework.pdf

Katz, E. (2015). Firing line. *Government Executive*. Retrieved from www.govexec.com/feature/firing-line/

Kent, D. (2020, December 14). Microsoft Teams statistics. *Tom Talks*. Retrieved from https://tomtalks.blog/microsoft-teams-statistics

Loubier, A. (2017, July 20). Benefits of telecommuting for the future of work. *Forbes*. Retrieved from www.forbes.com/sites/andrealoubier/2017/07/20/benefits-of-telecommuting-for-the-future-of-work/?sh=15d387cf16c6

Maurer, R. (2020, September 16). Study finds productivity not deterred by shift to remote work. *SHRM*. Retrieved from www.shrm.org/hr-today/news/hr-news/pages/study-productivity-shift-remote-work-covid-coronavirus.aspx

McLaughlin, M. (2020, June 15). Reforming FedRAMP: A guide to improving the federal procurement and risk management of cloud services. *ITIF*. Retrieved from https://itif.org/publications/2020/06/15/reforming-fedramp-guide-improving-federal-procurement-and-risk-management/

MeriTalk. (2022, July 18). *Improving the user experience to address the human element of cybersecurity*. Retrieved from www.meritalk.com/articles/improving-the-user-xperience-to-address-the-human-element-of-cybersecurity/

Mitchell, B. (2022, July 22). OPM director says telework flexibility needed so agencies can compete for talent. *FedScoop*. Retrieved from www.fedscoop.com/to-compete-for-talent-in-and-outside-government-agencies-need-telework-flexibility-opm-director-says/

Moffett, M. (2022, June 13). Hybrid work in government—why it's a good thing. *Cisco Blogs*. Retrieved from https://blogs.cisco.com/government/hybrid-work-in-government-why-its-a-good-thing

Montgomery, T. (2020, March 27). Why your data is safer in the cloud than on premises. *TechBeacon*. Retrieved from https://techbeacon.com/security/why-your-data-safer-cloud-premises

Naylor, B. (2020, March 13). In reversal, trump administration now urges agencies to allow telework. *National Public Radio*. Retrieved from www.npr.org/2020/03/13/814543505/in-reversal-trump-administration-now-urges-agencies-to-allow-telework

Newport, C. (2020, May 26). Why remote work is so hard—and how it can be fixed. *The New Yorker*. Retrieved from www.newyorker.com/culture/annals-of-inquiry/can-remote-work-be-fixed

Office of Management and Budget. (n.d.). Strengthening and empowering the federal workforce. *Executive Office of the President*. Retrieved October 14, 2022, from www.performance.gov/pma/workforce/

Office of Personnel Management. (2018). *Status of telework in the Federal Government report to congress: Fiscal year 2017*. Retrieved from www.telework.gov/reports-studies/reports-to-congress/2018-report-to-congress.pdf

Office of Personnel Management. (2021a). *2021 guide to telework and remote work in the Federal Government*. Retrieved from www.telework.gov/guidance-legislation/telework-guidance/telework-guide/guide-to-telework-in-the-federal-government.pdf

Office of Personnel Management. (2021b). *Status of telework in the Federal Government report to congress: Fiscal year 2020*. Retrieved from www.telework.gov/reports-studies/reports-to-congress/2021-report-to-congress.pdf

Ozimek, A. (2020). The future of remote work. *Upwork*. Retrieved from https://content-static.upwork.com/blog/uploads/sites/6/2020/05/26131624/Upwork_EconomistReport_FWR_052020.pdf

Telework Enhancement Act. (2010). No. 111–292 124 Stat. 3165. Retrieved from www.congress.gov/bill/111th-congress/house-bill/1722/text

Telework.gov. (n.d.). *About*. Office of Personnel Management. Retrieved October 21, 2022, from www.telework.gov/about/

Telework Metrics and Cost Savings Act. (2022). H.R. 7951.117th Cong. Retrieved from www.congress.gov/bill/117th-congress/house-bill/7951/text

Thibodeau, P. (2022, July 28). Republicans criticize remote work, White House defends it. *TechTarget*. Retrieved from www.techtarget.com/searchhrsoftware/news/252523283/Republicans-criticize-remote-work-White-House-defends-it

Wagner, E. (2022, June 15). A house panel advances legislation encouraging telework at agencies. *Government Executive*. Retrieved from www.govexec.com/workforce/2022/06/house-panel-legislation-telework-agencies/368185/

Young, S. (2022a, January 26). Moving the U.S. Government toward zero trust cyber-security principles (M-22–09). *Executive Office of the President, Office of Management and Budget*. Retrieved from www.whitehouse.gov/wp-content/uploads/2022/01/M-22-09.pdf

Young, S. (2022b, July 20). FY 2024 agency-wide capital planning to support the future of work (M-22–14). *Executive Office of the President, Office of Management and Budget*. Retrieved from www.whitehouse.gov/wp-content/uploads/2022/07/M-22-14.pdf

Chapter 12

State and Local Governments as Employers, Information and Communications Technology Roles, and Developing the Future Public Workforce

Joshua Franzel[1]

Content

DOI: 10.1201/9781003369783-12

The past decade has presented many challenges to state and local governments and their workforces, including those serving in information and communications technology (ICT) roles. Public entities of all sizes continue to focus on becoming employers of choice in order to recruit and retain a talented workforce that can continue to provide a wide range of important public services and programs. These labor force development efforts are set against the backdrop of the longer-term lingering impacts of the 2007–2009 recession (National Bureau of Economic Research, 2021),[2] the implementation of new approaches to providing public services, underlying workforce age demographics, stagnant wage and benefit structures, increased competition for workers with other sectors, and having recently navigated through the COVID-19 pandemic (Franzel, 2022b).

This chapter will explore what is known about the recent (2021–2022) employment levels of the state and local sector overall as well as the public sector ICT workforce more specifically. Employment projections for the next decade and ongoing occupational and skillset needs for U.S. states and localities will then be outlined. Finally, based on survey, case study, and focus group research, public management considerations and strategies that can be implemented to recruit and retain this future essential workforce will be explored. The workforce development practices implemented today will have long-lasting effects on how well state and local governments will be able to maintain an effective workforce that is able to comprehensively provide essential services, especially at a time of increased automation and the expanded adoption of technology-centered methods of administering public programs.

12.1 The Current State and Local Government Workforce

12.1.1 The Overall Workforce

According to the U.S. Bureau of Labor Statistics (BLS) Current Employment Statistics Survey, as of September 2022, there were approximately 5.3 million state government and 14.2 million local government employees across the United States (BLS—Current Employment Statistics, 2022). To put these numbers into recent historical context, during the recession of 2007–2009, when many public employers laid off or furloughed staff across the government enterprise, it took over 11 years (until 2019) for employment levels to return to their pre-recession points (Center for State and Local Government Excellence and ICMA-RC, 2020). As of October 2022, these numbers remain between 1% to 3% below where they were just prior to the start of the COVID-19 pandemic in February 2020.

When looking at the sector by industry, as of September 2022, within state government (see Figure 12.1), there were approximately 2.6 million education employees (49% of total state employment), 414,000 hospital employees (8% of total state employment), and 1.8 million general administration employees (34% of total state

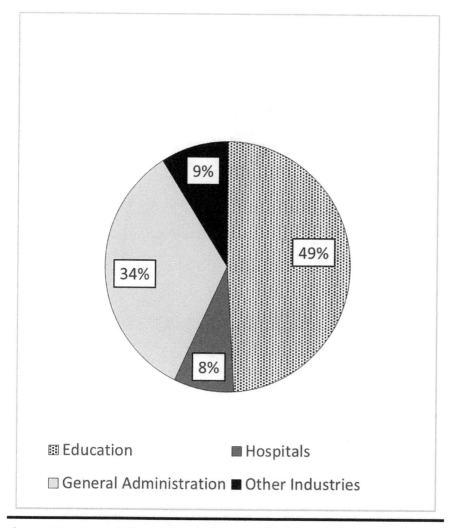

Figure 12.1   State employment by industry: September 2022.

Source: BLS, Current Employment Statistics Survey.[3]

employment), with the remaining 9% of state employees working in a variety of smaller industries. Within local government (see Figure 12.2), there were approximately 7.8 million education employees (55% of local employment), 246,000 utility employees (2% of local employment), 277,000 transportation employees (2% of local employment), 679,000 hospital employees (5% of local employment), and 4.2 million general administration employees (30% of local employment), with the remaining 6% of local employees working in other industries (BLS—Current Employment Statistics, 2022). With the exception of state government education

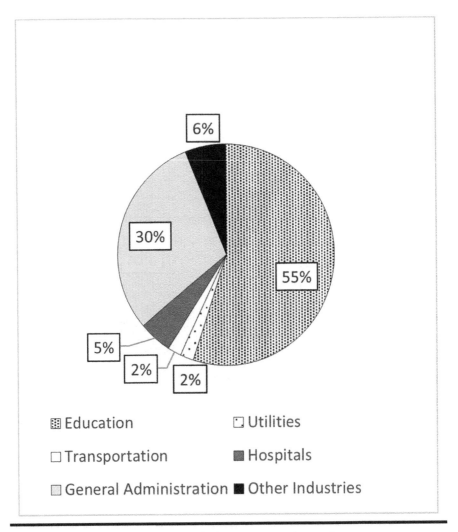

Figure 12.2   Local employment by industry: September 2022.

Source: BLS, Current Employment Statistics Survey.[4]

and hospitals, both of which have recovered from initial declines and now exceed pre-pandemic totals, the rest of these state and local government industries have followed the trends of the sector overall, having yet to return to their pre-pandemic employment levels.

Driving these overall employment levels are several notable labor turnover rate[5] trends, as offered in the BLS's Job Openings and Labor Turnover Survey (JOLTS) (BLS—Job Openings and Labor Turnover Survey, 2022) (BLS—Data Tools, 2022). First, while the layoff and discharge rate had averaged 0.5 between January 2001 through September 2022, in March, April, May, and June 2020, the rates significantly increased to 1.3, 1.8, 1.0, and 0.9, respectively, having since returned to (or fallen below) their two-decade average. Also, quits, which have averaged a rate of 0.7 between January 2001 and September 2022, never rising to 1.0 or higher for the two-decade timeframe prior to 2020, have stayed between 1.0 and 1.2 for most months (18) in 2020, 2021, and 2022.[6] At the same time, other separations—a primary component of which are retirements—spiked in the April to August 2020 time period. These turnover rates align closely with the MissionSquare Research Institute ongoing survey series, conducted in collaboration with the International Public Management Association for Human Resources and the National Association of State Personnel Executives, of state and local government human resource directors. In the 2022 edition of the survey (State and Local Workforce 2022 Survey), fielded in March and April 2022, 69% of HR directors reported that their governments had experienced higher quits in 2021 than in 2020, 60% reported higher retirements, and 41% reported lower levels of layoffs (Young, 2022).

At the same time of these separations, the job opening rate from the BLS JOLTS,[7] which had averaged 2.2 overall from January 2001 through September 2022, averaged 3.0 in 2019 and 2020, 3.9 in 2021, and 4.5 in 2022.[8] Relatedly, the hiring rate was up in 2021 (at a 1.7 level) and for much of 2022 (at 1.9) relative to the average hiring rate overall of 1.5 since 2001. Again, this data aligns with the State and Local Workforce 2022 Survey of public sector HR directors, in which 55% reported hiring more full-time employees in the past year than in 2020, and 38% answered that their full-time workforce increased in size over the past year.

12.1.2 Information and Communications Technology (ICT) Occupations

When focused specifically on computer-related occupations, according to the BLS's Occupational Employment and Wage Statistics program (BLS—Occupational Employment and Wage Statistics, 2022), in May 2021 there were 149,450 state government employees and 171,410 local government employees in these computer occupations. Table 12.1 offers a roster of the four broad categories of positions at the state and local levels for computer-related occupations.

Similar to the state and local sector overall, as of May 2021, computer-related occupations are below their pre-pandemic levels (May 2019) by 2,370 positions (-1.6%) at the state level and by 6,460 (-3.8%) positions at the local level.

According to the previously mentioned State and Local Workforce 2022 Survey, 69% of human resource directors reported having a hard time filling information technology (IT) positions over the past year, with 73% answering that they are receiving fewer qualified applicants than there are IT positions available. More generally, 52% of HR directors list technology skills as one of the skills most-needed in new hires.

Table 12.1 **Selected State and Local Government Computer-Related Occupations with Highest Employment Levels (Broad Categories), May 2021**

Occupation	State Level Employment	Local Level Employment
Overall computer occupations	149,450	171,410
Computer support specialists	47,600	71,750
Computer and information analysts	32,010	28,790
Software and web developers, programmers, and testers	31,660	21,360
Database and network administrators and architects	29,170	38,720

Source: BLS—Occupational Employment and Wage Statistics (2022).

12.2 Future Employment Projections and Occupation Needs

Based on a blend of labor force characteristics, industry demand and output, and the aggregate economy overall, along with occupational and industrial employment, the BLS Employment Projections program offers 10-year projections for industries and occupations across and within the entire U.S. labor market, including state and local governments (BLS—Employment Projections, 2022).[9] For 2021–2031, state government employment overall is estimated to contract by 6%, while local government employment is expected to expand by 1.4%.

When looking at examples of positions expected to increase the most, often they are knowledge worker positions and/or those that require postsecondary education or specialized training (Liss-Levinson, Franzel, and Young, 2019).[10] For example, between 2021 and 2031, at the state level, epidemiologist positions are expected to increase by approximately 35%, management analyst positions by 15%, and operations research analyst positions by 11%.[11] Other examples of positions expected to experience notable growth between 2021 and 2031, at the local level, include medical and health science manager positions by 25%, construction manager positions by 14%, and civil engineers by 9%.[12]

When looking at examples of positions expected to decrease the most, often these positions are those impacted by automation, the adoption of IT applications, and outsourcing, among other factors. For example, between 2021 and 2031, at the local level, parking enforcement worker positions are expected to decrease by approximately 38% and switchboard operators by 27%. State-level payroll and

Table 12.2 State and Local Government Computer-Related Occupations (Broad Categories), 2021–2031

Occupation	State Level Employment, % Change	Local Level Employment, % Change
All occupations	-6.0%	+1.4%
Overall computer occupations	-2.9%	+3.5%
Computer support specialists	-1.7%	+0.8%
Computer and information analysts	-0.4%	+5.9%
Software and web developers, programmers, and testers	+0.3%	+10.5%
Database and network administrators and architects	-0.9%	-0.5%

Source: BLS—Employment Projections (2022).

timekeeping clerk positions are expected to shrink by 23% and executive secretaries and executive administrative assistants by 28%.

Table 12.2 offers expected growth percentages for the broad categories of computer-related occupations for 2021–2031. With a couple of exceptions ("software and web developers, programmers, and testers" at the state level and "database and network administrators and architects" at the local level), the projected employment levels for these broad categories follow similar growth and decline expectations for the state and local government sectors overall.

Within these broad categories, examples of occupations expected to see the largest percent employment increase between 2021 and 2031 are data scientists (by 20% at the state level and 30% at the local level), information security analysts (by 15% at the state level and 25% at the local level), and web developers (by 6% at the state level and 14% at the local level). Examples of computer-related occupations expected to decrease over the same timeframe are computer programmers (by -21% at the state level and -15% at the local level), network and computer systems administrators (by -9% at the state level and -1% at the local level), and computer user support specialist (by -8% at the state level and no change at the local level).

12.3 Developing the Future Public Sector Workforce

In order to develop the future state and local government workforce, including those in ICT roles, what are some of the drivers behind what attracts talented

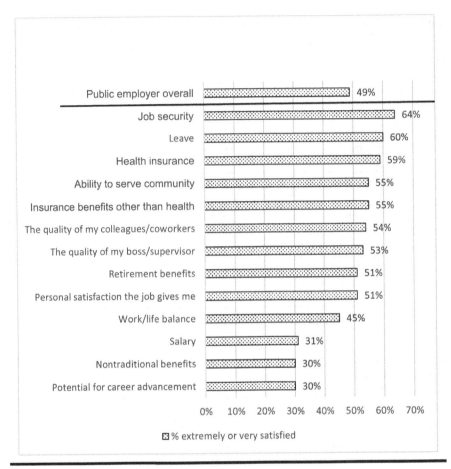

Figure 12.3 **Employee satisfaction with job elements, November/December 2021** (*n* = 1,100).

Source: MissionSquare Research Institute, Survey Results: Continued Impact of COVID-19 on Public Sector Employee Job and Financial Outlook, Satisfaction, and Retention, March 2022.

professionals to the state and local sectors? What are the key aspects of public service that can be used to recruit and retain the needed talent to the sector over the next one, five, and 10 years? And what are some of the management strategies and considerations that have been found to be most effective in these efforts?

From an *employee perspective*, since the start of the COVID-19 pandemic, MissionSquare Research Institute has been surveying state and local government employees regarding their satisfaction with their current jobs, workplace morale, career outlooks, and other related topics (Liss-Levinson, 2022). The findings from this polling provide insights into how employees prioritize various aspects of their public employment. As noted in Figure 12.3, as of late 2021, while 49% of state and local government employees are extremely or very satisfied with their employer overall, over half are satisfied with their position's job security, health and retirement benefits, quality of colleagues, and their ability to serve the community, among other considerations.

When employees were asked about what their organization could do to retain more employees, 62% answered "Improve salaries," followed by "Offer/improve bonuses" (50%), "Show more appreciation and recognition of employees and the work they do" (38%), "Improve benefit package" (32%), "Increase amount of leave allowed" (30%), "Offer more flexible work schedules" (27%), and "Offer more opportunities to work remotely" (25%), among other less selected options.

In 2021 and 2022, in an environment of overall robust tax and fee revenues, along with unprecedented levels of intergovernmental transfers from the federal government (U.S. Department of Commerce, 2022),[13] many public employers were responding to these considerations by re-evaluating salary schedules to remain competitive with other sectors (in addition to remaining competitive within the sector); implementing enhanced employee hiring or retention bonus programs; considering and/or adopting more flexible work arrangements when possible; and exploring the incorporation of "nontraditional" benefits,[14] such as subsidized childcare and commuting, student loan repayment, and enhanced wellness and employee assistance programs, into overall compensation packages.

Often included in the "nontraditional" or "quality of life" benefits category are programs focused on financial planning. Center for State and Local Government Excellence (now the MissionSquare Research Institute) survey research from 2019 found that 83% of state and local government employees worry about their finances and financial decisions, with 66% doing so while at work—potentially impacting productivity (Liss-Levinson, 2020). At the same time, less than a third (29%) had access to an employer-provided financial literacy/education program to help assist in their financial well-being,[15] while 68% would likely participate if offered a program. This is a benefits component that continues to receive increased attention in the public sector context to help employees optimize and effectively manage their current overall compensation when public employers may not have the budgetary or statutory flexibility to quickly adjust wages and benefits to remain competitive with other employers, especially from a staff retention perspective.

From an *employer perspective*, many insights can be gleaned from the State and Local Workforce 2022 Survey of public sector HR directors. When asked about how competitive state and local government wage and benefit compensation is relative to the broader labor market, 44% of HR directors thought their public employer's wage compensation was competitive, while a large majority (85%) thought their benefits compensation was competitive. Given the comprehensive nature of state and local government retirement, leave, health care, insurance, and quality of

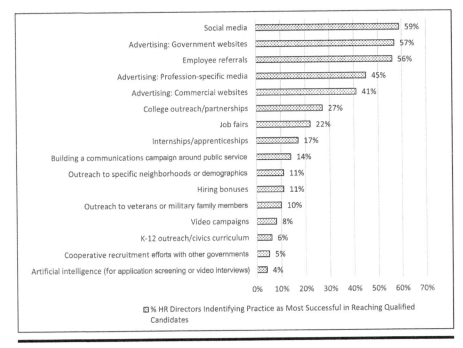

Figure 12.4 Effective recruitment practices (*n* = 261).

Source: MissionSquare Research Institute, Survey Findings: State and Local Workforce 2022, *June 2022.*

life benefits, these nonwage compensation components often are key to remaining competitive for talented staff, including technology professionals (Franzel, 2022a). Also, 54% of the HR directors surveyed answered that their governments are offering regular hybrid scheduling for eligible positions, 51% flexible scheduling, 38% flexible work hours, and 22% regular full-time telework for eligible positions.

When asked about effective approaches for recruiting employees, a blend of technological (social media and website postings) and interpersonal (employee referrals and college outreach) approaches surface as the most effective (see Figure 12.4).

Regarding retention efforts, in the State and Local Workforce 2022 Survey, over half of the HR directors listed the following as initiatives used for retaining employees: employee assistance programs (EAPs)/mental health support, exit interviews, funds/reimbursements for training/tuition, expanded leave benefits, in-house trainings, wellness programs (informational), recognition programs, and leadership development.

While a lot of these important recruitment and retention approaches focus on compensation structures, how and where work is conducted, and expanded education and trainings, the concept of recognition has continued to surface in MissionSquare Research Institute surveys, case studies, and focus groups. For example, as of November/December 2021, 47% of state and local employees surveyed believed that the pandemic had made the public more aware of the importance of what they do, a percentage that had remained stable throughout the pandemic (Liss-Levinson, 2022). This is in addition to the 38% of employees, as discussed earlier, who thought employers could show more appreciation and recognition of employees and the work they do in order to retain more employees. This recognition, in addition to helping with retention, also helps governments and their staff communicate the important work, roles, and job opportunities of state and local government to those who perhaps would not have otherwise considered working in the sector. Before and continuing through the pandemic, many innovative state and local governments (of all sizes) have positively leveraged their mission-driven, public service brand to attract employees, including technology professionals. Many have woven this messaging into job announcements, community outreach efforts, and social media engagements (Kellar & Young, 2018).

12.4 Looking Ahead

While the past decade has posed challenges to states and localities as employers, looking ahead, there are many available opportunities for these governments to continue to develop an effective and comprehensive public service workforce—including those in ICT roles. These efforts will likely be conducted in an environment of heightened labor turnover, expanded competition for talent across sectors, and evolving approaches pertaining to how and where the work of the public sector is conducted.

As this chapter has explored, how well governments are able to develop their workforces of the future will be linked to a variety of factors. These factors include, but are not limited to, how public entities manage their overall wage and benefit compensation packages to meet the evolving needs of current and future employees; how they communicate the important work their employees carry out on a daily basis to both internal and external stakeholders; how they comprehensively support employee health and financial wellness; and how they conduct employee recruitment outreach to all communities, including to those who typically would not have considered a career in public service. The workforce plans state and local governments develop today will have long-lasting impacts on the staffing and quality of essential public services and programs residents depend on and increasingly engage with via ICTs.

Notes

1 The author would like to thank Rivka Liss-Levinson, PhD, and Gerald Young of the MissionSquare Research Institute for their review of and input on this chapter.

2 See: National Bureau of Economic Research, *US Business Cycle Expansions and Contractions*.

3 Some percentages in figures may shift ±1% due to rounding.
4 Some percentages in figures may shift ±1% due to rounding.
5 From the BLS Data Tools website: ". . . data element rates (hires, total separations, quits, layoffs and discharges, and other separations) are computed by dividing the data element level by employment and multiplying that quotient by 100." Thus, a turnover rate of 1 would represent one person per 100 employees.
6 Through September 2022.
7 From the BLS: "The job openings rate is computed by dividing the number of job openings by the sum of employment and job openings and multiplying that quotient by 100."
8 Through September 2022.
9 Note: Occupational projection details offered in this chapter section are sourced from the BLS Employment Projections program. Excludes education and hospitals.
10 See the "Workforce Size and Key Demographics" section of Center for State and Local Government Excellence, *Financial Literacy Programs for Local Government Employees*, January 2019.
11 Note: These positions are expecting increases at the local level too, but at different rates.
12 Note: These positions are expecting increases at the state level too, but at different rates.
13 See: U.S. Department of Commerce, Bureau of Economic Analysis, *National Data: National Income and Product Accounts—Table 3.3 State and Local Government Current Receipts and Expenditures*. October 27, 2022.
14 See: MissionSquare Research Institute, *Benefits of State and Local Government Employees*, February 2022.
15 See: Center for State and Local Government Excellence, National Association of State Treasures Foundation, International Public Management Association for Human Resources, and Wells Fargo Foundation, *Financial Wellness Programs for State and Local Employees: A Quick Reference Guide*, July 2020.

References

Center for State and Local Government Excellence and ICMA-RC. (2020). *Infographic: State and local employment*. Washington, DC: Center for State and Local Government Excellence and ICMA-RC.
Center for State and Local Government Excellence, National Association of State Treasures Foundation, International Public Management Association for Human Resources, and Wells Fargo Foundation. (2020). *Financial wellness programs for state and local employees: A quick reference guide*. Washington, DC: Center for State and Local Government Excellence, National Association of State Treasures Foundation, International Public Management Association for Human Resources, and Wells Fargo Foundation.
Franzel, J. (2022a). *Benefits of state and local government employees*. Washington, DC: MissionSquare Research Institute.
Franzel, J. (2022b). The Public Sector Workforce of tomorrow: Key management considerations for recruitment. *Government Finance Review*, 42–45.

Kellar, E., & Young, G. (2018). *Workforce of the future: Strategies to manage change.* Washington, DC: Center for State and Local Government Excellence and Kronos.

Liss-Levinson, R. (2020). *Survey results—A focus on public sector financial wellness programs: Employee needs and preferences.* Washington, DC: Center for State and Local Government Excellence and Wells Fargo Foundation.

Liss-Levinson, R. (2022). *Survey results: Continued impact of COVID-19 on public sector employee job and financial outlook, satisfaction, and retention.* Washington, DC: MissionSquare Research Institute.

Liss-Levinson, R., Franzel, J., & Young, G. (2019). *Financial literacy programs for local government employees.* Washington, DC: Center for State and Local Government Excellence and Wells Fargo Foundation.

National Bureau of Economic Research. (2021). *US business cycle expansions and contractions.* Retrieved from www.nber.org/research/data/us-business-cycle-expansions-and-contractions

U.S. Bureau of Labor Statistics—Current Employment Statistics. (2022). *CES national databases.* Retrieved from www.bls.gov/ces/data/

U.S. Bureau of Labor Statistics—Data Tools. (2022). *Help and tutorials.* Retrieved from www.bls.gov/help/def/jt.htm

U.S. Bureau of Labor Statistics—Employment Projections. (2022). *National employment matrix.* Retrieved from www.bls.gov/emp/

U.S. Bureau of Labor Statistics—Job Openings and Labor Turnover Survey. (2022). *JOLTS databases.* Retrieved from www.bls.gov/jlt/data.htm

U.S. Bureau of Labor Statistics—Occupational Employment and Wage Statistics. (2022). *National industry-specific and by ownership.* Retrieved from www.bls.gov/oes/tables.htm

U.S. Department of Commerce, Bureau of Economic Analysis. (2022, October 27). *National data: National income and product accounts—Table 3.3 state and local government current receipts and expenditures.* Retrieved from www.bea.gov/data/government/receipts-and-expenditures

Young, G. (2022). *Survey findings: State and local workforce 2022.* Washington, DC: MissionSquare Research Institute.

Chapter 13

Data Ethics and Social Responsibility

Jennifer Koester

Content

In 2021, President Biden declared that the "first step to promoting equity in Government action is to gather the data necessary to inform that effort." Included in the *Executive Order on Advancing Racial Equity and Support for Underserved Communities through the Federal Government*, in addition to President Biden's stance, is a series of recommendations and considerations for data use in the context of equity and transparency (The White House, 2021a). Similarly, Biden's 2021 *Memorandum on Restoring Trust in Government through Scientific Integrity and Evidence-Based Policymaking* argues that expanding access to secure and transparent data will help researchers evaluate policies while also encouraging public empowerment via information (The White House, 2021b).

Indeed, state and nongovernmental organizations (NGOs) share similar perspectives. The State of Delaware, for example, has committed to the "timely and consistent publication of public information" as an "essential component of an open, accountable, and effective government." Governor Carney's 2018 signing of Executive Order 18 also established the creation of an Open Data Committee to ensure data sharing is ongoing and expands over time to meet the needs of residents and stakeholders ("Executive Order 18, State of Delaware").

As the commitment to disclose increasingly large datasets expands, additional consideration must be made regarding data ethics and social responsibility. Put simply, data ethics are "the norms of behavior that promote appropriate judgments and accountability when acquiring, managing, or using data, with the goals of protecting civil liberties, minimizing risks to individuals and society, and maximizing the public good" ("Federal Data Strategy"). Providing more information to more people, while ambitious, also opens additional possibilities for misuse. For example, variable names may be misinterpreted, thus leading to incorrect analysis. If, perhaps, a medical dataset includes a variable, "tested," that variable may mean something very different to the data owner than a layman. To the data owner "tested" may be a date field that represents the last time a patient was tested, regardless of result. However, a layman could misconstrue the presence of a date to indicate there was a positive test result (instead of a null or blank field). There are ways to ameliorate that, including making data definitions available, but as the number of datasets increase, so too do the possibilities for misinterpretation.

In addition to variables being misunderstood, expanding the transparency and availability of data also increases the chances of inconsistency in reporting. Take, for example, COVID reporting. At its height, several different organizations were reporting on COVID results and trends. However, not all sources had access to the same integrated database or used the same definitions for reporting (e.g., COVID deaths per week may mean Sunday-Saturday for one partner or Monday-Sunday to another). Therefore, one could receive very different results if they viewed data from a state's health department versus an institution of higher education. One of several ways to assuage this issue is to simply title and identify the data, while including all relevant information (e.g., metadata or variable definitions).

Another concern regarding increased collection and public access to data focuses on deidentification. One common way to promote anonymity is to suppress data by cell size. For example, a publicly available dataset that reports crime may include sensitive information a victim would prefer not to disclose, like sexual violence. If the cell size is low enough and a layman knows some level of detail about a particular person/incident (e.g., the date, location), they may now be privy to very sensitive information about a specific person. However, if cell size (N count) is high enough, it should mask personal identity. Additional confidentiality protocol should be included and will vary according to agency roles or best practices.

Misrepresentation or bias in data collection, another potential threat accompanying expanded dissemination of information, may perpetuate rhetoric promoting social inequalities. It is possible to collect and share data that only supports one particular perspective, either intentionally or not. For example, if data collection related to education occurred only during after school programs, the sample would likely exclude those with after school jobs or other responsibilities. In this way, data is only reflecting the experience and perspectives of a select group. In these instances, it is important to publish information related to collection, including who collected the data and which groups were (over/under) represented.

13.1 Fair Information Practice Principles (FIPPS)

There have been several efforts to address such ethical concerns in data collection and dissemination. The Federal Government, Non-Governmental Organizations (NGOs), institutions of higher education, and various other administrations have derived principles for ethical data use. One popular tool, identified in the 1973 Federal Report "Records, Computers and the Rights of Citizens," is known as the Fair Information Practice Principles, or FIPPS ("Records, Computers, and the Rights of Citizens | Office of Justice Programs"). FIPPS focus on nine key ideas:

1. *Access and Amendment*: Personally identifiable information (PII) must be provided only to appropriate individuals. They have the onus to edit PII, as needed.
2. *Accountability*: Organizations and agencies should be held accountable for proper adherence to privacy rules. It is the responsibility of the agency to provide training and define responsibilities for all individuals with access to PII.
3. *Authority*: PII should not be stored, distributed, or analyzed if authority has not been provided, as deemed by circumstances.
4. *Minimization*: PII should only be collected and stored if and as long as it is relevant to accomplish a specifically identified and authorized purpose.
5. *Quality and Integrity*: PII should only be collected and used if it is both accurate and strives for fairness to individuals.
6. *Individual Participation*: Individual consent and input should be used during the collection and usage of PII, whenever possible.
7. *Purpose Specification and Use Limitation*: Organizations should identify the purpose of PII collection/use and remain dedicated to that specific intent.
8. *Security*: Safeguards of all types (technical, role-based, etc.) must be established with use of PII. Consideration to depth of security should be commensurate with the size of risk resulting from disclose or misuse.
9. *Transparency*: When PII is collected or used, agencies should disclose information regarding purpose, collection, and logistics.

13.2 Federal Data Strategy: Data Ethics Framework

Over time, and as data collection and sharing increased in complexity, additional considerations concerning data ethics arose. Expanding roles to include responsibilities throughout the entire data lifecycle, was one such reflection. Released in 2019, *the Federal Data Strategy: Data Ethics Framework* helps identify responsibilities and best practices for an ethical data user. The report also provides recommendations for implementation, many of which will be discussed in this chapter ("Action Plan—Federal Data Strategy"). Within the framework, seven data ethics tenets are described:

1. Uphold Applicable Statutes, Regulations, Professional Practices, and Ethical Standards

2. Respect the Public, Individuals, and Communities
3. Respect Privacy and Confidentiality
4. Act with Honesty, Integrity, and Humility
5. Hold Oneself and Others Accountable
6. Promote Transparency
7. Stay Informed of Developments in the Fields of Data Management and Data Science

The first tenet, uphold applicable statutes, regulations, professional practices, and ethical standards, accurately identifies the importance of aligning all actions to legal specifications. However, regulations can take a long time to enact, and technology evolves quickly. It is, therefore, the onus of agency data leaders to support preexisting statutes, while also considering modern data ethics that may not yet be official.

The Data Ethics Framework offers several recommendations regarding implementation. First, it is crucial that all regulations and standards are clearly identified by leadership. There should be no ambiguity about ethical standards and a person should be identified to act as lead. It should be clear who the data professional should turn to with questions and that leader should have the proper knowledge and authority to respond. Additionally, professional development should be offered that is specific to the role of the employee and the status of the data (i.e., position in data lifecycle). This would include assigning database roles (e.g., read/write) appropriately, as to retain the integrity and privacy of the data. Furthermore, reporting of unethical behavior should be encouraged and codified. Each agency must have a whistleblowing policy, or similar strategy, to protect those reporting.

Tenet two, respect the public, individuals, and communities, posits that "data initiatives should include considerations for unique community and local contexts and have an identified and clear benefit to society" (Data Ethics Framework). Even in the earliest stages of the data lifecycle, including collection, this tenet can be considered. For example, data should be representative of the population it describes. Thus, if collecting community data, effort should be made to include input from all applicable parties, instead of favoring specific sources. Relying on the experience of only a selection of the reported population will lead to misrepresentative data. It would be impossible to fully understand and research the context, population, and/or dataset with only a narrow understanding. For example, if analyzing access to public transportation, a data professional may choose to include those who do not use public transportation. It may seem unnecessary or even burdensome, but it is important to gather as many community perspectives as possible and realistic. This group may have interesting insight related to resource access or limitations.

Additionally, organizations should be mindful of the impact data analysis could have on the public and take steps to mitigate negative consequences. Perhaps data analysis at a state Department of Transportation indicates that there is a significant number of drinking and driving occurrences in a specific town. This information should be released while masking personally identifiable information

(PII). The analysis should also include additional context and information (including statistics from nearby areas). In this way, one entity (person, town, agency, etc.) can be identified for intervention by an agency, but not maligned by the public.

Respect privacy and confidentiality, the third tenet, asserts that "privacy and confidentiality should always be protected in a manner that respects the dignity, rights, and freedom of data subjects." Data collection should not be a burden or intrusion for subjects. This may include making special arrangements for data collection or omitting personal details. Additionally, all efforts should be made to avoid negative consequences through data sharing and analysis. Several actions can be taken to mitigate these concerns. Privacy training should be developed, administered, and updated for data professionals. The federal government, as well as several organizations, provide privacy and confidentiality training that is easily accessible. Trainings that identify the importance of privacy as solely a technological imperative should incorporate discussion prompts regarding fairness and dignity, as those can be more difficult concepts to explain.

Additionally, the Data Ethics Framework recommends that agencies monitor new technology to proactively avoid disclosure, establish a communication standard upon potential breach notification, and limit disclosure when applicable. This can be a difficult balance; on one hand the data professional strives for transparency. On the other, they have an obligation to mask findings (e.g., cell suppression). For this reason, it is important that privacy and confidentiality protocol are codified; it should not be the interpretation of one data professional to decide how much data, and at what level, to release.

Tenet four, acting with honesty, integrity, and humility, may seem obvious, but those with experience in data-related fields often experience how challenging this can be. Regardless of pressure to publish erroneous or biased data, it is the ethical responsibility of the data professional to resist such demands. In this situation, the data professional should consult human resources or designee. Sometimes, a data professional will be asked to push ethical boundaries in seemingly innocuous ways. For example, when presenting a visualization, feedback may indicate that a tool would be clearer if outliers were removed. While this may make the data more aesthetic or help focus on the majority of the population, it could easily lead to erroneous understanding. In such cases, it would be wise to present the entire visualization and include filters or magnifications of particular sections. Additionally, any biases or concerns with the dataset should be disclosed. This may include sampling technique, low response rate, or other applicable detail.

Holding oneself and others accountable, tenet five, promotes transparency in data practice and

> includes the responsible handling of classified and controlled information, upholding data use agreements made with data providers, minimizing data collection, informing individuals and organizations of the potential uses of their data, and allowing for public access, amendment, and contestability to data and findings, where appropriate. (Federal Data Strategy, p. 14)

There are several distinct sub-recommendations in this tenet:

- Responsible handling of classified information: This includes developing a data security plan and series of best practices for sharing and storage.
- Upholding data agreements: Modifying signed data-sharing agreements without agreement from all partners can jeopardize the right to use data, as well as dissolve trust between sharing agencies.
- Minimizing data collection: There are several views regarding this point. From a technologist's view, it would be wiser to collect as much as possible, as to limit table appending, thus decreasing the likelihood of integration errors. However, as data collection can place some (however small) burden on respondents, it is wise to consider the usefulness of collection. Additionally, it is important to minimize collecting data that is already collected/reported. This could lead to inconsistent reporting and confusion. If data is reported in multiple places, it should all query from the same source, whenever possible.
- Informing individuals and organizations of data use: This process should be codified in data-sharing agreements, memoranda of understanding, or another agreed-upon document. If the intended use changes, it should be either approved or acknowledged by the data-providing agency, according to agreement specifics.
- Public access and interaction with data: Many individual states and municipalities have formed open data initiatives. Delaware's Open Data Portal (see Figure 13.1) is one example of government-supplied data that is available for public consumption and interaction. There are options to suggest a dataset, search by agency, create visualizations, and export.

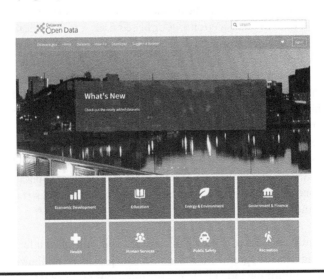

Figure 13.1 Delaware's Open Data Portal landing page is shown. It includes a search bar for accessing data, as organized by domain. Domains include education, health, recreation, and more.

CASE STUDY: TRANSPARENCY, DELAWARE OPEN DATA PORTAL

Signed in 2021, Delaware Senate Bill 28 required the publication of a variety of traffic data ("Delaware Data—Delaware.gov"). This information was requested by several residents and advocacy groups to petition for stop lights and other public safety resources. This tool is also provided for agencies to use regarding outreach and intervention purposes. While it does filter down to single incidents, special consideration was spent on deidentification efforts. This was accomplished by a diverse committee, composed of individuals from various agencies and legal authorities.

Data was pulled from several disparate agency datasets to create a comprehensive view for the public (see Figure 13.2). Individuals can search by street or other variable to receive a variety of information, including if a seatbelt was used and the weather conditions.

In addition to empowering individuals and agencies with information, Open Data initiatives also cut back on FERPA and additional requests. Instead, one source of continually updated information is available for all to download or view. This will limit miscommunication and help the state with regard to transparency initiatives.

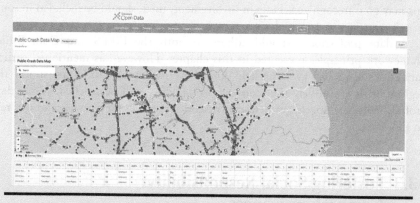

Figure 13.2 **The Open Data feature includes crash information in both table and map form. There are search and export functions.**

Promoting transparency, the sixth tenet, posits that clear communication regarding data use enables stakeholders to make better-informed decisions. Stakeholders can be residents, service users, board members, or other concerned individuals. Feedback from stakeholders should be valued and included, when possible. For example, if a state's Department of Housing reports on annual average home electricity costs but uses a fiscal calendar, that may be difficult for the public to understand. Feedback may request that data be presented in a calendar year order/format. This simple revision would take little time for a data professional to accomplish but may have a big impact on public understanding. Another aspect of transparency is progress reporting. This could include disclosing data quality concerns or simply providing updates on use. The Data Ethics Framework also discusses the importance of documentation for transparency. Documentation should be encouraged when describing datasets, detailing analyses, and making modifications to existing datasets or reports.

The final tenet, staying informed of developments in the field, is critical in the sphere of data science. Technologies, analysis methods, and best practices are constantly changing. This may introduce new, unimagined threats to datasets or analyses. Data professionals should undergo training each time a new technology is introduced to their data stack. Even if the technology is an update to an existing or familiar product, it may introduce opportunities for error or misunderstanding.

The Data Ethics Framework concludes by offering some considerations for the future. Key among these is the important role emerging technologies will have. By employing increasingly advanced technologies, we are trading some of the manual work that serves as a data quality check. For example, facial recognition may rely on algorithms that employ bias. Without some level of manual human involvement, this may go unrecognized. Human involvement, then, should be included in some form in all types of data analysis.

A data professional should adhere to both the FIPPS and Data Ethics Framework principles presented in this chapter. However, as mentioned earlier, data ethics is an ever-evolving field, and those recommendations are simply the beginning. It is unlikely that consensus or finality will be reached. Many data professionals have specific or field-centric codes of ethics for data use and will rely on those.

13.3 Fostering Social Responsibility: Comprehensiveness

Most versions of data ethics focus on appropriateness and legality. Matters of social responsibility, like striving for equity, are often mentioned but not emphasized. There are several reasons for this, including wanting to remain focused on science, not politics. However, data science has the unique ability to show empirical truth. As such, data professionals have a responsibility to provide that truth to the greatest accuracy and robustness possible. This chapter will refer to this additional potential data ethic as "comprehensiveness."

An approach to comprehensive data can be difficult to envision. Imagine trying to solve a puzzle, but only with edge pieces. A full picture could not possibly emerge. The middle of the "puzzle" is unknown to us; therefore, so is a complete understanding. That is what it is like to attempt to answer large-scale (social) problems with only a fraction of the necessary information.

Similarly described by David Pozen in 2005, mosaic theory details a basic precept of intelligence gathering: Disparate items of information, though individually of limited or no utility to their possessor, can take on added significance when combined with other items of information. Combining the items illuminates their interrelationships and breeds analytic synergies, so that the resulting mosaic of information is worth more than the sum of its parts. (Pozen, 2005)

This approach applied to data science, often used to describe the need for an integrated data system, is made increasingly possible with new technology and increasingly imperative with modern concerns.

Imagine, for a moment, the role a comprehensive data mosaic could have filled during the height of the COVID pandemic. A Department of Education cabinet secretary would certainly need to know the impact of COVID on student achievement. However, if analysis only included education data, potentially significant factors would be ignored. After research is consulted to help determine necessary analytical variables, as many measures as possible should be included in a data mosaic for initial analysis (to determine eventual model inclusion). It may be that housing is an important consideration. Perhaps parental guardians losing housing during COVID's acme had a significant impact on a child's education . . . even more than any educational variables. Unless a robust and integrated data mosaic is employed, many potentially significant variables would be ignored, as they are not even accessible.

The 2022 article "A Linked Data Mosaic for Policy-Relevant Research on Science and Innovation: Value, Transparency, Rigor, and Community" asserts several important points regarding data mosaics (Chang et al., 2022). Primarily, the authors identify that data mosaics are not decentralized data infrastructures. Such decentralized systems typically divide data according to overly narrow access, thus only presenting part of the solution (or the edges of a puzzle).

Following pre-established data ethics is imperative, but they alone are too passive to cultivate the increasingly complex realm of data mosaics. Current data ethics stress the need for the protection of data but not the responsibility to strive for ever-improving data. In other words, current guidelines support data protection but not deeper dives into more robust data. Indeed, an additional ethical guideline, comprehensiveness, could help promote this form of analysis and lead to tremendous improvements for people and communities.

CASE STUDY: COMPREHENSIVENESS, FEDERAL FIRST RESPONDER INTEGRATION

In 2015, the Next Generation First Responder (NGFR) program, housed in the Federal Department of Homeland Security, partnered with various first responders to better understand the successes and limits of associated technology regarding safety (DHSST). This required a good bit of up-to-date data to accomplish:

> Fifteen different NGFR technologies were assessed for their first responder support capabilities to: (1) provide or enhance network capability; (2) route or manage data; and (3) enhance situational awareness, which included (4) geo-location, (5) monitoring physical health and (6) video dissemination. These capabilities and sub-capabilities were integrated into an ad hoc (i.e., non-permanent) architecture.

Following integration, NGFR was able to view physiological data in the context of real-life situations. A collection of data points were joined and enabled new technologies, like streaming capabilities. This in-depth and multilayered analysis simply would not be possible using data from one source. It was necessary to integrate and analyze as a comprehensive full picture. Put plainly:

> It is crucial for public safety agencies to maintain effective real-time situational awareness in the execution of their various law enforcement, emergency medical care and fire safety missions. Data integration is an essential part of enabling situational awareness, including providing the location of first responders, their physical condition, and any exposure to HAZMAT. This awareness helps command staff make informed decisions that both protect first responders and improve their effectiveness in serving their communities. (DHSST, p. 10)

CASE STUDY: COMPREHENSIVENESS, IOWA'S INTEGRATED DATA SYSTEM FOR DECISION MAKING

As is true in many states, Iowa's early childhood data traditionally existed in disparate, difficult-to-join databases. This made robust analysis of child background, outcomes, limitations, and program participation impossible. To correct this, Iowa developed an Integrated System for Decision Making (I2D2). This allowed for simultaneous analysis of human services, education, and health data, thus presenting a more comprehensive picture of Iowa's youth (Gabay et al., 2022).

Data privacy, legal agreements, security, and sustainability complicated development. However, all large-scale integration projects should plan for unforeseen rises in cost, time, and effort due to the large number of potential complications. Overall, the system persevered through technical and political difficulties, due to its clear benefit to stakeholders:

> (U)sing I2D2 benefits both data users and data owners. It allows for a more focused use of cross-program data to achieve Iowa's goals for children and young families while improving the privacy and confidentiality of program data and the quality of program data available to data users. (Gabay et al., 2022)

In contrast to serving youth with only a partial understanding of circumstances, I2D2 can now provide a full picture of a child's development, needs, successes, and outcomes. A selection of a few projects I2D2 has enabled is shown in Figure 13.3.

Project Title	ECI Longitudinal Study	Family Support, Home Visiting, and Community Risk	Substance Use Among Iowa Families with Young Children
Objective	Use I2D2 to analyze child and family characteristics, service participation, and kindergarten outcomes	Use I2D2 to understand more about families served by Iowa's home visiting programs with a focus on children aged 0-3	Explore the capacity for a statewide IDS to inform program and policy efforts related to family substance use in a popular home visiting program
Datasets Integrated/Data Owners	• IDPH Birth Records • IDE Kindergarten and Preschool Enrollment • Teaching Strategies GOLD® Assessment • IDHS Childcare Subsidy Receipt	• IDPH Birth Records • IDPH DAISEY Home Visiting Records	• IDPH Birth Records • IDPH DAISEY Home Visiting Records
Primary Data Elements Used	**IDPH Birth Records:** Child demographics (gender, race, birth order); Low birthweight; Preterm birth; Inadequate prenatal care; Low maternal education (<12 years); Birth to teen mother; Birth to single mother; Poverty (WIC/Medicaid enrollment) **Iowa Department of Education (IDE):** Child demographics (age, gender, race/ethnicity); Free/reduced price lunch status; English language learner status; Kindergarten enrollment (location & dates); Kindergarten attendance rate; Kindergarten literacy assessment; Had DE-funding preschool experience **Teaching Strategies Gold:® Assessment:** Enrolled in a participating preschool program **IDHS Childcare Subsidy Receipt:** Used a Child Care Assistance subsidy	**IDPH Birth Records:** Preterm/low birthweight; Teen mother; Low maternal education (< 12 years); Single mother; Inadequate prenatal care; Poverty (WIC/Medicaid enrollment); Tobacco use in pregnancy **IDPH DAISEY Home Visiting Records:** Child age at enrollment; Prenatal enrollment; Successful completion; Enrollment duration; Average number of visits per month	**IDPH Birth Records:** Child demographics (gender, race, birth order); Poverty (WIC/Medicaid enrollment); Tobacco use; Unmarried mother; Low maternal education (< 12 years); Teen mother; Pre-term/low birthweight; Inadequate prenatal care **IDPH DAISEY Home Visiting Records:** Enrolled in MIECHV; Substance use history; Completion of home visiting program

Figure 13.3   Examples of analyses made possible by I2D2. A chart is displayed with some examples of successful initiatives Iowa has been able to pursue, thanks to its integrated data system (I2D2).

Without integrated data, a data professional will often answer questions based on convenience. Urgency, capacity, and existing data architecture can all limit the ability to conduct thorough analyses. However, with an established integrated data system (IDS), an analyst is empowered to use more data, probe deeper, and make better recommendations. Put plainly, this case study demonstrates how comprehensive data is an imperative for ethical data analysis because relying on incomplete information can have a negative or misleading impact on the public.

13.4 Summary

Data ethics is an increasingly complicated and important field. Ethical guidelines will vary according to one's specific position or role. However, core ethics mentioned in this chapter serve as a good starting point for any data professional. Additionally, professional associations germane to one's field will often suggest a series of ethical data guidelines.

Regardless of an organization's finalized code of data ethics, the data professional must adhere in all cases. Operating without ethics can have dire consequences. It can lead to the identification of individuals or inappropriate allocation of resources or even have legal ramifications. If a data professional is pressured to break or bend any codified—or potential—data ethics, they should report the conflict to the appropriate person(s). This may be human resources, a board of trustees, or a supervisor.

Adhering to data ethics can lead to great benefits. The public will have greater confidence in the quality and findings of data due to transparency, safety/confidentiality, and integrity. Ensuring data is easily understood, available, and not conflicting with other sources is crucial. Although it is difficult to build and maintain a broad set of data ethics, they can be broken quite easily. It only takes one unethical analysis or misleading report to jeopardize the public's trust. Data's truth and authority will become increasingly valued only through consistent and widespread ethical use. Therefore, it is a definitive role for the data professional to cultivate and follow a formal, but fluid, set of data ethics.

References

Carney, J. (2018). *Executive order 18—Governor John Carney—state of Delaware*. governor. delaware.gov/executive-orders/eo18.

Chang, W.-Y., et al. (2022, April 28). A linked data mosaic for policy-relevant research on science and innovation: Value, transparency, rigor, and community. *Harvard Data Science Review*. hdsr.mitpress.mit.edu/pub/u073rjxs/release/2.

Department of Homeland Security Science and Technology. (2017). Next generation first responder Apex Program Technology experiment after action report. *DHSST*.

Retrieved from www.dhs.gov/sites/default/files/publications/NGFR_GrantCounty-TechEx-AAR_1709-508.pdf.

Department of Technology and Information. *Delaware data—Delaware.gov: Official website of the State of Delaware | Delaware Open Data Portal.* Retrieved September 30, 2022, from data.delaware.gov

Federal Data Strategy. *Action plan—Federal Data Strategy.* Retrieved September 30, 2022, from resources.data.gov/assets/documents/fds-data-ethics-framework.pdf.

Gabay, M., Krenzke, T., Bennici, F., & Machado, J. (2022). *Case study report, Iowa's integrated data system for decision-making: Creating a data sharing initiative intentional* (OPRE Report 2022–33). Washington, DC: Office of Planning, Research, and Evaluation, Administration for Children and Families, U.S. Department of Health and Human Services. Retrieved from www.acf.hhs.gov/sites/default/files/documents/opre/case-study-report-i2d2-mar-2022_0.pdf

Office of Justice Programs. (1973, January 1). Records, computers, and the rights of citizens. *Office of Justice Programs.* Retrieved from www.ojp.gov/ncjrs/virtual-library/abstracts/records-computers-and-rights-citizens.

Pozen, D. (2005). The mosaic theory, national security, and the freedom of information act. *Yale Law Journal, 115.* Retrieved from https://scholarship.law.columbia.edu/cgi/viewcontent.cgi?article=1527&context=faculty_scholarship.

The White House. (2021a, January 21). Executive order on advancing racial equity and support for underserved communities through the Federal Government. *The White House.* Retrieved from www.whitehouse.gov/briefing-room/presidential-actions/2021/01/20/executive-order-advancing-racial-equity-and-support-for-underserved-communities-through-the-federal-government.

The White House. (2021b, January 27). Memorandum on restoring trust in government through scientific integrity and evidence-based policymaking. *The White House.* Retrieved from www.whitehouse.gov/briefing-room/presidential-actions/2021/01/27/memorandum-on-restoring-trust-in-government-through-scientific-integrity-and-evidence-based-policymaking

Index

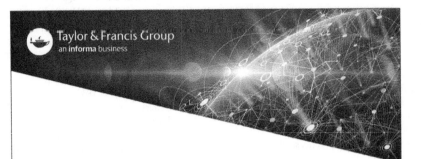